Waiting to Fly

Also by Ron Naveen

Wild Ice: Antarctic Journeys
The Oceanites Site Guide to the Antarctic Peninsula

Waiting to Fly

My Escapades with the Penguins of Antarctica

Ron Naveen

Quill
William Morrow
New York

Grateful acknowledgment is made to reprint from the following:

"Antarctica," in *Canto General* by Pablo Neruda (edited/translated by Jack Schmitt) © 1991 Fundacion Pablo Neruda, Regents of the University of California.

"The Lives of Penguins," in *Collected Poems* by Amy Clampitt, © 1997 by the Estate of Amy Clampitt, reprinted by permission of Alfred A. Knopf, Inc.

"East Coker," in *Four Quartets* by T. S. Eliot, © 1943 by T. S. Eliot, renewed © 1971 by Esme Valerie Eliot. Reprinted by permission from Harcourt Brace.

"Things Men Have Made." in *The Complete Poems* by D. H. Lawrence, edited by V. de Sola Pinto & F. W. Roberts. Copyright © 1964, 1971 by Angelo Ravagli and C. M. Weekley, Executors of the Estate of Frieda Lawrence Ravagli. Used by permission of Viking Penguin, a division of Penguin Putnam, Inc.

Logbook for Grace by Robert Cushman Murphy. Copyright 1947 by Robert Cushman Murphy, renewed © 1975 by Grace E. Barston Murphy. Reprinted by permission of Simon & Schuster.

Love and Garbage by Ivan Klíma (translated by Ewald Osers), reprinted by permission of Alfred A. Knopf, Inc.

Two Men in the Antarctic by T. W. Bagshawe, reprinted by permission of Cambridge University Press.

Text from a telegram sent by Hubert Wilkins to Frank Debenham, reprinted with permission of the Scott Polar Research Institute.

Lyrics from "Truckin'" (Grateful Dead) words by Robert Hunter, used by permission of Ice Nine Publishing Company.

Lyrics from "Penguins" (Lyle Lovett) © 1994 Michael H. Goldsen, Inc./Lyle Lovett. All Rights Reserved. Used by permission. International Copyright Secured.

All photographs by Ron Naveen.

It is the policy of William Morrow and Company, Inc., and its imprints and affiliates, recognizing the importance of preserving what has been written, to print the books we publish on acid-free paper, and we exert our best efforts to that end.

The Library of Congress has cataloged a previous edition of this title.

Library of Congress Cataloging-in-Publication Data
Naveen, Ron.
Waiting to fly : my escapades with the penguins of
Antarctica / Ron Naveen. — 1st ed.
p.   cm.
ISBN 0-688-15894-3
1. Penguins.   2. Penguins—Counting.   3. Naveen, Ron—Journeys—
Antarctica.   I. Title.
QL696.S473N38   1999

598.47—dc21   98-28539
                                                                CIP

Paperback ISBN 0-688-17573-2

Printed in the United States of America

First Quill Edition 2000

1 2 3 4 5 6 7 8 9 10

BOOK DESIGN BY BERNARD KLEIN

www.williammorrow.com

To Michael Paul Cyprian, forever locked in my memory as a true believer in humankind's best instincts. Michael had unflagging confidence that all of us could—and somehow would—establish better connections with one another and with the biological and physical systems of which we are a part. I miss him deeply.

Contents

Contents

INTRODUCTION

······················

Racing from the Cold

But it feels its life as boundless,
unfathomable, and without regard
to its own condition: pure, like its outward gaze
And where we see the future, it sees all time
and itself within all time, forever healed.
                                    —RAINER MARIA RILKE

This very early October morning—Washington, DC, circa late in
the twentieth century, one of my introspective moods churns. A
restless night has evolved to a throbbing headache, helped little by
the sharp rain pinging noisily, forcibly, against the kitchen alcove
windows. Soggy leaves swirl like miniature tornadoes around my
little backyard. Feebly, I waken. The coffee flows in gulps, but
proves a sparse antidote. The cats, now fed, lie content and plump

in different parts of the room. This month of contradictions, as always, arrives briskly, groggily. Fortunately, a glimmer parses through. I know the routine all too well. Invariably and soon, penguins will be parading across my radar screen.

The difficulty is that I'm half here and half in the region comprising the Antarctic Peninsula and South Shetland Islands—my spiritual home. While I'm fumbling around, trying to focus, millions and millions and millions of Adélie and chinstrap penguins are massing and restlessly moving, their hormones running, aroused to long jaunts back to breeding territories hundreds of miles south. The push is on and I'm barely to the starting line. Proust drifted asleep dreaming of storm-petrels snuggled in rocky crevices. He was lucky. I can't sleep or snuggle because it's that time of year. I endure a schism of venues, split between homes—one close, the other so far, far away. But inner juices kindle and I get the message: Like the short-feathered, blubber-layered, human-like objects of my work and affection, I, too, am ready to migrate.

Outside, at latitude 37 degrees north, the biting wind and cold rain quickly nullify this calendar year's last warm glory days. Seven thousand miles away, at latitude 62 degrees south, below the Antarctic Convergence, incessant winds and relentless currents fracture the winter's newborn ice. Here lies true Antarctica—biological Antarctica, where the water's always freezing and penguins begin filling the early springtime leads. Their warm glory days are just ahead. Mine, too. We're on the verge, racing from the cold.

For me, one incentive is getting back to work. I'm already mulling the censusing and mapping I'd like to accomplish in the coming field season and dreading all the gear that I haven't packed. Clothes and kit have to be pruned and arranged. I've got to check whether the repair patches on my windproof pants and parka are holding. There are myriad logistical details: Which ships will be able to carry me and my field teams? Can they drop us at a specific location on a particular day, retrieve us around the glacier a few days later? The work schedule requires that we transfer from one platform to another to keep our censuses going—to secure nest counts and chick counts at the appropriate times. Will we be able to lay over for a couple of days with colleagues at Copacabana Field Station in Admiralty Bay? Will a flying schedule work this season with the Royal Navy and HMS *Endurance*? Data sheets must be printed, field notebooks set up. Batteries in the handheld radios, GPS machines, and cameras must be checked. Film canisters must be assembled and marked.

But for Antarctic Peninsula and South Shetlands penguins, the imperative is acute and somewhat more compelling. It is a matter of evolutionary success or failure. They hear, see, feel the beltway of ice surrounding the continent cracking and receding—a clarion to commence their homeward sprint. There's no time for kissing and other foreplay, no time to think, no time to devise new ways of avoiding predators. They have the shortest of short windows to porpoise south, mouths agape, day after punishing day—to find mates, set up shop, court, lay eggs, raise chicks, and then get out before frigid weather locks in once again. I'm sure all of their systems are "go" and on fast forward: Feathers preened, cleaned, oiled, and waterproofed. Internal rangefinders set. And layered with sufficient blubber to stoke and fuel the long journey south.

Sections of the morning's *New York Times* and *Washington Post* sprawl across the table. Recently, both have featured a slew of front-page stories about global warming. What positions will be taken at upcoming international negotiations? Business leaders say this, environmentalists say that, and the governments and politicians spin in varied directions. Who will take the lead? Who won't? Adding to the spice, the articles briefly mention penguins—a modestly rare event. This is because the winter ice ring surrounding Antarctica has been smaller than usual—continuing a recent trend. As a result, there will be a smaller nursery for larval krill that use the underside of this fast ice to hide from predators, as well as to find phyto-plankton to eat.

Krill, scientifically known as *Euphausia superba*, is quite literally the "power lunch" of the Seventh Continent. Everyone from penguins to leopard and crabeater seals to whales eats krill, which is highly nutritious and spectacularly abundant. There may be a standing krill stock of more than 6.5 billion metric tons, but no one knows what might happen if many future winters are as ice-free as this one. Or if we start craving krill burgers. Up to five hundred million tons of krill may be taken annually by penguins, seals, and whales. Another hundred thousand tons may be taken by international fishing operations. Krill also is an extraordinarily long-lived crustacean, having a lifespan of perhaps seven years. Krill swarm in large patches, some of which may be many miles long. The bottom line is simple: If Antarctica's wintry, icy day-care center becomes leaner, there will be a smaller *year class* of krill and, down the road, less hearty banquets for those desperately seeking this salubrious little shrimp. So few links in the chain—and so many complications.

When I first went to Antarctica in the early 1980s, the Seventh

Continent's vast, 5.4 million square and desolate miles were expected to double in size during the frigid austral winter. Lean-ice years were relatively infrequent, occurring perhaps no more often than two in five. But according to this latest news the weather's changed. One consequence is that chinstraps and Adélies will have a shorter trek home. And if it's been this warm, there's likely been sufficient open water for gentoo penguins—the third species I know well—to have wintered in the South Shetlands or the Peninsula, heartily fishing away their bleak gray days.

The reduced amount of sea ice can be discerned from ice charts and schematic diagrams I've downloaded in recent weeks from the Internet. These arrays are as clear as my years of experience in The Ice. I now walk many beaches where glaciers once impeded my steps. I now witness more precipitation in Antarctic springtimes—freak snowstorms that bury penguins and their eggs and rainstorms that drench their feathers and flood their nests. I'm also aware that Antarctic penguin populations appear to be sliding downward. How do these indicia fit together? Is any of it or all of it somehow connected? Are we seeing natural variations or do we humans somehow cause or exacerbate these changes? Penguins are on the front lines of global climate change, and now they've made the front pages of the papers. I'm cheered that this difficult issue is causing ripples. Finally. Stories about geologic time usually don't sell a lot of newsprint. Not that we'll be able to do much to quell these trends, but it's a welcome relief from the usual litany of stories about crime, entertainment, and politics.

We'd probably be better off as penguins—who really don't spend a rash of time reasoning, planning, pondering, or worrying too much about anything. It's our curse to be rather obsessed about the here and now. Penguins lead frenetic, action-packed lives and they're very, very busy—with tons of work to do and very little time to get it done. So they just do it. Our blessing and bane run toward the other end of the spectrum—too much time to think about immediate needs and not wishing to think too excessively about the next generation or about many generations to come. Geological, long-term propositions are more than we'd like to handle. So, no matter how the global warming debate resolves as a diplomatic and political matter, my gut—my penguin barometer—tells me that tough choices will be put off until I'm long gone from the equation.

But penguins nesting in the Peninsula and the South Shetlands don't have these kinds of choices. There is slim leeway because, for better or worse, they're preordained to stick with a rather specific program. If dazed and confused, they lose. These penguins spend their entire lives in frigid water, see mates for only a few weeks each year, and endure some of the worst winds and harshest weather imaginable. Being a penguin is hardly a picnic. As a consequence, they've become evolutionarily wired to predictable behaviors and chores, with very little intuitive freedom. But the specialized hardware and dedicated software work substantially well. Only three of the world's seventeen species of penguins are considered to be in any degree of environmental difficulty—and none of these is in the Antarctic. So while penguins constantly amuse us, their comically deceptive exterior belies the reality that, over geologic time, they've succeeded and perhaps mastered survival a little bit better than we have.

October focuses these contradictions, though the easy course is to tune out and stop listening to the messages. But I'm doing better. I'm starting to grasp the nuances—for example, that the lives of these penguins revolve almost exclusively around food, sex, weather, and defending one's turf. If all four are good and in synch, chinstraps, gentoos, and Adélies will survive quite nicely. Actually, whether we admit it or not, it's much the same with us—or should be, given our status as ordinary biological creatures. No doubt, for many in the western world, the first three are in pretty decent shape. Unfortunately, the last is distorted too often to mean economic security and material wealth, which, penguins might say, makes it harder to separate the krill from the kelp. In evolutionary terms, the number of toys we possess is wholly irrelevant. Fortunately, chinstraps, gentoos, and Adélies have their priorities straight. These highly charged, hardwired breeding and feeding machines make a lot of noise, but they don't whinge and squawk unnecessarily about their possessions—the pebbles they steal relentlessly for nests, or their homes—some of the most crowded housing developments imaginable.

Soon and for weeks of magic moments in time, these broader questions will fade and I'll be at peace, slogging through snow, mired in penguin guano, or shivering in katabatic winds—intent on gathering data, drawing maps, and taking pictures—just trying to move my work along. My experience with penguins has been rich, spread across sixteen austral spring and summer field seasons. I've been extraordinarily lucky—one of the very, very few people who's logged the equivalent of three to four entire years working in this dream location, firsthand, with marquee animals. Field researchers only reluctantly reveal the intense attachment they have for the subjects of their investigations. It feels almost petty, perhaps even childish, but I'm not ashamed to rave on about penguins. I can't help it. They've grabbed me and simply won't let go.

So up north, in October's material world, the big news this morning is that my hiatus is shortly going to end. For months we've hidden from one another. I've been cranking out reports, analyzing data and maps—simply dealing with the grunt work tied to my research project. The time's come: I'll return to the penguins, they'll show more of their lives to me, and I'll continue being confused about their and our roles in this curious drama called Life on Earth.

The chinstraps and Adélies also have been north—Adélies on the edge of the fast ice ring, chinstraps in the open water beyond. Adélies use the pack ice as a home base for their feeding runs, while chinstraps prefer a more pelagic, or open-sea, existence. With glimmers of the approaching long days' light, they're off—Adélies first, the chinnies a few weeks later. With both species, mates apparently don't stay together in the off-season. Chinstraps and Adélies aim for the same precise nest site they used the previous season. By contrast, gentoo mates might stay together in the Peninsula and South Shetlands during the winter. And while gentoos may return to the same general area to breed, they change nest sites readily. Adverse weather might delay their courtship rituals. Perhaps there's been some disturbance or predation. Sometimes it happens for no apparent reason. Gentoo pairs also may construct a number of pebble nests before the female makes her choice and, finally, lays.

The massive caffeine ingestion kicks in with absolutely perfect timing, as my radar crowds quickly with the expected—and this now unstoppable—stream of penguin consciousness. I'm used to it.

Once it starts, thoughts swing south and everything seems penguin-esque.

Hobbes—otherwise known as "Fat Boy"—has his overweight thirteen-pound and two-foot-long cat girth lolled across the cushion next to my hip. He looks like an Adélie penguin gorged on too much krill. He simply doesn't want to start *his* spring trip home, however shortened this season's journey might be. Moose, the slimmer, nine-pound, two-and-a-half-foot version, jumps to the window and sits, stirred by something moving outside, bobbing his head from side to side. He looks like a trim Adélie two weeks into incubation, starving, resting on his stones, alertly, anxiously, waiting his mate's return. The cats' basically black color assists the illusion. When they stand upright, stretch their length, and paw my upper leg, the size comparison to Adélies and chinstraps is striking. Fortunately, they don't bite like a berserker male Adélie, lunging at my privates, totally annoyed I've invaded his personal space.

Moose and Hobbes also are fortunate they weren't roaming the Antarctic with the British sealing captain Robert Fildes. He was perhaps the most ill-fated sealing master to work the Peninsula and the South Shetlands in the early nineteenth century. Fur seals were overrunning the beaches of the South Shetlands, tempting a stream of British and American competitors. All sailed across the Drake in small craft, driven by dreams of inflated profits from valuable furs. These were dangerous voyages. There were many shipwrecks and deaths, and many of the beaches in the South Shetlands became crude campsites for the starving, shivering, and sometimes hopeless men stranded onshore. The human toll, though, was modest. The seals were the really big losers.

During the sealers' salad days in the 1820s, the prevailing philosophy was single-minded: Kill everything and anything that moves, give 'em a few years to recover, then return and wipe 'em out once again. Fildes first came in December 1820 and, in the midst of the slaughter, noted huge numbers of what he called "half form'd birds"—penguins. But Fildes's success was rather short-lived: His first vessel, *Cora*, foundered and wrecked within a month. Fildes and his men camped on Livingston Island for weeks until they were rescued. And remember: This was long before our days of comfy, lightweight, warm, and breathable outergear. We know little about these crazy ventures because sealers' logbooks were routinely destroyed by customs officials after a few years' of record-keeping. Yet, as British researcher, writer, and historian L. Harrison Matthews describes, Fildes is an important historical figure because two of his logbooks somehow survived this ruinous fate.

After *Cora* wrecked in early 1821, Fildes's log notes that the ship's cat came ashore. In these sad moments, some of the islands were dotted with caves that provided needed shelter from the profusion of storms. In Fildes's situation, the men were destitute and lived in a makeshift accommodation—a patchwork tent concocted from sail, other available canvas, wood, and rocks. The design included many large puncheons, or casks, which were used by the men for sleeping and for keeping warm and dry. One of the spare puncheons was occupied by Fildes's cat, who didn't mind sharing space with a couple of penguins who repeatedly returned after long feeding runs for some rest and relaxation. What a scene: cat and penguins napping side by side. Fildes reports the penguins' persistence in returning to their purring companion, relentlessly exploring for any possible opening or crack in the canvas, and assiduously avoiding the sealers' efforts to keep them out of the tent. I can't imagine Hobbes, our alpha cat, abiding the presence of penguins in the house. It would be a battle royal. After returning to England—and despite his profound failure—Fildes was given another command, *Robert.* Sealing fever was high and it was rather irrelevant that Fildes had just run one vessel onto the rocks. In Round Two, he did slightly better, keeping *Robert* afloat for three months before it, too, was gone.

Luckily, during my times in The Ice, I've endured less agonizing conditions than Fildes and his cat. I've faced relatively few crises: Snagging on an assortment of ledges and outcrops while chasing chinstraps. Having my face blown to frozen contortions by katabatic winds. Occasionally soaking in frigid water to my hips.

So October dawns and another field season begins, part of an extended trip I never expected—and one that I hope will never end. Thousands of miles of distance have collapsed and one home now merges with another. Sights, sounds, and places converge. The spots of leaves in my backyard could be a neat array of penguins, with backs to the gale, guarding their evolutionary investment, protecting a few inches of personal space. Washington could be Petermann Island, Waterboat Point, Copacabana Beach, Paulet or Heroína Islands, Baily Head, the whalebone beach at the Aitcho Islands, or the sealers' digs at Yankee Harbor. I'm privileged to be working in a dream location, to go toenail-to-boot and face-to-face each season with literally hundreds of thousands of penguins. We are racing back to one another. I'm tuning to their clues and trying, always, to discover more of their secrets. There will be dirty fingernails, unavoidably long hours in the field, lots of slogging through guano pools, and more than a little huffing and puffing to reach some isolated census colonies.

Strung together, these snapshots articulate an intricate and complicated story—an amalgam that's been swelled by years of incidents, flavors, sights, smells, sounds, and other details. I no longer simply see a chinstrap, an Adélie, or a gentoo. Each snapshot becomes a moving picture of an entire, manic life—and *all* of it, the entire cycle, passes before me. Tick, tock, up and down and forward we go, marching to a special drumbeat.

I've been there, when they stream back in droves, returning home, searching for mates, ready to set up shop and commence another breeding season. I've been there when they hustle after me, chattering aggressively, unsure whether I pose any additional dangers.

I've been there when one of these potbellied, almost human characters, in haste, falls flat on its face, then stares down the stones that caused its inelegant missteps.

I've been there when fledglings tiptoe to the brink, look left, look right, and then take to the sea for the first—perhaps, sadly, the last—time.

I've been there in the late-season chill, when chinstraps huddle protectively in streambeds to molt, strewing the landscape with a broad swath of white, shorn feathers.

I've been immersed, lost, in a sea of tuxedoed penguins that's never been surveyed.

Alone. Me and them.

And I've been there after they've left, assimilated in the same landscape, still alone, clasping dreams of seasons to come.

With astonishing swiftness Antarctica returns to inanimate calm. Exposed and fulfilled, I'm part of this overpowering cinema.

I've been to penguin paradise, I've had many adventures—and there are many more stories to tell.

ONE

All Time, Penguin Time

What a long, strange trip it's been.
—*Grateful Dead*

This penguin addiction has curious roots.

And leaves many footprints.

I can't elude them. These playful, human-like creatures we call penguins. Or my recurrent visions of penguins. I sometimes rouse from sleep dreaming I'm a penguin. The physical reality may be that penguins live thousands of miles distant. But in a weird metaphysical sense, they're never quite gone from my sight, never quite removed from consciousness. Indeed, I suffer a peculiar, albeit curiously uplifting malady—and I've been thrust center stage, into many dramas and tales. Of life and death. Love and lust. Of penguins surviving the worst conditions on the planet. And of a growing number of us humans who have become utterly fascinated by these compact, upright packages of feathers, fat, and muscle.

I see penguins everywhere.

Imagine the crowded Leicester Square tube stop at the height of a spring morning's commuter romp. The lifts are chockablock full of furiously rushing Londoners. I savor my four inches of personal space and realize there's no quick way out. I'm resigned to an endless procession and tumult, which surely repeats itself morning after morning. The escalator's long, slow ride to the top simply must be endured. One step above, a scruffy woman carries three heavy clothing bags and annoyingly shifts them from hand to hand, and in the process keeps bumping me in the chest. A step down, an immaculately dressed businessman clutches his leather briefcase for dear life and pompously bobs from side to side, trying to find an opening to scoot on past. All of us consult wristwatches, swing elbows, huff and puff, and seemingly sweat whether we're going to make it on time, wherever we're going. Tick, tock, up and down we go like tuxedoed penguins on parade, marching to a special drumbeat. To the call of the breaking Antarctic ice. Somewhere, maybe at another tube stop, my mate also races home. Another breeding season is about to start.

Or picture a midsummer's day in downtown Manhattan. The bright sun lures everyone to the street, swirling here, swirling there—an effervescent, almost musical flow of people in all directions. In similar traffic, Piet Mondrian envisioned colorful, fast-moving rectangles, dots, dashes, boxes, and lines. In my mind's eye, I see the traffic of 'guins chasing food for days on end, before returning home to feed their anxious, fragile chicks. Just another trip to the supermarket.

But it also could happen on a frigid, snowy mountain peak—anywhere on the planet where it's blowing fifty knots and no one's in sight. There's a desolation of white in all directions. Winter plunges forward and penguins shiver on the beach or on the fast ice surrounding the Antarctic continent. A painful feather molt is mercifully finished and it's time to rest or frolic at sea for eight long months, sometimes meandering, but mostly feeding. Winter's important for them and a big mystery to us. We don't know precisely what they're eating during these months and how far they roam to find it. We speculate it's the same diet they pursue when we can see them firsthand—mostly krill, occasionally fish, and very rarely copepods. And no doubt, as is the game, they'll still need to avoid predators, constantly. These penguins must migrate home each spring fattened to the hilt. Without this energy to burn, penguins can't consummate the long fasts that inaugurate each breeding cycle, in which case nests will fail—and no chicks will be produced. But we don't encounter them in *their* winter. We're never there. It's too bloody awfully cold and dangerous. To be blunt: A successful return to breeding territories isn't assured. That contemporary, nihilistic pop adage intones that life's too short and then penguins—and we—die. But one penguin-counter isn't quite ready to check out—and won't—without some proper reflection.

I'm affected on various and sundry levels. Superficially, I'm lured like everyone else: The penguins' upright stance and animated behavior reminds me too much of my own waddling around, sometimes unsteadily. This lure has attracted many Antarctic explorers and scientists. Apsley Cherry-Garrard, the youngest member of Robert Falcon Scott's British Antarctic Expedition of 1910–13 and the author of *The Worst Journey in the World*, writes that penguins "are extraordinarily like children, these little people of the Antarctic world, either like children, or like old men, full of their own importance and late for dinner, in their black tail-coats and white shirt-fronts—and rather portly withal."

But the infection runs deeper. Consider where chinstraps, gentoos, and Adélies live: Antarctica. It's the one spot on the planet that no human rules, that no ownership possesses—a strange location where people from more than forty countries, representing 75 percent of the world's population, work together harmoniously. Antarctica is the last frontier on the planet—a mix of unspoiled beauty, heart-tugging wildlife, and history, which has been explored only within the last two or three generations, essentially within the time frame of our parents and grandparents. So in my complicated view, chinstraps, gentoos, and Adélies stand before me as research subject, as messenger, and as symbol—and they continually lure me back. They keep me on my toes, keep me thinking, and force me to wonder how it might be, if I—if all of us—had a less dominating view of the planet.

Sixteen years of penguins provides me different antennae. Perhaps it is a gift. I see and hear differently—can understand that nothing stays the same. Take this Antarctic photograph: A chinstrap penguin colony with more than seventy-five thousand nests, in an amphitheater stretched across a green, black, and pink volcanic mountainside. On closer examination the picture continually changes, over and over, like some vibrant undulating organism. There are clues in every corner: Filthy penguins, just relieved at their nests, pompously ambling downhill toward the sea, hungry and ready to eat. Sparkling clean penguins, having just returned from feeding and preening, weaving uphill toward waiting partners. Some chinstraps are incubating eggs, a few inexperienced birds are still courting, and a fair number are blowing off snowy sheathbills who are trotting around, trying to find some eggs to peck and slurp.

By sitting and taking a discerning look you'll notice an entire cast of characters, moment-to-moment drama, and roving clouds and weather that mutate incessantly. Because my work requires a considerable amount of penguin-watching, I have a special opportunity. Patience allows me to see more clearly their habits and behavior, perhaps to examine something new: The purple color of a chinstrap's brood pouch. The spiny bristles lining their mouths, which allow them to hold prey tightly, aim food down their gullet. The curiosity of young gentoos, who are rather content to sit in your lap.

A semblance of patience also helps when answers seem totally impossible and questions percolate exponentially: Why do chinstraps sometimes expel their yellow stomach linings? How do they compete with one another—as well as with other predators—for conceivably limited resources? How is their dietary staple, krill, affected by increased ultraviolet-B radiation seeping through the planet's thinned ozone layer? How do they cope with changing weather conditions—freak snowstorms and drifts, unexpected katabatics? If more icebergs are calving, does this increased freshwater cause a salinity imbalance that may affect krill and phytoplankton stocks? It's impossible to work on penguins if one's looking for easy solutions. The penguins'—indeed the planet's—mysteries don't resolve in an instant and may never be known, even in few lifetimes. The penguins help me realize that it's complicated out there and that change is inevitable—but also that change may be nurturing.

Admittedly, examining penguins' lives with a clear lens means getting down to basics—getting one's fingernails dirty with a few inconvenient details. Many say it's a very *simple* ecosystem: Harm the phytoplankton and krill fails. Knock down the krill and there's theoretically less food for penguins and others higher up the food chain. And the consequences might take years to play out, until penguins presumably won't be able to find the right size of krill in the right places at the right time of year. Yet it remains entirely possible that they'll be able to switch to krill of different sizes and ages, perhaps start eating more fish and copepods. I remember summers when research trawlers couldn't find any krill swarms, but chinstraps, gentoos, and Adélies were repeatedly returning with loaded bellies. So another message is that these apparently short links may generate an abundance of myths and a paucity of facts—that natural variations can't be reduced to neat little equations. Which probably explains why we avoid grandiose matters like global climate change and decreasing Antarctic penguin populations. It's so painful to be reminded, even in seemingly elemental situations, that we don't steer the planet. By the same token, I've come to relish these complications and embrace a humility inevitably attaching to closer looks at penguins—that we can be happy, irrespective of our cosmic and not-so-cosmic concerns.

The environs where the sealers once roamed might just as easily be called Penguin Central. They lie within my study area in the South Shetland Islands and northern Antarctic Peninsula—and I know them well, as familiarly as the buttons and levers on my cameras. It's a very seductive region, overloaded with snowcapped peaks and expansive glaciers squirming sinuously seaward. Colossal tabular icebergs bob the watery horizon like broad corks. The sensory overload includes guano fumes wafting through the air, sometimes many miles from penguin colonies. The Shetlands and the Peninsula lie more than five hundred miles below South America. There aren't any airports. So to get to work, I must suffer the infamous Drake Passage—two days rocking and rolling south, and two back.

The Peninsula lies astride the volcanic Scotia Arc, which sits like a crooked left arm waving alluringly to the northeast, extending to the South Shetlands, South Orkneys, and South Sandwich Islands. The geological history is that the Transantarctic Mountains, the Peninsula, and these nearby island groups have long been separated from the Andes Mountains of the South American continent. The Drake fills the breach. I recall being told that if you're going to pick a research project—especially if the hours are long and the work difficult—at least pick a location that's worth the investment. The Peninsula and South Shetlands certainly fill the order. The rest of the Antarctic continent—an area the size of the United States and Mexico combined—has relatively sparse wildlife, a brutally inhospitable climate, and weeks of permanent winter darkness south of the Antarctic Circle. By contrast, the Peninsula and South Shetlands are truly paradisiacal—a Banana Belt full of penguins.

At Yankee Harbor on the southwest end of Greenwich Island, a rusting old try-pot is the sole, vestigial artifact remaining from the region's tortured sealing history. On that sad score, the good news is that fur seals have returned, building in droves as summer progresses. Above Yankee Harbor's protected anchorage, gentoos adorn the uplifted beaches and extend well into the highlands. Save for the try-pot, there's an air of unspoiled beauty—of how it surely appeared for aeons, before its discovery. This is a common Antarctic thread—being surrounded by land and ice and glaciers that are more than 99.9 percent untouched by us. It's as if Captain Kirk of the starship *Enterprise* has beamed me back to that special moment when continental drift forged the Peninsula's present identity and nature. Time feels blotted out. These look like the same penguins I saw in photos from the Second French Antarctic Expedition, which spent the winter in the Peninsula in 1909. They also fit the sealers' descriptions from the middle of the last century. I can't tell the difference and I have an eerie feeling of being exposed—a time traveler who's taking a special trip through history.

But truth be told, it's been a long, strange trip for a second-generation kid, a grandchild of immigrants who settled along the banks of the Susquehanna River in the United States in the early 1900s. I grew up in a situation where my parents' fondest dream was for my and my sister's future security and ease—something they didn't come close to enjoying. Both of my parents' families were large and the general malaise was that they always were scraping to survive. The Great Depression hit hard and some mild successes were erased by the meager World War II economy. One family operated an automobile sales and repair shop, the other a neighborhood grocery store. The small plot of dirt adjoining grandfather's market was an occasional playground in my early years, but for Dad this polygon had been the full and sum total of his outside world of dreams. He often told me that his toys—his *only* toys—were irregularly shaped blocks of wood, which one day were trains and automobiles, the next day soldiers and warriors. My bequest was supposed to be different, but the stability my parents wished, I rudely and realistically learned, isn't the norm.

My folks weaved dreams with a simple premise that my sister and I would "have it better" than they had managing the booming American Dream. Which clearly suggested something about college and graduate school, having an adoring spouse and 2.3 children, a very comfortable home in the suburbs, an unspecified number of household pets, a station wagon for a second car, one job forever, and an Ozzie-and-Harriet life that would be happy ever after. Mom and Dad repeated one particular metaphor about life being an open book, and how I had so many blank pages to fill. Well, of course, it didn't quite happen that way. In fact, it seems totally implausible that I wound up working in Antarctica. This was far out of my *expected* line, but fortunately, a few key influences greased the way.

The gloss on my blank pages begins with Terry Baltimore, a friend who was the first bird-watcher I'd ever met. He must have been seeking a Boy Scouts badge in birds, and I tagged along out of sheer curiosity. Soon, an entirely new set of adventures opened up, far removed from the preordained notions of success my family encouraged. There was something special about these outdoors jaunts and chases, all related I'm sure to carving my own identity. I pestered Mom and Dad for a pair of six-power binoculars and soon my lifelist was full speed ahead. Actually, the term "bird-watcher" was then the height of derogation. But nobody accused Terry and me of such weirdness because, outside of our immediate families, we kept our little secret close to our vests. We were in the closet with birds. Bird-watching just wasn't in vogue. In fact, it was so far removed from vogue that even a minimal association with such aberrant activity might totally cripple our chances of relevant, 1960s-type bonding with our adolescent cronies. We lugged binos and our bible—the third edition of Roger Tory Peterson's *A Field Guide to Eastern Birds*—everywhere, trying at every waking moment to "one-up" the other.

As my birding chases blossomed, so did tensions with Mom's and Dad's expectations. More and more they talked about careers and more and more I chased new ticks for my lifelist. It got to the juncture where I believed outside counsel was needed. And I could fathom no better savior than my guru, Roger Tory Peterson himself. With great nervousness, I wrote and asked for any possible guidance to foist on my unsuspecting parents. It was simple: "Mr. Peterson, they want me to go off to college, but I'm not sure. Or should I go after what I really want—birds? I mean, I take your field guide everywhere, I really like birds, and I don't see why I couldn't get along like you have—perhaps even study at Cornell's Laboratory of Ornithology." My burden was in his hands. With a letter from Mr. Peterson in hand, my parents definitely would understand.

Weeks and weeks passed. Finally the response arrived, shockingly: "Dear Ronald: What do you mean: *'Go into birds'? Are you kidding? Listen to your parents. There's no money in birds!*" Oh, no. Hmmm. I was stopped dead in my tracks. But in another blink, taking full advantage of more than thirty years' distance, I laugh at the irony. While editing *Birding* magazine, I got to know Roger and realize now, on reflection, that his advice was only half right. It was too early for him, for anyone, to realize that the burgeoning "field guide" revolution he had fostered would enable many of us to realize our wildest dreams—even to make a living at it. Not that we'd be able to make a lot of money—on that he was absolutely correct—but at least we'd manage to survive economically.

So, somewhat reluctantly, I followed my folks' suggested path and went to college, keeping my restlessness tucked in an easy-to-reach side pocket. Then came Vietnam. I marched against the war and avoided service, first by attending law school and taking advantage of a one-year student deferment, then permanently via the blossoming Crohn's disease in my colon. This led to three years with a law firm in Florida, which confirmed in loudly blinking lights that I wasn't cut out for a lifestyle of constant time pressures and clients whose values I didn't respect. I returned to Washington for a stint with the US Environmental Protection Agency, then concluded my traditional résumé with a stint as the "marine mammal lawyer" in the US National Marine Fisheries Service, back in Washington.

It was a heavenly job—for a while. I felt I'd revolved full circle, back to animals—to those defining moments chasing birds along the red, muddy shores of the Susquehanna River. And the birding, which had been minimal while testing fate in private legal practice, returned to my front burner. I started going offshore on the pelagic birding and whale-watching trips my friend Rich Rowlett was conducting out of Ocean City, Maryland. It was the mid-1970s and Roger Peterson's field-guide revolution now was booming: Increasing numbers of binocular-toters were chasing lifelists in more and more obscure locations, including the open ocean. Pelagic trips were operating on both coasts in North America and at a few locations in Europe. But comparatively little was known about the offshore quarry we sought. Even the newest field guides lacked adequate details. I dug for better sources and information.

The beacon was Robert Cushman Murphy's *Oceanic Birds of South America*—a classic, two-volume magnum opus from 1936, written by the late curator of oceanic birds at the American Museum of Natural History in New York. I'd been exasperated spending so many long, rough, seasick days on the ocean, with the birds whizzing by faster than even a good field birder could keep up with correctly. The diagnostic field marks mentioned in the guides were oftentimes meaningless. The seabirds seemed too mysterious, and their lives and identification too difficult—until delving into Murphy. But *Oceanic Birds* was no ordinary bird book and my eyes opened to a whole new world. To Murphy, these creatures were much more than objects of our vision and commodities for cold, scientific analysis. They were fellow denizens of the planet, worthy of respectful study, not passing glances. I discovered a seabird connoisseur who was an articulate, impassioned writer. I was hooked deeply by Murphy's graceful, literary style, his descriptions such as that of an albatross "on the invisible currents of the breeze" who appears "merely to follow its pinkish bill at random." Or, describing Southern Ocean seabirds called prions: "When the air is filled with a flock of whale birds careening in the breeze, rising, falling, voplaning, twisting, sideslipping above the sea, now flashing their white breasts, now turning their almost invisible backs—they resemble the motes in a windy sunbeam."

Murphy became a hero. I learned about El Niño warming periods that occurred sixty years ago along the western South American coasts. And I learned much about other seabirds that lived thousands of miles away from my coast. I was especially intrigued by penguins because they'd taken their flying skills underwater. I wanted to see them, too. The science seemed inexorably mixed with romantic adventures. After all, his was the era of Amundsen and Scott, when "men" still explored and sought adventure, and often turned to Antarctic waters for wealth, fame, and, of course, the last great geographical goal on this planet—crossing the great ice sheet and reaching the South Pole. Murphy's work in the Southern Ocean fit this questing pattern. Leaving his new bride, Grace, behind, the zestful, twenty-five-year-old opportunistic scientist joined the whaling brig *Daisy* in 1912–13 and set sail to the Roaring 40s and Furious 50s. The main objectives, both commercial and scientific, were centered at South Georgia, below the Antarctic Convergence.

Murphy's recollections of these heady days were inspiring, full of discoveries: How do you skin a slew of chunky, forty-pound king penguins? By employing special help, of course. Murphy enticed a band of scavenging skuas—the gull-like birds who are rapacious scavengers at penguin colonies—to assist him in skinning and defatting a large number of penguin specimens. How do you study the little seabirds called storm-petrels? Well, you bring *them* to *you*. Murphy recounts the escapades of Rollo Beck, who did extensive fieldwork for the California Academy of Sciences, and who first discovered that storm-petrels could be attracted to chum lines—strings of food cast behind or alongside the boat. Beck actually discovered a new species, Hornby's storm-petrel, off Peru in this fashion.

And how do you learn more about these penguins—the "half-formed birds"—that Fildes saw? Murphy sat and watched their rou-

27

tines very carefully: Gentoo penguins—Johnnies, in the parlance of the day—are a case in point. Murphy found their disposition gentle, their curiosity more than slight, and he describes playing children's games with them: "On the afternoon of this day I walked to a glacial pond on the far side of which stood a group of Johnny Penguins. As soon as they saw me, one of their number swam across under water and walked toward me. When I moved quietly it followed, and when I stopped it did likewise. Then, one by one, it was joined by the other penguins from across the pond. It was whimsical to see this troop of mimicking small brothers with no other wish than to keep me company." This sounded like the best employment in the world. If penguins were the research subjects, who could resist being a biologist?

Oceanic Birds was my precious lodestone, a magic flare kindling dreams of days to come. Murphy spun me in a different direction. He was a terribly exacting scientist—a seabird Sherlock Holmes— and he spent laborious moments, whatever was needed, to discover the intimacies of these creatures' lives. The work was hard—all science is—but Murphy's affectionate and respectful approach made it seem so worthwhile because there was so much to savor. One favorite passage was Murphy's analysis of gentoo penguin breeding shenanigans. He describes lady gentoos awaiting gifts of pebbles or ancestral bones from suitors:

> Cocks sometimes make mistakes, with dire results, by offering pebbles to other cocks. The presentation to a hen is a pantomime of bowing, accompanied by soft hissing sounds and later by either angry or joyous trumpetings, according to the outcome. The hen is the

builder of the home, the cock the bearer of bricks, and acceptance of the first pebble is the symbol of success in wooing. Today a cock laid a pebble at my feet, a compliment properly followed by ceremonial bowing and, I hope, by mutual sentiments of high esteem. That, I believe, is an expression to be expected from an ambassador.

These entrées were powerful—and penguins began rising over my horizon.

The Murphian connections were nurtured further by Tom McIntyre, who was one of my close compatriots on the Ocean City pelagic trips—and the only whaler I've ever known. In 1969 and 1970, Mac had worked in the last, US-based whaling station at Richmond, California. He was struggling to earn money for his family. When I met him, he was working out of the marine mammal office of the Fisheries Service in Washington. A number of years into this job, the Service had sent him to the Antarctic to observe whaling activities on a Japanese mothership, a floating factory. This was great fodder for discussion and we spent oodles of hours chattering through the dead time on the offshore Ocean City trips. I spun seabird stories and Mac covered the whale and dolphin side of life. I was impressed with his knowledge—in fact, he could have handled the seabirds just as well, especially the Antarctic ones. He knew *Oceanic Birds* inside out and kept mentioning snippets I'd missed in Murphy's text: The complex discussion of ocean currents and the movements of prey stocks. The derivations of the penguins' names. Murphy's poking holes in specious theories already cluttering the literature.

Mac discerned my emerging dreams and took special joy niggling them forward. His kidding revolved around the notion that penguins were actually marine mammals. "After all, Navarinsky," as he'd often called me, "They don't fly—do they? And what about that blubber? They've got it too, you know. But the big thing, don't forget, is that they *porpoise* through the water." We had immense fun and our interests aligned like stars in a constellation. Chasing a lifelist started feeling irrelevant and nowhere near as challenging as chasing secrets: Why were these seabirds found at particular places or at particular times of the year? What were they eating? How were their lives complicated—or ended—by the vagaries of wind, weather, predators, illness, or other unforeseen calamities? I began to see complications, not clarities. "Water covers seventy percent or more of the planet," Mac intoned, "and the Antarctic drives it all—its surrounding Southern Ocean, the winds that blow unimpeded around the continent. That's where it all begins. Yeah, you should get there."

When I ultimately joined the general counsel's office of the Fisheries Service in 1978, Tom was ensconced right down the hall—a very fortuitous break for me. All the legalities hinged on whether the marine mammals in question were at an acceptable level of health deemed an "optimum sustainable population." Every issue—from regulations about the incidental capturing of dolphins in the tuna fishery to the then-operative fur seal treaty in the north Pacific Ocean to conflicts between salmon fishermen and Dall's porpoise— revolved around a seemingly straightforward matter: How many animals existed and would the species still be at healthy levels when the proposed taking was concluded? There were myriad texts, theories, and buzzwords permeating these matters—and Mac helped me through quite a bit of the morass. In the end, my tenure was tantamount to earning an advanced degree in biology and population dynamics.

If I needed information on the distribution of Pacific *Stenella* dolphins, Mac knew which papers to consult. If the issue was Pribilof Island fur seals, Mac had many of the scientific references at his fingertips. He had this penchant for dropping manuscripts on my desk to peruse. How did he know all this stuff? Something wasn't exactly clicking. One day I took him aside and asked where he'd gotten his Ph.D. "*Rrrrgh, Rrrrgh*" was his unintelligible reply. "I don't have one."

"OK, then, so where'd you get your Master's?" More harrumphs and grumphs erupted. In fact, Mac finally admitted, there was no advanced degree. He'd learned it all by getting his fingernails dirty, literally from the skin of the whales down to their guts and back out again. The Richmond whaling station was just the beginning of his hard-knocks path. I then knew little about the exploits of Antarctic explorers and researchers like Cherry-Garrard, Bagshawe, and Lester, all of whom, I'd discover, were cut from Mac's kind of cloth—self-taught, not afraid to ask questions, and willing to spend hours searching for clues. I admired this spunk and determination enormously. Another wrinkle developed: Mac took a brief sojourn to work as a lecturer on the *World Discoverer*, one of the expedition ships that operated in the Antarctic Peninsula and South Shetlands each November to February. I listened intently to the details, salivating, thinking this might become my eventual route south. Mac willingly shared relevant contact numbers and addresses.

My marine mammal days flew, accumulating more quickly than

I'd realized to four and a half years. Workdays grew increasingly stale. I'd had enough, done just about everything a staff lawyer possibly could do. And despite the overtures, I certainly didn't want to be "bumped upstairs" to some management position—to push paper and worry about budgets, hiring freezes, layoffs, and—worst of all—a new administration that would likely place a lower emphasis on the issues I'd found so fascinating.

Leaving this chapter of my life wasn't complicated: Rich Rowlett had left the area, I'd inherited his pelagic trip business, and I thought that by adding trips to other locations—like the Galápagos—I could survive, without being a lawyer. Best of all, after years of phone calls, letters, and pleading with Mac's contacts, I was hired to work as a lecturer on the *World Discoverer* for a short, weeklong visit to the South Shetlands and the Antarctic Peninsula.

They'd come, finally.

Well past the horizon. Into the foreground.

Now flooding my vision.

Flying in water, waddling over ice.

All time, my time.

Penguin time.

TWO

· · · · · · · · · · · · · · · · · · · ·

Stonecrackers

[W]e live so that we should pass on a message whose significance we cannot quite fathom because it is mysterious and unrevealable . . . because there are a number of encounters ahead of us for the sake of which living is worthwhile. Encounters with people who will emerge when we least expect them. Or else encounters with other creatures whose lives will touch ours with a single shy glance.

—IVAN KLÍMA

To the starting gate. Then, beset with frustration.

Finally, fifty minutes that changed everything.

My days of penguins and Antarctica had a messy inaugural. At the time, the *World Discoverer* was one of only two expedition ships regularly visiting the Antarctic during the austral spring and summer.

Our run through the Drake Passage started easily enough, but Day 2 brought overcast, rain, snow, drizzle, and fog. The sea got rough and there was a high, rolling swell. The *Disco* pounded forward, but the blustery east winds refused to quit. At times, there was very uncertain motion, the ship's 285-foot-four-inch length not fitting neatly between the swells and producing a nauseating mix of rolling and pitching. The sensation reminded me of "green days" off of Ocean City, Maryland, when the seabird-watching had to be commingled with seasick trips to the rail.

Reaching the South Shetlands, icebergs bobbed in all directions. And the windy blasts continued. Forget Nelson Island—landing scrubbed. Sorry, no Deception Island. What I'd heard about the highly variable Antarctic weather wasn't holding true. Ours was constant: wind, wind, wind—with the barometer staying depressed.

Desperately seeking penguins, but flummoxed by weather I'd never anticipated.

We kept moving south down the Bransfield Strait, trying to buy some lee, and finally headed into Port Lockroy at the southwestern end of Wiencke Island. But no dice. The Zodiacs—the rubber inflatable boats that take people ashore—would have spilled everyone into the water. Palmer Station and Paradise Bay were the next stops, and both suffered from the continuing plague of high winds, rain, and choppy surf on the beaches. The landings had to be cut short and were very unsatisfying. I wanted some unfettered, Robert Cushman Murphyesque moments with the penguins and all I could muster were dribs and drabs. It wasn't until the fifth day in the Peninsula when the clouds parted, the swells died, and we glimpsed slivers of blue sky. By this time, we'd returned north to Deception

Island, a haven stuck in the middle of the Bransfield Strait, technically part of the South Shetlands. Deception is one of only three volcanic centers in the region, having previously erupted—as far as we know—in 1842, 1871, 1912, 1956, 1967, 1969, and 1970. In the 1970 blast many people were killed. Let's hope it doesn't erupt today—replacing weather as our most dreaded foe.

Deception is shaped like a donut with a bite taken out of its southeastern end—an opening called Neptune's Bellows, which leads into the most protected and, perhaps, the most famous anchorage in the region. The island's circumference is approximately twenty-five miles. The early sealers gave Deception its name because the narrow opening is so easily missed. The entrance has been called Hell's Gate, Dragon's Mouth, or Challenger Pass—and gained its present appellation from early American sealers impressed by the howling wind funneling through this crack. When entering the caldera it's imperative to stick to the starboard side of the Bellows because of the submerged rock in the middle of the channel. The hazard caught a spate of victims before it was charted and word of the danger spread. Off to port, one casualty—a wrecked whale catcher, *Southern Hunter*—lies rusting and crumbling on the shoreline.

This precise spot is called Entrance Point and I hardly notice the few hundred chinstraps nesting on the higher slopes. A squadron of pintado petrels leads us forward, as they have for most of our time in the Peninsula. These fifteen-inch-long, black-and-white fulmarine petrels are obvious and regular ship-groupies in the Antarctic, and many nest on the yellow-brown cliffs above the Bellows. The donut surrounds Deception's circular, sunken caldera—called Port Foster, which is now filled with seawater. Henry Foster was the British navy scientist who conducted magnetic, astronomical, and gravity observations at Deception from the vessel *Chanticleer* in 1829. This vast, protected anchorage is six miles long from northwest to southeast and up to three and a half miles wide. After passing the Bellows, we turn to starboard and enter Whaler's Bay. The French explorer Charcot gave the bay its name, memorializing its heavy use by whalers at the turn of the twentieth century.

The Whaler's Bay beach is a typical Deception landscape: volcanic ash and cinders of various sizes, strewn for miles on end. Several meltwater streams descend from snow and glaciers topping the donut, cutting channels through the ash. Strong, sulfurous steam rises from hot springs along the shoreline. The off-and-on volcanic activity has occasionally heated the water in Port Foster to extreme levels. Indeed, there are records of superheated water stripping paint from ships lying at anchor. Onshore, rusting boilers and dilapidated buildings date from shore-based whaling operations that began here in 1912 and ended in 1931. There also are remnants of the British base destroyed in the 1970 eruption. But penguins are rather scarce *inside* Deception—the water's too warm. Any passing krill is likely to be boiled. The prime penguin breeding locations lie on the *outside* of Deception's ring, where there is much better access to the sea. My frustration mounts. When will my magic penguin moments finally come?

The unmodulated black-and-white scenery is awesome, with Deception's higher reaches enveloped in fog and mystery. The high rim of the island has an average elevation of almost a thousand feet. The highest points are Mt. Pond at 1,798 feet to the east, and Mt.

Kirkwood at 1,522 feet to the southwest. Above an elevation of 300 feet, the cinder motif yields to glaciers and ash-covered ice, which reach the sea at many places along the coastline. History oozes from Deception's volcanic pores: Nathaniel Palmer, the famous Yankee fur-sealer, likely made the first detailed examination of Deception's shoreline in 1820. Louis Gain and Jean-Baptiste Étienne Auguste Charcot visited here in 1909 in the midst of the penguin-prominent Second French Antarctic Expedition. Thomas Bagshawe and Maxime Lester, who would complete the first natural history study of brushtailed penguins, communed with the chinstrap penguins on the *outside* of Deception in 1920. Hubert Wilkins made his Antarctic flight from these shores in 1928.

I'm glad the skies have cleared, but I don't want to squander another day within the caldera. The general plan was to take passengers to Whaler's Bay, then up to the north end of Port Foster to visit Pendulum Cove and the site of the 1970 eruption. Frank Todd, who'd lectured many times on the *Discoverer*, was similarly rasping at the bit—and he had a plan. He'd arranged a little side excursion for the two of us. While passengers were ashore, we'd be whisked by Zodiac back to the Bellows, to explore the small chinstrap colony at Deception's entrance. There wasn't enough time to get to the *really* huge chinstrap colonies located here—especially the Baily Head colony at the southeastern side of the donut, but I appreciated Frank's generosity. He was the dreamer who'd planned and developed Sea World's *Penguin Encounter* exhibits, and now he was facilitating my first bout of quality penguin time.

I recall everything: In a flash, we're on the *Discoverer's* loading platform, then off and away. Speeding across the bay, we aim for the wrecked whale-catcher just inside the Bellows. About twenty chinstraps are scattered across the Entrance Point beach, with single animals and occasionally pairs coming ashore all the time. We off-load quickly and the Zodiac speeds back to the ship. If there are no snags, Frank and I will have three or four hours until the passengers are finished. There's little wave action, just a slight ripple, and it's easy to see the chinstraps swimming-in underwater as they reach the beach. On the edges of the beach, two southern giant petrels drool over a fresh penguin carcass that's just washed ashore. Soon, the GPs will be immersed, bloodying their faces with penguin gore.

Frank quickly races uphill, but I start much more deliberately. I remove my life jacket, placing it safely inside the catcher, and begin to pull my camera gear, field notebook, and binoculars from my backpack. I'm ready for penguin adventure. This is what I've been waiting for—and I don't want to miss a thing. A chinstrap swims in and jumps out, landing at my feet. No matter. It utters a growling *oork* and moves upbeach, stops, and begins squeegeeing seawater from its right wing. It turns to me, then continues its preening. It will have a steep climb back to its nest. The slope rises quickly to an angle exceeding 30 degrees. The upper reaches are extensively pock-marked by huge volcanic bombs and debris. The lowest chinstrap nests are more than a hundred feet above the beach. One prominent feature is a huge, thirty-foot-tall tuff boulder, which stands alone and has a circular gouge cut right through its middle. It lies upslope to my right. Chinstraps are descending and rising on either side of the tuff boulder.

I'm quickly taken by these chinstraps. They're a bit smaller than

I've imagined—two feet tall and rising to just above my knee cap. Much is going through my head—too much to process, as I try to remember all I've read in Murphy and elsewhere about these guys. Plunging out of the water, they quickly assume an upright position, showing off the neat black line running across their throat, from one side of their black head to the other. Emile G. Racovitza, on Gerlache's *Belgica* expedition, thought the cheek-line was reminiscent of "the sketchy moustache of a musketeer" and noted that this penguin was "a bad and boisterous neighbor and a strict individualist, constantly quarreling over its personal property." Murphy thought the cheek-line gave the chinstrap a "truculent look quite in keeping with its character," which differs from the more docile Johnny—or gentoo penguin—who "exhibits the wisdom and calm of a philosopher, and enjoys the opportunity for leisure that always results from a well-organized social system."

Chinstraps have this curious gait composed of quick, hobbling movements. It's not one loping step, then another. Rather, their feet, bobbing heads, and flippers are coordinated in a short, two-step swagger, with waddling and rocking from side to side—*ta-doo, ta-doo, ta-doo.* I guess they can't help their lack of knees. In Murphy's words: "When hurrying along a more or less level surface, it usually brings its wings into play synchronously instead of alternately. The result is a form of progression that resembles rowing. With each stroke the body of the bird bobs up and then falls forward." The term *pompous gait,* coined by penguin researcher Dietland Müller-Schwarze, refers to a chinstrap who is foot-stomping and waddling around a nest in front of its mate.

Murphy reports that the bossiness of chinstraps was noted as early as 1902–4, by naturalists on Bruce's Scottish National Expedition, which spent considerable time among chinstraps in the South Orkney Islands between the South Shetlands and South Georgia. The chinstraps were always jockeying both the gentoos and the Adélies. Murphy, working at South Georgia, found the chinstraps to be totally fearless: "It is the only penguin that cannot easily be outmaneuvered by a smart dog and the only one that will deliberately attack a dog. It believes equally in getting in the first blow against man and will often open fire without provocation, either on land or ice-floe. Sometimes a bird will rush forward furiously, jump, and fasten on to a human intruder well above the tops of his sea boots. The visible expression of ferocity is similar to that of an Adélie Penguin, an enraged bird raising its bristling mane, and 'growling.' A visit to a colony of this species is always likely to be a parlous adventure."

OK—I'm ready for chinstrap danger. As I walk uphill, I'm accompanied by one of the returning chinnies. I'm a few feet ahead and every time I stop, it stops. Like walking your dog. A Pavlovian game. No problem if I keep moving, but the chinstrap doesn't want to miss a thing—and it halts if I momentarily catch a breath or turn to check something along the route. After the fourth of these stops-and-starts, it bows low, utters a low hiss, raises its beak skyward, then leers at me with its penetrating gaze. It is very curious. It must be a totally different experience among thousands of these jaunty characters. I recall accounts of locations that had huge numbers of chinstraps. In 1922, Hubert Wilkins reported extreme numbers of them at Zavodovski Island, which lies in the South Sandwich Islands, well beyond the South Shetlands at the far end of the Scotia

Arc. Zavodovski is a conical, volcanic island, with rising blue vapor that Wilkins reported having absolutely no effect on the chinstraps. It's a colony presently estimated at a half a million breeding pairs. Wilkins found Zavodovski and nearby icebergs jam-packed with chinstraps. He observed chinstraps crowding along the waterline, leaping more than three feet to gain a better foothold—and in so doing, often pushing others into the water. There will be many fewer today at Entrance Point—but no complaints. The footing is thus far excellent and the steep climb is easily negotiated. To starboard, I pass an undulating line of chinstraps descending to the beach. The moment tingles, weirdly. I think of all the time I've spent doing *something other than chinstraps*. How could I have waited so long? I have a feeling I'm staking some new claim, leaving behind the fog of too many years dealing with other people's presumed aspirations for me.

My reverie is interrupted by a single, boisterous chinstrap that breaks from the first nesting group. It saunters immediately to my feet, and begins squawking wildly and loudly, checking my bona fides. It waves its head energetically left and right and approaches closer and closer, until it is forcibly stabbing my boots and leg— just as I'd been led to believe they might. *Hell-o*. Bold and pugnacious, this pompous chinstrap is giving me a thorough going-over— a border guard inspecting my passport and ID card, attempting to verify whether I have any legitimate reason for entering this country, this nation of noisy, squabbling, raucous, smelly penguins.

My boot-grabbing, two-foot-tall chinnie weighs about eight or nine pounds. Its five-inch-long tail, which can have twelve to fourteen feathers, quivers left and right, then is lowered to the ground for a little balance. The toenails are two and a half to three inches long, clawing right into the ground. The exposed part of the bill is about two inches long, with another inch, back to the gape, densely clothed with dense, short feathers.

The white breast and chubby belly aren't covered with too much guano and grime, so I guess it's recently returned to relieve its mate. It also finds my presence to be a totally intolerable intrusion. I remember Murphy's description of these stiff-tailed penguins—the three species that were about to take over my life: "Nor is the noisiness all bluster, for the Ringed Penguin has the universal reputation of being the boldest, most pugnacious, and most agile member of its genus, if not, indeed of the whole penguin tribe. The relative reactions of the three species of *Pygoscelis,* when brought face to face with man, might be broadly characterized as follows: the Johnny Penguin turns tail, the Adélie stands his ground; the Ringed Penguin charges." The din is earsplitting—yells of *duh-ARGH'-ARGH'-ARGH', duh-ARGH'-ARGH'-ARGH'* erupting from many of the adults. An incredible racket. A quick glance at the nests reveals a slew of two- to three-week-old chicks, all freestanding and no longer able to fit within their parents' brood pouch.

I think, too, of L. Harrison Matthews, who cleverly recounts in his book *Penguin, Whalers, and Sealers* when he saw his first penguin—a stray magellanic penguin—on a warm, lovely beach near Rio de Janeiro. But reading on, the gist is that this penguin-in-the-surf had interrupted Matthews's time with a strikingly beautiful woman named Dolores. Throughout his book—and especially when he's describing how the slime and grime of working with whales and seals got to be a bit nasty—thoughts of this once-in-a-lifetime lady keep erupting in Matthews's head. Matthews had worked on the

British Discovery Investigations, and had visited Deception in 1927. I really don't know the sex of my new friend, but for some reason I start addressing it as Dolores.

Dolores backs off a bit and stops screaming altogether when I sit down, effectively reducing my height closer to chinstrap eye level. The atmosphere changes—and I gain a better look at Dolores's particulars—black on the back, white in front, and that thin black line traversing its white chin, very reminiscent of Buckingham Palace guards. More of Murphy pops forward: The salt water dripping off the tips of Dolores's bill, indicative of penguins' built-in osmosis system, which allows them to drink and process seawater. The extremely short feathers packed close to the body, which trap air and keep the birds insulated. Dolores is feathered everywhere and its problem won't be the cold. It will be overheating. The only vents for excess heat are the feet, the small bare area at the base of the bill, and the veins running close to the feathers on the undersides of the wings. Dolores circles me clockwise. A few additional chinstraps race over, but none stays as transfixed or as close as Dolores. I'm pleased its aggression has loosened, replaced by an abundance of bows and stares, and occasional pokes and now gentle nibbles at my parka.

Then, this invitation: Dolores lifts from a very deep bow and aims its thick beak toward the crowded assembly of nesting chinstraps. Dolores begins ascending, at first leisurely, looking back one time at me, then bursts forward into a full scamper. I'm not sure chinstraps have thoughts, but the behavior suggests something like: *OK, I've shown this guy—now I'm outta here before there's real trouble.* I follow Dolores uphill. All around, chinstraps. I sit again and find it ridiculously easy to examine them closely, discern their penguin attributes: Bristly tongue and mouth for holding prey. Pinkish feet. Meager stone nests. Fat, tightly feathered bellies hiding a thin blubber layer.

One chinnie backsteps over the edge of its low pebble nest, slowly lifts and raises its tail, then casually blasts its nearest neighbor with pinkish guano, which spews in a long, milky stream from its black cloaca. Why black-colored cloacae? They are pinkish in gentoos and Adélies. The pearly-gray chicks look fat and healthy. Arthur G. Bennett, the acting government naturalist on the Falklands from 1924 to 1938—who also worked in the Peninsula—noted that chinstrap nests could be flooded with meltwater and eggs would still hatch successfully. Murphy found that, unlike Adélie and gentoo chicks, chinstrap chicks were less prone to gathering in large groups when fully grown, and stuck closer to their home territories: "Such behavior is perhaps to be associated with the prolonged state of dispute concerning property rights, the eager pugnacity, skill in combat, unequaled vociferousness, and generally dominating personality of the doughty little species." I want to know more about chinstraps' breeding strategy.

Frank is at the top end of this small colony, notebook in hand, busily counting nests and recording the ages of the chicks. Over his shoulder, out in the Bransfield, huge tabular icebergs gleam. The entire hillside is stained with pink penguin guano. The chinstraps' krill-fishing obviously has been good. Large patches of the green algae, *Prasiola crispa*, bloom profusely and claim ground the chinstraps haven't appropriated. But these are distractions. I can't turn away from the penguins. I've never had wild animals walking—or more accurately, charging—right up to me, trying to take control. They may be a bit smaller in stature than I'd conjured—but they are at least two orders of magnitude louder. Many believe they're the noisiest voices in penguindom. James Weddell, who explored the South Shetlands, South Orkneys, and South Georgia in the early nineteenth century, called the penguins he encountered *stonecrackers*. They must have been chinstraps. I am surrounded by a howling potpourri, all seemingly unglued, screaming at maximum volume, each one trying to outyell the other. It's a disease spreading quickly from one nest to the next: One adult raises its beak skyward, spreading wings, waving its head violently back and forth as its lungs loosen with its cadenced *duh-ARGH'-ARGH'-ARGH'*, *duh-ARGH'-ARGH'-ARGH'*. Then its closest neighbor picks up the chant. Soon, two thirds of the throng is screaming. It's a competition—none in unison, all of them informing others: *This is my space, dammit—don't even think of coming near me*. Their piercing brownish-yellow eyes ooze a demonic chinstrap rage. Perhaps next time I'll remember earplugs.

These raucous, picturesque, wing-waving exhibitions are *ecstatic displays*. Edward Wilson, the esteemed biologist who perished with Scott on their return from the South Pole in 1912, first coined the phrase. In chinstraps, the ecstatic display is both an advertisement for mates, performed by both sexes, and a territorial claim. Chinstraps announce their respective ownership claims deafeningly. With them, I'd prefer calling it a *volcanic* display. A big photograph of raucous chinstraps should go right next to the definition of *cacophony* in each and every dictionary.

It is an amazing neighborhood. A chinstrap returning to its nest in the middle of the colony runs a gauntlet. The incubating chinstraps it passes defend their nests like fictional superheroes. There's only a small zone of comfort between nests—no more than a flipper length. One returning chinnie tries standing as tall as possible—a *slim walk*—to get through unscathed, it hopes. But tempers are hot. If there's a misstep, neighbors pummel the returning bird relentlessly with their hard wings, stab it with their beaks—quick as cobras. I see one chinstrap being pulled away by the lips. They are the neighbors from hell.

All the neighbors appear to shoot their guano randomly. One incubating chinstrap ejects right into a neighbor's face. The penguin on the receiving end immediately shakes the pink mess away, or at least, as much as it possibly can. But there's no retaliation. This goes on all of the time, obviously—just part of the routine.

My first moments with these up-front, in-your-face penguins defined an indelible attachment. You've got to love an animal that makes no bones about sussing you out from top to bottom—and who then, thankfully, leaves you in one piece. They brim over the top with sass, noise, curiosity, and *attitude*. If I reincarnate somehow as a penguin, I want to be a chinstrap.

I want to sort through more chinstrap behavior. And I greatly want to check out the additional groups that extend into the distance, around Deception's western perimeter. It is such an eerie place: a black-and-white, sleepy volcanic behemoth, ready to blow again at any time, with steep and evil terrain everywhere. Beyond and upslope, the footing is more challenging. I later discover that these exact same chinstrap groups were regularly visited by whalers and explorers who came to Deception early in the century. Louis Gain had recorded macaroni penguins at Entrance Point in 1909, but none are now present. Thomas Bagshawe was plagued with a horrible case of vertigo among these chinnies. He recounts extreme difficulty getting to the higher reaches at Entrance Point. He was egging at the time, sweating profusely and visibly shaking, quite fearful he and his basket of penguin eggs might go plummeting over the side. He admired the chinstraps' predilection for higher ground, as well as their mountaineering skills, neither of which he could fairly emulate. In this regard, the most apt description comes from L. H. Valette, who'd worked extensively at Argentine meteorological stations in the South Orkneys. Valette knew chinstraps well and had written in 1906 that they were the alpinists among the Antarctic penguins.

It was a shame Bagshawe couldn't enjoy his Deception egging as others had. Arthur G. Bennett would always carry bread and butter in his boat when he went to collect. After gathering his prizes, he'd put two fresh eggs in a container, which he'd drop into Deception's boiling, volcanic water—and eventually produce some lovely fresh egg sandwiches.

The few hundred nests Frank and I peruse are many fewer than have existed in earlier times, when chinstrap eggs were filling the ships' larders. But an exact nest count proves impossible because the weather goes to hell in a handbasket. In less than an hour, with little notice and rather amazingly, the blue sky clicks over to dark gray clouds and a howling blow, announcing precipitation. The snow comes horizontally, quickly. Now, finally, proof of the adage I've heard: If you like the weather in Antarctica—just wait ten minutes. Our visibility reduces to zero in less than three. Through the blinding flakes, I see incubating chinstraps turning backs to the wind, sheltering chicks. Footing becomes horribly slippery almost instantly and we are very uncomfortable, totally bared to the elements. Frank suggests retreating to the wrecked whale-catcher on the shoreline, which still has enough metal sheeting to protect us from the gale. We slip-slide away and downslope, not too embarrassed by the endless procession of chinstraps continuing to move up and down, oblivious to the storm: Surefooted. Taking advantage of their long toenails. Unperturbed, in their pompous procession.

We stand for hours, shivering—with penguins running over the beach and filling my brain. I am consumed, trying to compare the reality of the last fifty minutes with my years of reading and preparation. The three brushtailed, northern Peninsula penguins share a similar black-and-white coloration. Gentoos are actually the third largest of all penguins, ranging up to thirty-five inches tall and between ten and nineteen pounds. The other two brushtaileds are slightly over two feet tall, chinstraps up to thirty inches and seven to eleven pounds, depending on the season, and Adélies up to twenty-eight inches and eight to fifteen pounds, at varying times during the year. They all exude a certain chubbiness, though chinstraps seem the trimmest and least bulky of the three. Adélies are the ones who look like little tuxedoed animals: Prominent white eye ring set against an all-black head, and a sharp division between the white of the belly and breast and the black of the head and back. Chinstraps also bear the basic black back and white front, but the face is white and is bisected by its characteristic thin black strap. Gentoos bear white patches on their heads and a bright red-orange bill.

Through DNA analysis, there are presently believed to be seventeen species of penguins—the family known as the *Spheniscidae*. They're tucked in between loons and frigatebirds on the evolutionary chart, and closely related to their northern flying relations, the auks and guillemots. Five species—Adélie, chinstrap, gentoo, macaroni, and emperor—breed in Antarctica. Regarding Adélies, chinstraps, and gentoos, more than a quarter of each species' worldwide population nests in the Peninsula and South Shetlands region, according to estimates in the early 1990s: Adélies—692,536 pairs out of a worldwide population of 2,465,800 pairs. Chinstraps—2,189,640 pairs out of a worldwide population of 7,490,200 pairs. Gentoos—80,645 pairs out of a worldwide population of 314,000 pairs. Macaronis may be found at scattered locations—Elephant Island, Livingston Island, a few are still rumored to be found at Deception Island—but their breeding stronghold, almost twelve million pairs, is at South Georgia, just below the Antarctic Convergence. The world's 195,400 pairs of emperor penguins breed mostly on the eastern side of the Weddell Sea and on the Ross Sea side of the continent, though a small group of less than a hundred pairs nests at the Dion Islands, south of Adelaide Island, below the Antarctic Circle. One recent estimate suggests that the five species normally inhabiting the Antarctic region have a combined biomass of greater than three hundred million metric tons.

Penguins were undoubtedly first seen by non-Europeans—Fuegians, Tasmanians, or other aboriginal peoples. There are suspicions of seventh-century, far southern journeys by Polynesians. But nothing was recorded. All of this is an oral history that has passed and been spun from generation to generation. We'll never know when that first sighting precisely occurred. Because of the many fossil penguin discoveries in the Australian–New Zealand region, as well as the long tradition of Maori names for these animals, one might surmise that these people were the first to know penguins well. Many Maori names survive, including one of my favorites—*hoiho*—for the forest-dwelling, yellow-eyed penguin. By contrast, it wasn't until the late fifteenth century, when Portuguese expeditions explored navigable routes around the Cape of Good Hope, that Europeans likely saw their first penguin, in this case the African black-footed penguin.

The Maori also generated the first fossil penguin discoveries. In the 1860s, south of the village of Oamaru on the east coast of New Zealand's South Island, the quarrying of limestone beds for building materials began, ultimately assuming some economic importance. The area's name is Kakanui. Non-natives had certainly known about these quarries from earlier Maori activity, which had proceeded in this area on a much smaller scale. In the late 1850s, a Maori discovered a fossil bone in the Kakanui beds, which was transferred to a local authority, Dr. W. B. D. Mantell. His expertise was fossil moa bones. Suspecting something unusual, Mantell in turn transferred the specimen to Thomas Henry Huxley at the British Museum in London.

What Huxley then described copiously in an 1859 article was the wholly unique, primary foot bone of penguins, called a *tarsometatarsus*—and a totally amazing extinct penguin, *Palaeeudyptes antarcticus*, from the Early Oligocene, about thirty-five million years old. It probably stood around four feet tall. The tarsometatarsus is a compound, fused bone that is found at approximately the location where ankle and heel connect to our tarsus. Each and every penguin species has this characteristically shaped tarsometatarsus. Later on, while rummaging through various and sundry penguin colonies to do censuses, I've commonly found numerous tarsometatarsi—as opposed to complete penguin skeletons, which are impossible to discover. If they're going to die on land, penguins are usually scavenged and pulled apart, leaving little intact, except their fused foot bones.

The name *penguin* is an outright misnomer. It was first applied to the great auk of the northern hemisphere, *Pinguinus impennis*, now extinct. The derivation may come from the Welsh *pen gwyn*—white-headed—but great auks were black-headed. The name more likely derives from the Latin *pinguis*, meaning fat. This has some sense to it. Louis Gain claimed the name was first used by Spanish navigators of the seventeenth century, who called them *pinguinos*, which comes from *pengüigo*, meaning grease—of course, referring to the abundance of fat they possess. The more recently used Spanish word *pingüe* refers to the fat profit one might make from a business transaction.

For unrecorded, quite unknown reasons, the name then transferred to the southern hemisphere flightless animals we now know as penguins, a currency that certainly was in fashion during Thomas Cavendish's third circumnavigation of the world, 1586–88, on *Desire*. By the seventeenth century *penguin* was in full usage and has now become the standard. The eighteenth-century French naturalist Comte de Buffon thought it quite ridiculous to name southern hemisphere birds for a northern hemisphere species, and thus, he proposed the name *manchot*, meaning one-armed, undoubtedly referring to the penguins' flight-deficit disorder. But of course, they have two arms—wings, sometimes called flippers. The French also use *pinguoin*. The Spanish—reported by Gain—*pingui-*

nos has become *pingüino*. And there are the Portuguese *pingüim*, the German *pinguin*, the Italian *pinguino*, and similar-sounding words in Greek, Russian, and other languages. The Czech word for penguin is *tucňák*, the fat one.

All penguins are southern latitude animals, though the small, black-and-white Galápagos penguin straddles the Equator and fairly regularly crosses north of the line. There are various breeding strategies: Emperor penguins lay a single egg annually, king penguins a single egg semiannually, and the others lay two eggs. However, in the group of crazily plumed penguins called the *Eudyptes*, the crested penguins, the first egg is much smaller than the second and this *alpha* egg or the chick from this first egg quickly succumbs—often to its more dominant sibling.

No doubt, when Antarctica was much younger—and when it possessed a much warmer climate—penguins had a much different lifestyle. The fossil record is incredible, suggesting more than forty prior species. The *Spheniscidae* probably erupted in the Late Cretaceous period, anywhere from 60 to 140 million years ago. Moving forward, there is evidence of penguins from the Late Paleocene or Early Eocene periods, 50 to 60 million years ago. By the Late Eocene, 40 million years ago, many ancestral penguin species had evolved. The only fossil found thus far in the Peninsula region is from Seymour Island in the Weddell Sea, *Anthropornis nordenskjoeldi*. It was collected by Gunnar Andersson during Nordenskjöld's 1903–5 Swedish Antarctic Expedition. This brute of a penguin dates from the Late Eocene and stood between five and five and a half feet tall. The eminent paleontologist and penguin paleobiologist George Gaylord Simpson estimated that a well-fed *nordenskjoeldi* might have weighed three hundred pounds. Of today's penguins, the emperor is the largest, weighing in at about ninety pounds and four feet tall, and the smallest is the little penguin, which is not bigger than a backyard starling. Among chinstraps, Adélies, and gentoos, the range is from seven pounds—a slim chinstrap female that's just completed her clutch—to just under nineteen pounds—a fattened gentoo that's about to molt.

Weights aside, the seventeen species break into six genera: emperor and king penguins, the *Aptenodytes;* the four *Spheniscus* penguins, vernacularly known as jackass, banded, or black-and-white penguins; the six *Eudyptes*—or crested—penguins, which have wild orange or yellow plumes flowing from their heads, devilish red eyes, and who resemble barflies who have had one too many drinks at the local pub; *Eudyptula,* the little penguin; *Megadyptes,* the unusual yellow-eyed penguin; and the three *Pygoscelids*—the chinstraps, Adélies, and gentoos, which I know best of all. In Greek, *Pygoscelis* means "rump-legged," which, George Gaylord Simpson notes, also makes us humans *pygoscelids*—whose legs erupt from our bums. The three *Pygoscelids* possess stiff tails and are collectively referred to as the *brushtailed* penguins.

In the winter of 1911 three members of Scott's *Terra Nova* Expedition—Edward Wilson, Birdie Bowers, and Apsley Cherry-Garrard—unlocked the breeding secrets of emperor penguins. Sadly, Wilson and Bowers would die during the following austral summer, along with Commander Scott, Titus Oates, and Edgar Evans, on their return from the South Pole. Cherry-Garrard dubbed the exploratory venture to Cape Crozier *The Worst Journey in the World,* which became the title of his classic Antarctic book. Cherry-Garrard's writing is characteristically humble and the reader understands why he was Wilson's "right-hand man" and the number two biologist in rank on the Scott Expedition. Through guts and hard knocks—not a university Ph.D. in biology—Cherry-Garrard had earned the admiration of the others, and had advanced to an outstandingly high position under Commander Scott.

The Crozier story is remarkable: This historic emperor trek transpired in the dead of the Antarctic darkness. It had been believed that emperor penguin embryos would increase our understanding of evolution. Alas, the three tromped and trudged through many weeks of hardship to reach the Cape, collect their eggs and, somehow, return to safety. As it happened, the emperor eggs unlocked no particular evolutionary mysteries. In fact, Cherry-Garrard had difficulties getting the British Museum to accept the eggs.

The very substantial upside, however, was our first detailed information about this penguin's strange habits. Nearing the onset of winter, the female lays a single egg and immediately transfers it to her mate. In this species, the male is solely charged with incubation duties during the long Antarctic winter. What a deal: The males get to endure the most extreme and harshest circumstances of any animal on the planet. Huddling in large crèches— or *tortues*—to keep warm. Losing a third or more of their body weight. Shivering and shrinking, while the emperesses are far to the north, presumably enjoying better and warmer weather, eating fish and squid and getting fat and happy. The females won't return until the chicks hatch in the early austral spring, in October. If they're late, the males must nourish the chick with a reserve of stomach oil. When the female finally makes it home, he'll take to sea to fatten, and then return to assist in rearing the chick. But again, she takes the first long stint, to two weeks or longer. The bottom line: The females set the agenda, and I don't think it's off base to argue that a more apt, vernacular name for this penguin would be *emperess* penguin. The females are fully in charge—and have been for a long time, perhaps the planet's first truly liberated feminists.

By contrast, the brushtailed mates share the family-planning and child-care arrangements. It's hard work and they operate on a tight, two- to three-month schedule, which necessarily dictates feverish activity. As the pack breaks, chinstraps and Adélies must furiously race home. The geographical range of Adélies includes the entire Antarctic continent. Chinstraps concentrate on the northwestern side of the Antarctic, on the exposed ocean edges of islands on which they breed. The gentoos, whose southern limit is Petermann Island, range all the way north, across the Drake Passage, to South Georgia, the Falkland Islands, Kerguelen Island, Heard Island, and Macquarie Island. There are two gentoo subspecies—the smaller *ellsworthii* in the Peninsula and South Shetlands, the larger *papua* at the northern outposts.

The brushtaileds breed on land. Nests are mere scrapes on the ground, which often are ringed with greater or lesser numbers of pebbles and stones. The Adélies are rigorously site-specific, returning to the exact location where they bred the previous season—but they often change mates. Timing is everything with Adélies: The male needs to return plumped and ready to go as soon as the snow clears, and the female needs to get back in very short order—because he won't wait for her. No second chances: If last season's mate doesn't show quickly, he'll pair with any available female he can find. The pair bond is fragile. The gentoos' relationships, however, are the most stable among the brushtaileds: There are relatively few divorces. The mates often move their nesting sites, but they'll do it together. They also may stay with each other during the winter. Chinstraps are more like Adélies—married to pebbles, but with a slightly stronger pair bond, allowing some leeway to females in timing their returns. As for breeding sites, certain preferences emerge. Chinstraps are the mountain climbers, often taking the loftiest sites, hundreds of feet up. Adélies take slightly lower sites, and gentoos most often seem to take the lowest levels. However, there's much overlap and, at some places, gentoos may claim sites at least two hundred feet above the tide line.

Arthur G. Bennett describes the penguin's short time ashore as moments consumed with "feeding, fighting, courting, thieving, and philandering." Female brushtaileds normally lay two eggs, which commences their similar, shared incubation and feeding routines. Gentoos, unlike chinstraps and Adélies, will lay again if the first clutch of two eggs is lost. The brushtailed chicks hatch after slightly more than a month of incubation. Adults brood and guard the chicks for two to three weeks, the chicks then assemble in crèches, and parents continue feeding them for at least six to seven weeks. After seven to eight weeks, Adélie and chinstrap chicks leave the breeding grounds and take to sea, no longer fed by their parents, and presumably migrating as self-sufficient birds. Gentoo chicks are much less independent. Young gentoos gradually learn to forage on their own, going to sea at about eight weeks, but continue to return each night to be fed by one of their parents. By their tenth week of life, they must be fully independent because both parents then come ashore to molt, and can no longer provide any more food. The vast majority of chicks never return. A 20 percent return at age three would be high.

On land, penguin adults and chicks often have to run the gauntlet of marauding sheathbills and skuas, but there aren't any polar bears or arctic foxes to wreak havoc in their land-based colonies. The planet's divergent evolution took the land predators in one direction, so northern birds adapted, growing wings. South, the worst predators were at sea, so the penguins learned to fly through the water. After the chicks leave, the parents get a much deserved chance to rest, to feed and replenish their own energy, and then to molt before leaving for the winter. Adding up the days, the brushtaileds spend only about a fourth of their lives on land.

Finally the *World Discoverer* rounds the corner, turns out into the open ocean, and drops a Zodiac to reenter the Bellows and retrieve us. I am numb and soaked—and totally jazzed. It's been a great first blast, fifty solid chinstrap minutes that changed everything. It was a sealed deal from that point forward, a commitment to spreading the word about this special place and these very exceptional animals. I've never shaken Cherry-Garrard's notion about that special band of people he dubbed *Antarcticists*—all mercilessly afflicted with the Antarctic bacillus and possessing unremitting confidence about changing the world. It was conviction tagged to a lofty ideal: "For we are a nation of shopkeepers, and no shopkeeper will look at research which does not promise him a financial return within a year. And so you will sledge nearly alone, but those with whom you sledge will not be shopkeepers: that is worth a good deal. If you march your Winter Journeys you will have your reward, so long as all you want is a penguin's egg."

I, too, was infected and my intentions had certainly clarified, though I had no illusions about changing the world.

I wanted more stonecrackers.

And, ultimately, to contribute something to Antarctica.

THREE

Fistfuls of Penguins

[M]an can behave arrogantly not only by deifying his own ego and proclaiming himself the finest flower of matter and life, but equally when he proudly believes that he has correctly comprehended the incomprehensible or uttered the unutterable, or when he thinks up infallible dogmas and with his intellect, which wants to believe, reaches out into regions before which he should lower his eyes and stand in silence.

—IVAN KLÍMA

I count penguins.

Not the most common profession, admittedly—and I suspect no more than a relative handful claim this line of work. And certainly not, when I was fourteen, what I expected to be doing when I hit thirty and forty.

My shipboard lecturing had moved quickly to expedition-leading and, when I burned out at that, to writing books and newsletters, participating on the U.S. delegation to the Antarctic Treaty meetings—and now, compiling baseline information about locations I'd been visiting for years. The project is called the Antarctic Site Inventory and relates to the *Protocol on Environmental Protection to the Antarctic Treaty,* which entered into force in January 1998. The new accord commits participating countries to environmental assessments of *all* human activities before they take place. The expectation is that an a priori vetting of possibilities allows an activity's proponent to take steps that will reduce potential adverse environmental impacts to a minimum—or avoid them altogether.

The Antarctic Treaty entered into force in 1961. It is a testament to humankind's best instincts and a masterpiece of brevity, a mere fourteen articles contained in three pages of text. At present, forty-three countries, representing more than 75 percent of the world's population, subscribe to it. Twenty-seven of these parties are original signatories or undertake significant science operations, and all must reach consensus before any Treaty-wide action is taken. Of course, consensus often means that action and progress is painfully slow. But the Treaty has endured and prospered for more than thirty-five years, maintaining the Seventh Continent and the waters below latitude 60 degrees south as a bastion of peace, science, and now sensible environmental awareness and conservation. All territorial claims are held in abeyance. Access is guaranteed to all who can get to Antarctica safely and responsibly.

All told, the Treaty and adjunct agreements like the *Protocol* ensure that 10 percent of earth—what I consider to be the planet's most emotionally stirring wilderness—remains a shining jewel. Hopefully, data and information being compiled for the Inventory will assist the effort. But the questions are hard and may be difficult to answer: Are penguin and seabird numbers going up or down? Are moss beds expanding or being trampled by visitors? How does any or all of this relate to natural fluctuations in weather and climate, the extent of winter sea ice, the distribution and abundance of prey species and food sources, or changes in ocean currents?

There'd been no compilation of site-specific information before the project started, and the objective is to have these baselines in place so useful comparisons can be made in future years—so any potential changes, up or down, may be detected. If changes are found, the next and much harder line of inquiry is to pinpoint the reasons, which becomes extremely complicated because these sites, mirroring the Antarctic as a whole, likely experience a variety of natural perturbations and variations. I've seen an entire cohort of penguin chicks at one location collapse—bodies strewn everywhere, death in the air. Next season, though, all had returned to some semblance of normality. Actually, I'm not sure that *normal* is a word that can be used in any of these discussions. We've been visiting the Antarctic for less than a century, and the geological record suggests that the changes have been enormous and have transpired over many centuries, literally over aeons.

Presumably, to the extent that tourism locations are involved, part of the analysis will require some assessment of how penguin, seabird, and seal populations and floral communities—lichens and mosses— have fared, referring to some extent back to the baselines being collected. This applies the pressure. It's important to ensure that the data we're collecting are assembled rigorously and systematically, and made readily available to be used down the line. Censuses need to be repeated from season to season, so ebbs and flows over time may be identified. The project's site descriptions and penguin counts are painstaking efforts, often requiring many visits before a site's orientation map can be satisfactorily drawn, or until a site's penguin populations are properly scoped out, identified, and mapped.

When the project began, there was a broad initiative to identify appropriate *indicator species* that could be readily followed and censused, and whose changing or constant populations would offer some insight into the nature of the location, and potentially allow changes to be spotted. In general, Adélies, chinstraps, and gentoos that are *recruited* to their respective populations return to breed where they were born—their natal colonies. When the time comes and the hormones start to run, they'll always head home. The new breeders will fill in along the edges and periphery, ultimately moving to interior and more established sites as other pairs die or split. But there were important differences affecting whether these three species would be useful indicators.

The precise bit of ground where a penguin decides to breed is, obviously, called a *nest site*. A number of nest sites may form a discrete *colony*, and a collection of these colonies at a particular location composes a *rookery*. An important key for our project is that Adélies and chinstraps are very tightly tied to a precise nest site—specific stones and turf that were the focus of their fevered breeding activity the previous season. Adélies are a bit more site-specific than chinstraps, but the generalization holds. If the pair fails, that season's breeding effort is abandoned and the mates will proceed to molt, head to sea, enjoy their winter vacation—and then return to the exact same nest site the following season. Gentoo mates, by contrast, are much more wedded to each other than to any particular nest site. If a first set of two eggs is ruined, the mates may re-lay. If disturbed altogether, they'll just move to another nest site around the corner, which may be in the same colony or in an altogether different colony within the rookery at that location. Presumably, at their new home, the gentoos will encounter fewer skuas, people, or other disruptions.

For a census project like the Inventory, therefore, these proclivities meant that we could obtain useful data on Adélies and chinstraps even if we couldn't count all of the colonies at a particular location. Their site-specific tendencies meant that we could proceed with regular censuses of countable colonies and, over time, still determine whether or not changes were occurring. It also meant that we could establish on-site comparisons between chinstrap and Adélie colonies located near a site's landing beach, which would necessarily be visited by any and all visitors, vis-à-vis *control* colonies of Adélies and chinstraps located a mile or so distant, which would receive no visitor traffic at all. Then, what potentially gets teased out are changes caused by the visitors. But this plan doesn't necessarily work for gentoos. They tend to move around, thus requiring that *all* gentoos at a particular location—that is, all colonies of them—have to be counted to gain some temporal understanding of changes that are potentially occurring.

Against this framework, there are two important censusing periods during each field season. The first is the peak of egg-laying, generally in mid-November to early December, when nest counts need to be accomplished. The second important time frame is about seven weeks later, early January to the beginning of February, when the chicks hatched that season have crèched together in large groups. They are best counted before they move to the beach and head off to sea. To facilitate reaching the sites as often as possible at these peak times, I've relied on ship-hopping between and among a number of expedition ships during their five- to seven-day expeditions, and on the British navy ice patrol ship, HMS *Endurance*.

It is a good routine: Out and about as much as possible during the eighteen- to twenty-hour-long day, carrying a basic complement of hat, sunglasses, neck gaiter, gloves, parka, layers of easily peeled, lightweight clothing, and rubber or hiking boots. The layers of T-shirts, turtlenecks, overshirts, and fleece are adjusted depending on body temperature, which scrambles constantly based on the interplay between the frigid, windy air and the overheating that naturally comes with vigorous hiking and climbing. When done, it is back to the ship to complete data sheets, revise orientation maps, tally census numbers—and, eventually, to sleep. An occasional layover at a field hut yields long moments stretching legs on stable ground, watching light dusk settle over the elderly earthscape after 11 P.M., before snuggling into sleeping bags for the short night, on unheated bunks, dreaming of a 3:30 A.M. dawn.

Yet even the most carefully arranged schedules and logistics may be easily scrambled by weather and ship breakdowns, and there are bona fide risks of missing connections altogether. But for the most part these relatively well laid plans have worked. I and my Inventory colleagues have huffed and puffed to collect as much information as possible, sometimes over miles of distance with as little time as an hour or two, occasionally having a half day or longer. I've been down and dirty with more penguins than I could ever imagine. Hustle and bustle aside, we penguin-counters are blessed with ring-side seats—the great fortune to observe the penguins' entire on-land cycle. That alone makes it an amazing job, with a suite of impressive attributes and perks.

Imagine the *noise*. It can be deafening if every chinstrap nest starts erupting in ecstatic display. My hearing was bad to begin with. Now it's worse. You can shout them down a bit, and bewilderingly, they'll settle—at least momentarily, perhaps wondering what it means to have a large visitor yelling: *Be quiet, you guys. I can't take it anymore.*

And the *smell*. It can be overpowering if you're downwind from tens of thousands of breeding penguins. In late summer, when the snow has melted, the guano mixes with mud and runoff and some locations become indescribable cauldrons of muck. This pungent brew infiltrates your gear—seemingly, to waft nasty fumes forever. On two occasions, I've offended others with my newly acquired perfume. One captain came into my quarters and started spraying deodorant around the room. In the second instance, the officers simply closed the door and ordered me to keep it shut.

Or the *sights*. The penguins are enticing in and of themselves. There's an immediate connection simply because these little guys resemble our waddling ways so much: The pompous gait of chin-straps. The tuxedoed appearance of Adélies. The gentoos who *hee-HAW* back and forth like friendly donkeys. And how 'bout those pudgy bellies? They're not bulimic, but if they didn't regurgitate the one- to two-pound loads they keep bringing to the kids, they'd explode. Add in some absolutely totally out-of-the-way, rugged landscapes and there's literally more to take in than the eye, mind, or brain can accommodate.

My knowledge of—and curiosity about—penguins' lives, habits, foibles, and tendencies has grown enormously since I first visited the Antarctic in 1983. All of my counting and censusing embellishes a matrix that grows more and more complicated. And raises the stakes. I realize that the data we collect today others will presumably use in the future. So care and accuracy are undeniable watchwords. Stripping bare the intricacies and details of the work, there is the phenomenon of connecting to the same penguins, visit after visit, season after season. Because they tend to reinhabit the same colony and nest site from the previous season, I *know* some of these chinstraps, Adélies, and gentoos very well. I therefore appreciate what Wayne and Sue Trivelpiece mean when they talk about *their* penguins at Copacabana Beach in Admiralty Bay. I've become very, very interested in the status and whereabouts of *my* study penguins. And beyond this attachment, there are new envelopes to open—the thrill of reaching locations I've never visited, sites that possibly have never been censused at all, the prospect of new data expanding the database even further.

At the end of the day, the analyses boil down to how well we penguin-counters are doing our job. I'm at the bottom of the pyramid, attempting rigorously and systematically to note where these penguins are located and to count them at key times each breeding season. I'm asked myriad reasonable questions about these efforts:

How do you count them?

The basic implement is your handheld *tally-whacker*. Slip your index finger through the loop, and your thumb lines up against a flange that pops out from the top of the counter. You depress the flange for each tally you want to make—click, click, click. A dial on the face of the counter jumps a digit every time you click. When you're finished, a spindle on the side is twisted to reset the counter to zero.

How do you keep track of penguins you've already counted? How reliable are the counts?

I keep my field notebook raised over my left eye and count by moving counterclockwise around the group or colony in question. The penguins to my right are ones I've already tallied. I try to line them up in rows, spying them with my right eye, and count either from top to bottom or bottom to top. I point my index finger at each penguin in the row and for each nest or chick my finger "touches" I tap the flange on the tally-whacker—*ka-CHING*. With practice, I get fairly speedy—*ka-CHING, ka-CHING, ka-CHING*. For statistical accuracy, it's important to get three counts. The standard censusing protocol suggests getting three counts totaling within 10 percent of one another other. We've tightened this a tad for the Inventory project—three counts with the highest no greater than 8 percent above the lowest value.

Aren't there too many penguins to handle at times? What do you do when there's a gazillion penguins in front of you? You'd be there for weeks if you tried to count every single bird or nest individually.

Sure, it can be crazy at times. And I don't spend *forever* counting them. The animals or nests may bunch too tightly and it will be difficult to sort it out. You also need to have a decent vantage point, usually high enough so you can see all the penguins in the group you're counting. It would be ideal if you could walk the perimeter of the group, see all the animals at all times, and proceed slowly from one starting point to another. Sometimes a rock in the center or on one edge of a colony will be a convenient marker noting your starting point. Sometimes I've pounded stakes next to rocks or into the ground to assist the orientation. You can't efficiently tally-whack an assemblage of nests or chicks that's greater than a few hundred strong, or perhaps complicated by uneven terrain and a lack of vantage points. If you confront thousands densely massed together, you must resort to approximations—by counting *fistfuls* or *fingerfuls* of penguins, with each fistful or fingerful of penguins containing an estimated number of nests or animals.

The peculiarities of some of these sites becomes apparent after a few visits. One of the chinstrap colonies at Baily Head is best counted from the top of a lava boulder that sits in the middle of the throng of penguins. It requires a gentle tiptoeing into the colony and onto the rock, but once you're perched the penguins will settle immediately and you can get your counts quickly and efficiently. Some counts are difficult all the time: The perimeter of chinstrap colonies *A, B,* and *Beach* at Hannah Point can't be walked easily or completely. And there's no center rock to assist the effort. By continuing until there are three counts within the required variance, you therefore ensure that the mean values are statistically meaningful.

While the data collection has proceeded for the most part aboard expedition ships, the association with *Endurance* has produced an entirely different suite of experiences. Her helicopters provide an opportunity to take aerial photographs of many of our census sites and, occasionally, to accomplish some necessary *ground-truthing*—actual, on-site counts of these photodocumented locations. The aerial photography requires practice but has great promise. Ultimately ground-truthed nest counts and nest densities may be extrapolated to enable counts from photographic prints or from versions of the photos digitized into the computer screen. There also is the promise of censusing from satellites. Right now, only penguin colonies a few hundred yards in width can be detected from satellites. But if the imagery is refined, it's possible that remote sensing will make us on-the-ground penguin-counters totally obsolete. I hope not too soon.

I've experienced one day when, in a nine-hour stretch, we encountered about a half million penguin nests—or, if everyone had been at home and in sight, roughly a million penguins. There have been times flying in the helos, lost in the clouds, slipping in and out of the fog banks, then emerging over unworked territory, where penguins have never been counted before.

The day with penguin nests bursting everywhere happened in early December 1996, off of the *World Discoverer*. I have a fond affection for this ship, which I've used regularly since the inception of the Inventory project and which, years ago, had brought me south for the first time. Then it was painted red and white. Now it's blue and white. This day my *penguin-cognition delusion* struck fiercely: There was much to process and not a lot of available time. We were visiting these colonies right before the Adélies hatched, so for the most part, one of the mates at each nest was on a feeding run offshore. A half-million nests. Up to a million individuals. Like winning the lottery.

Mind-boggling. In wonderment, my colleague Steve Forrest and I toted the numbers again—not quite believing the results. Bang on. Two mornings earlier, we'd anxiously awaited the *World Discoverer* in the wee, wee hours of the morning at Copa Beach in Admiralty Bay. The scheduled pickup was at 4 A.M. but it was *blowin' a hoolie,* as my British navy friends would say—and a retrieval was hardly assured. The cobble beach out from the hut, the normal pickup location, was awash in white foam and pounding rollers. It was a better morning for surfing than for climbing into Zodiacs.

I knew the risks tied to using the expedition ships. Being stranded is one bit of jeopardy I'd accepted in planning the logistics. Occasionally, the transfers are made at sea, via Zodiac, as two ships pass, as we leave one ship that's now heading home and join another that's just made in across the Drake. Sometimes we rely on frequently visited research stations to make the changeovers. We've also used the Copa hut in Admiralty Bay as a layover point, because it conveniently lies along the route most of the expedition ships take to the south. If the ship-hopping works, the project avoids a lot of dead time unnecessarily crossing the Drake Passage—two days up, then two more on the return. The time is better spent counting nests or chicks. All's good in theory, but of course the weather is totally unpredictable. The risk of a busted schedule is real.

Indeed, the first year of the project, my colleague Brent Houston and I were mired at Copa for two weeks because of unforeseen ship-scheduling conflicts and foul weather. On this present round, Steve and I had worried from the start about the high surf in Admiralty Bay. From the moment we'd arrived, there was much wind and spray, waves pounding high over the cobble beach in front of the hut. We were expecting to stay only a few days, but if the rollers on the beach didn't subside, our chances of making the intended rendezvous with the *Discoverer* would be seriously diminished. Copa's leader,

Wayne Trivelpiece, optimist that he is, scoffed at the pending difficulties: "Just tell them to come around Copa Rock, a half mile up the beach. There's usually a little bit of lee, just around the topside of the rock. Even in the worst of storms. The Zodiac can tuck into the corner, right at the beginning of Ipanema Beach. You'll get wet, but what the hell. It's Antarctica."

Wayne had it spot-on. At 3:30 A.M., thirty minutes ahead of schedule, Captain Oliver Kruß came booming over the radio: "Copa, Oceanites, this is *World Discoverer*. Do you copy? Are you ready?" The ship was lying straight out from the hut.

"Yes, captain, but the breakers on the beach are miserable. If you're still game, can you send the Zodiac upbeach, just around and behind the big rock? We should be able to transfer there."

Or so I'd hoped. Oliver agreed and Steve and I scrambled to load our gear into Wayne's cart. At least we could roll the gear the mile we needed to go. Indeed, a hoolie was blowin'—about forty knots out of the southeast. We were bitterly cold making our way down the beach. All, the gentoos were prone on their nests, with backs turned to the wind, sheltering their nests and eggs. A few lifted and stared—not quite recognizing the three of us lumbering over the cold turf. It took ten minutes to reach the little cove, where we found the Zodiac and the ship's third officer, Carsten Brueninghaus, awaiting us. Carsten nosed the Zodiac toward a large boulder; we tossed our bags and jumped aboard. On with life jackets; goodbye waves and shouts to Wayne; and off we went. Once beyond the brash, about fifty yards offshore, it was a relatively smooth ride to the ship. The anxiety eased.

We went to the bridge to say hello to Captain Kruß and gleaned some unanticipated news. In a few hours, right after breakfast, we'd make a three- to four-hour landing at one of our key survey sites, Penguin Island. That had been expected. The site's just "around the corner"—a little more than an hour away. But then, a big surprise. Usually, when the expedition ships cross the Drake Passage and start a five-day sojourn through the South Shetlands and the Peninsula, they keep heading south, trying to cover as much territory as possible. But Oliver had a strange twist up his sleeve. Apparently, many in the group had been promised a visit to Elephant Island, well to the northeast. So, strangely, after Penguin Island, we were backtracking to attempt a landing at Point Lookout at Elephant Island the next morning, before once again heading south. A lot of driving and a lot of extra fuel to burn—but hey, let's keep the passengers satisfied. Given how tired we were, Steve and I relished the thought of some extra sleep after the Penguin Island gig. Then, an additional surprise: After Elephant, instead of heading straight back to King George Island and south, Oliver wanted to try going north and east around Joinville Island and then south into the Weddell Sea, around the top of the Peninsula, instead of attempting the usual, more southerly entrance through the Antarctic Sound. Ice-free conditions had prevailed thus far this season, so why not?

My eyes lit. If all went well, irrespective of making a landing at Elephant, that meant we'd be in the far northwest Weddell, a very special treat—with a potential reconnaissance of the Danger Island group in the offing. This small string of islands is not well known. There have been a few recorded visits, and the northwest Weddell is usually caked with copious amounts of ice. Only a very few ships have visited this area, with reports and rumors suggesting wall-to-wall penguins. But these were colonies that had never been adequately surveyed. So, if weather and seas cooperated, we'd have a chance to do some groundbreaking survey work.

I rushed to check *The Penguin Bible*—a site-specific compilation of Antarctic penguin survey numbers that Eric Woehler presently maintains for the bird biology subcommittee of the Scientific Committee of Antarctic Research. This slim monograph has the official title *The Distribution and Abundance of Antarctic and Subantarctic Penguins*. It was published in 1993 and succeeds an earlier reference work that John Croxall and Ed Kirkwood had compiled for the British Antarctic Survey. *The Penguin Bible* is a major research tool. There's been a long-held view—and I believe it's a very proper view—that the intricacies of the Antarctic ecosystem can't be understood without firmly understanding how all of the living marine resources of the Antarctic—its various predators and their prey—function. There's considerable dynamism in the system, and until there's some handle on how many penguins, seals, and whales there are and where they're located, it will be difficult for the Antarctic Treaty Parties to make any decisions about potentially managing these resources, if it ever gets to that. It's impossible to keep track of a dynamic resource without baselines. Ultimately, penguin counts tell us a story. New censuses and data may be compared to old, changes may be detected, and then the question of pinpointing the cause of any such changes can be tackled. New sites, new censuses—all of it adds to the knowledge base.

The Penguin Bible is arranged by species, listing all sites where Adélies, gentoos, chinstraps, macaronis, and emperors have been recorded breeding, the numbers of breeding pairs estimated at each site, and the quality of the estimate. The best counts—called *"N"* counts—reflect a census of breeding pairs during incubation. As *The Penguin Bible* notes, the *N* numbers may be underestimates of the total number of breeding pairs because many pairs may have failed before a census is made and there may be pairs attempting to breed after the time of the census. This reflects a natural aspect of penguin breeding: While there is a particular window of time within which the penguins breed, there will be a natural fluctuation within that period, rising to a peak of nesting activity, then sloughing off. If you visit a penguin colony within the nesting window, you're likely to see a range of behaviors: Penguins setting up. Penguins copulating. Others well into incubation. Early in the period, there is more fighting and sorting out of territories, and considerably more copulations than later on, once the majority of pairs have settled on mates, begun to arrange their nest, laid, and proceeded to incubation, hatching, and chick-rearing.

Chick censuses—called *"C"* counts—also are utilized in *The Penguin Bible,* and estimates of the number of breeding pairs is difficult because of annual fluctuations in breeding productivity. For about a ten-year period, the three penguin species at Copa Beach in Admiralty Bay averaged a productivity of approximately one chick fledged per nest, but there may be years when the figure is higher, and seasons when it is much lower. The brushtailed penguins lay two eggs and theoretically productivity can be as high as two chicks per nest, but this never happens. There always are losses. The productivity may hit 1.3 or 1.4 for a particular colony in a particular season, but it's extraordinarily rare to do better. Too many skuas. Too much variable weather. All kinds of reasons for losses.

On the other end of the spectrum, there can be chaotic years. In 1993–94, I experienced an abject breeding failure at an enormous Adélie penguin rookery that had always been bustling and healthy, full of life. That season, at two to three weeks of age, all the chicks crashed. It was a season with a considerable amount of ice just offshore. It is theorized that either the adults couldn't reach their normal feeding grounds—just couldn't find the krill they normally take at that time of year—or else the krill had moved. I have seen gentoo rookeries systematically plucked and plundered by skuas. In November full of gentoo nests. A month and a half later a desert.

The Penguin Bible also lists adult censuses in some instances—*"A"* counts—which are highly variable and not a good indication of a site's breeding population. There can be a wide flux in the number of adults present at any one time. With Adélies and chinstraps, there are long stretches when one of the mates is offshore, away and feeding, while the other is home tending to incubation or brooding the chicks. The two will be together for changeovers at the nest during incubation, which in Adélies could occur at two-week inter- vals, with chinstraps at ten-day intervals, but with gentoos, daily. Once the chicks are hatched, the feeding runs are intended to bring protein back to the chicks at regular times: With Adélies, every twenty-four hours, chinstraps every sixteen to eighteen hours, and gentoos every twelve hours. If the adult census takes place once the chicks have crèched, both members of the pair will be out feeding. So then adult censuses are very unreliable.

Then comes my favorite designation in *The Penguin Bible*—a simple letter *B*. This means "no estimate of numbers was available. In these cases a colony or colonies are known to exist at that locality, but no further data are available." Occasionally, a remark suggests that the unsurveyed site is a *large colony*. The point, though, is that these unknown areas make penguin-counters salivate: They are a chance to add to our overall knowledge of where these animals are located and how many of them exist at a particular location. The more information added to the database, the more we'll be able to understand, over time, whether fluctuations are occurring.

Each recorded count is coded in terms of its accuracy. An *"N1"* count, for example, means that nests or pairs have essentially been counted individually, and that the count is accurate to better than plus or minus 5 percent. An *"N2"* count means that pairs or nests have been counted in a smaller, known area, then extrapolated over the whole. These estimates also include head counts from aerial photographs and generate an accuracy of plus or minus 5 to 10 percent. *"N3"* means an estimate accurate to plus or minus 10 to 15 percent, *"N4"* an estimate only accurate to plus or minus 25 to 50 percent. An *"N5"* count would be a total guess, accurate to the nearest order of magnitude—a few hundreds or thousands. Alternatively, counts might reflect gross estimates, ranging from *"VS"* (very small, up to 99 breeding pairs) to *"L"* (large, 7,500 to 19,999 breeding pairs) to *"EL"* (extra large, greater than 100,000 pairs).

The hints were enticing. In February 1978 an American geology team aboard the research vessel *Hero* briefly visited the Danger Islands. As noted in *The Penguin Bible*, the team reported five or more colonies of Adélies, designated *B*—no proper estimates on file. The Dangers previously had been visited in the 1960s by a British Antarctic Survey team, yielding an *N4* estimate of fifteen thousand breeding pairs of Adélies spread over more than three colonies. But there was no indication where the colonies were specifically located. I'd vaguely remembered these counts but almost completely forgot the possibility there might be wall-to-wall Adélies. Ships rarely plied this route into the Weddell. The Dangers were too dangerous. Thus, Oliver's plan presented a unique opportunity.

It would be a long haul. We wouldn't make Point Lookout until late the next morning, and, if a landing took place, we'd have a two- to five-hour stay. The Dangers were more than 150 miles and at least twelve hours' normal cruising time from Point Lookout. So assuming that we weighed anchor from Point Lookout by midaf-ternoon, and if seas, wind, and weather were decent, we might expect to arrive very early the following morning at the Dangers.

The venture north to Point Lookout was a total bust. The weather was awful and, when we arrived, the usual landing beach was churning with a high surf. The chief mate, Robert Parthe, went out to scout the beach for landing possibilities, but it was impos-sible. We waited a couple of hours for a change, but none was forthcoming. The barometer continued bouncing around, so the de-cision was made to get out—and to give ourselves a little more time getting over the top of Joinville to the Dangers and the other side of the Peninsula.

The long route around and into the Weddell is fraught with all kinds of potential difficulties, from wind to enormous tabulars, too much open sea, more than a little uncharted water, and today, a barometer that keeps jumping up and down. The Dangers lay forty miles northeast of Paulet Island, a Weddell Sea visitor site with which I'm very familiar—but it is regularly ice-clogged and impossible to approach. The vast Larsen Ice Shelf to the south calves many bergs each season and recently has collapsed to a record extent, birthing more bergs than usual. So even though reports have been good—that the currents have kept the ice well to the east—it's always a treacherous consideration going this way into the Weddell.

Joinville Island is a big, fat blob of an island—about forty miles long, north to south, and about twelve miles across, sitting just above the tip of the Peninsula. It is separated from the Peninsula by the narrow Antarctic Sound, which is the usual route over to the Weddell Sea from the Bransfield Strait. Joinville was discovered and roughly charted by Dumont d'Urville in 1838, who named it for François Ferdinand Phillipe Louis Marie, the Prince de Joinville, who was the third son of the Duc d'Orléans.

I thought it was appropriate we were chasing Adélies, the penguin named for d'Urville's wife, and this French history was a nice overlay to our little quest. The Dangers were thirteen miles east-southeast of Joinville Island. They had been discovered by James Clark Ross four years after d'Urville's exploits. Ross called them the Danger Islands because they appeared among heavy fragments of ice and had remained mostly concealed until his ship was on top of them.

The nautical chart revealed additional details. The islands have strange monikers: Comb. Beagle. Platter. Dixey Rock. Darwin Island was the largest of the group, which Ross named for Charles Darwin, who never, of course, made it to The Ice. Heroína Island lay on the northeastern end of the group, and is named for an Argentine expedition ship. The chart indicated that Heroína had a height of about 250 feet and a navigation beacon or marker. David Elliot,

the lead geologist on the February 1978 expedition that briefly visited here, remembers those moments well. It had been another relatively ice-free year. Captain Lenie brought *Hero* as close as possible.
The strange-looking island named Comb revealed lateral striations
running along the entire face of the island, as if it had been gouged
by parallel spokes. David noted that penguins were "everywhere possible" on some of the islands, and "numerous" on Heroína itself.
He recalls the bay on the northwestern end of Heroína, which that
day was totally murky-brown from the guano runoff. The island
had a cover of orange-brown slime—guano—running from one end
to the other, insinuating to David the notion that Heroína's frigid
offshore water would be more appealing than the shore. The place
was crawling with nitrogen.

Steve and I were early to the bridge, as the *Discoverer* moved closer
and closer to Heroína. The bad weather held off and I was expe-
riencing one of my heart-pumping, previsit moments. The anticipation could be cut with a knife. There was a buzz of something
special in the air—figuratively and literally. The literal was an enormous flock of snowy sheathbills, about fifty of these white-
plumaged, chicken-faced scavengers, which hung in the wind right
in front of the ship. A gust of wind would rise, and the whole flock
would blow to port, then return to hang in front of the bridge
windows. Sheathbills are really weak fliers, constantly fluttering their
rounded wings. It's a wonder that these birds migrate the Drake
each year. The sheathbills' legs dangled underneath, showing off
their lack of webs—the only non-webbed-footed birds in Antarctica.
They aren't permanent Antarctic residents. But their presence was

an important clue: They're strongly associated with penguin colonies, coming for the guano, which they love to slurp. The plethora of sheathbills suggested a plethora of penguins.

Oliver inched the ship nearer and nearer, checking the sonar constantly, nudging toward the island's northwestern end. The navigation tower—or what was left of this slight metal—appeared on a tall rock, with "Viva Chile!" graffiti scribbled nearby. It was a very cold, dank morning. The air was heavy, there were banks of fog to the south, and the dark gray cloud ceiling was very low. Finally, palpably, the smell intruded. Yes, there are lots and lots of penguins. No doubt about it. Raising binos to eyes, we see slopes totally jam-packed, end to end, with Adélies. Sometimes dreams come true.

On this early-December day, much ice still rims Heroína, which from the chart and the radar appears to be more than a half a mile across and at least a mile long from north to south. We'll confirm once ashore, but the penguins seem to be tightly incubating. The birds are laid out on their nests, one after another, well into the distance. The slopes level off at the charted 250-foot elevation, and it's pure speculation what the terrain on top might be. We'll check it out, hopefully. The ambient is a miserable 24°F, with the wind gusting to thirty knots from the south. Translation: It's a damned bitter morning. No island-wide guano-slime is apparent. In this cold, the muck's likely confined and immobile because it's frozen in place, right at the penguins' feet. Ah, nothing better than being 7,210 miles from home, ready to tramp some frozen guano and tackle some totally new territory—if we can make it ashore. Robert calls the boatswain, orders a scout boat to be readied, and gives me and Steve the high sign: "Ten minutes. Be there." We hustle to our cabin, pack gear, and race to the loading platform. It will be a day for neck gaiters, gloves, and an extra fleece.

We jump into the Zodiac and quickly depart the ship. Robert cruises the northwest shoreline, slowly heading down the western side of the island. Adélies clamber over any available space, wherever a path to the water appears. We enter a small cove, which has a level interior landing area. Steve and I crane over the front edge of the Zodiac, yelling out where the rocks are. Puttering in, we pass one small berg topped with about twenty sheathbills, restlessly pushing each other for a comfortable foothold, perhaps the same birds we had in front of the ship thirty minutes ago. Robert's able to nudge the tip of the boat against the ice foot and we slowly exit—trying not to disturb the huge greeting party. We have to walk for about forty yards to reach the rocky beach, with about 150 Adélies in between. *Hello.*

We move very slowly, so they don't scatter, but they're obviously very restless. Lots of noise—*gork, gork, quark*—many vociferously displaying their annoyed, evil-eyed stares. Unlike chinstraps, which can charge unprovoked and unannounced, Adélies often give some warning they're perturbed. Most of the time, they give you a chance to back off. Their eyes roll downward, showing the white sclerae—and the short feathers on their heads rise. A few of the birds show a characteristic standing-in-place, wing-flapping, foot-stamping, and claw-scraping routine, suggesting some aggression. We kneel, trying to calm the crowd, and they oblige. Goodbye to Robert, who tells us to return in about two hours and to keep our radios *on*, just in case there's trouble. If bergs start moving too close to the ship, we'll have to depart earlier than expected for Paulet.

We rise, move slowly past the horde, and head toward the gully that drains the upper level of the island. It lies about four hundred yards distant. Ice and snow chunks cover the shoreline. We pass a big Weddell seal along the margin of the shoreline who awakes from its snooze, raises its head, and gives us a wide-eyed glance. The slopes rise slowly at first, then quickly angle to 30 degrees or more. It is Adélie City. They are unavoidable. The worst part of the climb will be the ice. Whatever melt has flowed in the ditch this spring has now frozen solid. The gully is packed full with slippery ice. I foresee a lot of hands-and-knees-on-ice scrambling. Penguin nests line either side of the ditch. It's going to be a slip-sliding affair, with Adélies scowling at every step. The gully seems to be the most reasonable way to the top, but we don't have crampons. There must be at least fifteen to twenty thousand nests in my peripheral vision. The place is loaded. We agree that there's no sense trying to count until we check the higher reaches, see what kind of view we have, and then work back down to the drop-off spot. It's likely the top will provide a higher and better vantage.

Trudging uphill I'm trying to stretch my height, to be as lean as possible to avoid annoying any of the nesting Adélies. But the ice in the shallow gully betrays my effort. I continually fall. Footholds are nonexistent and tiptoeing the edges means getting within peck-and-stab range of the penguins. Fifteen feet above me, an Adélie struggles up the gully, scratching its way forward and uphill on the ice. It probably can't believe what's happened: *A week ago, this was easy.* This one's a fighter: It has its beak jabbed right into the ice, its claws are scraping, and the wings are beating steadily, as it somehow maintains its balance, somehow inches forward. Chinstraps may be the alpinists, but all of them, and certainly these Adélies, can use their built-in crampons when they need to. I slow my pace because I don't want a stray guano shot in the face.

An endless series of nests extends outward from the gully. At their densest, the nests are spaced a mere twelve to eighteen inches apart, but along the edges, the interspecific nest distance may double. In one sense I'm dreaming—immersed at the junction of tens of thousands of tuxedos. All of them seem so immaculate, and at a distance, so peaceful. But up close and personally, these guys are ready for battle. The technical name for the aggression is *agonistic* behavior. Fighting. This may involve aggressive actions where one bird is threatening or confronting another, trying to secure or defend a mate or a territory. Or it may involve more submissive and defensive actions in an attempt to avoid unnecessary conflict—birds trying to pass each other in the midst of crowded colonies, or younger birds trying to avoid attack from adults defending nest sites. It also encompasses *displacement* behaviors that seem totally out of the ordinary—preening in the middle of a beak-stabbing contest, or wing-shaking behavior that seems to erupt out of the blue.

But today, it's mostly poses and postures, which only occasionally escalate to combat. If an Adélie wanders a bit too close to another nest, it can be beaked severely in the upper breast or charged and very quickly engaged in a wild bout of breast-thumping and flipper-beating. In many cases, the action is averted with ritualized stares. Space is minimal and what territory each pair has secured is precious.

Typically, the most experienced breeders will be in the middle of the throng, more inexperienced penguins on the edges. The feints and parries are designed to force intruders—usually other Adélies, perhaps a skua—to back off. Today, though, we humans are the opponents and there are more than a few stabs and pecks aimed in our direction. Every twenty seconds or so, despite our attempted quick pace uphill, we're nailed, mostly on the boots. However, one Adélie gets me right in the thigh. *Bang.* If I carefully and quickly move past the nests, the Adélies are quickly mollified and return to incubating. Which is fine until I slip on the ice, slump to my knees, and find myself face-to-face with a stabbing, bug-eyed Adélie. I have it coordinated: If I tumble, I remember to keep my head and neck back. I'm wearing shades, but still don't want to get hit near the eyes. My knees ache and the cold throbs.

This is an amazing colony, lying in the middle of nowhere, among many unexplored islets and crags, far removed from the regular science and tourism activity of a late-twentieth-century Peninsula spring and summer. Joinville Island lies a shag's flight west, Paulet Island forty miles southwest, and for endless hundreds of miles to the east and south the Weddell Sea stretches mightily—full of bergs and incipient danger. This is the white wasteland where Shackleton's ship *Endurance* was beset and sank. The massive tabulars of the Larsen Ice Shelf—the size of cities and small states—roam unimpeded and immutable. Today, this dreamland has turned from mirage to a personal field of dreams and questions.

Huffing and puffing, we're about thirty feet from the top. The Adélies are within a week or ten days of hatching another season's clutch of two eggs per nest. The males usually take the initial stint for up to two weeks, the females then return for the next week to ten days, followed by short changes until hatch, thirty to thirty-five days after laying. I can sense their irritation. They're well past peak—most nests have two eggs, and I find one nest with three, though the dirtiest egg is holed and likely dead. Why hasn't the bird removed the shell? The eggs are about to pop, there's little maneuvering room on the steep slopes, and we're in the way. At most nests, only one mate—the incubating penguin—is present. I observe only a few nests where both mates are present. Like another garden in another time, this Eden of frozen, upslope guano rocks lies virtually on the edge of consciousness, a pocket of life undoused by the hustle and bustle of humans. Hard to believe that in this day and age these outposts still exist.

I'm having a very nice reverie, pondering how lucky it is to be possessed by penguins—when I'm snapped to attention by one of the *berserkers*—a returning Adélie male who's just rejoined its mate and who's totally unglued by my presence. My efforts to tiptoe around him are fruitless. I've encountered these guys before: They're not happy and laid-back. It's probably just fed for the first time in weeks, its eggs are nearing hatch, and I've got no business in the homeland. It lunges upward, straight at my privates. The whites of its eyes are bulging and its head feathers are as erect as they possibly can be. This is my regular nightmare tied to working Adélie colonies. I dodge the blow, turning sideways at the last moment, leaving the berserker grabbing and stabbing my left knee. It locks on. With a quick shake, I disconnect Mr. Adélie from my wind pants—but he's not quite finished. As quickly as I can, I move the last few yards to the upper plateau, with my nemesis nipping deliriously at my heels, screaming loudly and passionately. I implore, just as loudly: *All right, guy. I'm outta here. Hey, back off. Take it easy.* It keeps chasing and finally, with about twenty yards of buffer, the tension eases. I bow to him, he leers back, lowers his head feathers, grunts loudly, then raises his tail and spews a stream of guano—just missing another nesting Adélie.

Now, to get back to the really important business. With little hesitation, he descends to his nest, calls to his mate, raises his beak to the sky. She returns the stance, and quietly they wave their chests back and forth. He's slightly taller and a bit larger around the head and beak. They bow, he parades halfway around the nest, they bow again and then change over. He rustles the eggs into his brood pouch. Two eggs, still warm. She preens a bit, shakes her filthy body—after all, she's been sitting here through sleet and mud for days on end. She rearranges a few stones and carefully starts down-hill to the shoreline. Neighbors peck and complain, but she moves fairly quickly and avoids any prolonged confrontations.

I suspect I've missed most of this season's knockdown, drag-out battles. When most of a colony's nests are established, there's much less fighting. There are a few battles erupting here and there, but these are likely between and among late arrivals or inexperienced breeders, and occur mostly on the edges. The incubators will con-tinue sparring at neighbors, one bird perhaps grabbing an adjacent penguin's beak, locking on, and doing some pushing and pulling. The gentoos are the ones who seem to do the most of this tête-à-tête-ing.

Twenty yards away, downhill and below my berserker buddy, two outliers are showing some antagonism. A standing Adélie leans forward at another walking uphill, averts its eyes downward, white sclerae showing, erecting its crest, and leaning its head and neck far forward toward the passing intruder. Its flippers are held tight to the body. As the intruder draws within two feet, the posturing Adélie rears back and starts waving its head pointedly from one side to the other, keeping a stare fixed and flashing the whites of its eyes, starting to wave its flippers slowly and growling. It now leans back on its haunches, lowers its body toward the ground, and seems about ready to spring at the intruding bird—but the intruder notices the threat and swerves sideways, disrupting an incubating bird, and quickly scurries off. Almost immediately the displaying Adélie relaxes. The threat's passed. It picks up a stone, walks over to its mate, and drops the stone in front of the nest.

Two other peripheral Adélies square off, breast against breast. One grabs the other on the neck and pushes it backwards, knocks it over. The loser starts to run away, but not too quickly. The winner, apparently incensed by the slow retreat, erupts suddenly and chases the other penguin for about fifteen yards, never quite catching it. The victorious Adélie snorts, shakes its wings, then returns to its nest. Both mates rise, face each other, lift beaks to the sky, and croak their ecstatic displays—though not as intently as the male would display earlier in the season, when reclaiming his territory and advertising his presence. The noisy, mate-to-mate reacquaintance gesture is called a *loud mutual* display. Often, it's done quietly, with only low growls and much bowing—a *quiet mutual* display. At this time of the breeding season, the wings are generally kept to the side.

Earlier on, when the males are in high sexual display, they'll stretch their heads and necks vertically to the max, shake their chests, clap their bills, and rhythmically thump a beat against their bodies with their wings—all the while booming their vocals, which crescendo, louder and louder, to a peak. They'll erect their head feathers and flash the whites of their eyes. Female Adélies, however, don't perform loud territorial ecstatics. They'll belly up to the males for mutual ecstatics during courtship and once the pair is bonded, but he's the one who stakes the noisy, ecstatic territorial claim.

We make the rim and, as suspected, the island is flat-topped. Steve and I reconnoiter the possibilities. How to proceed? The penguins extend in large groups all the way to the eastern and southern ends. The penguin density diminishes noticeably to the south, which is likely more exposed to the prevailing weather. They have it down: Place the nests to avoid the weather, which usually means north-facing. The algae *Prasiola crispa* erupts in the barren spots left unoccupied. Steve's already punching waypoints into the handheld GPS—that is, global positioning system—unit and starting to collect positions, actual latitudes and longitudes, at precise spots all over the island. When we return to the ship, all the data will be transferred to a grid and his rough field sketch will manifest to a more precise orientation map we can use in future surveys.

We'll double efforts. I'll hike to the far eastern end and work back, counting all the way. In one respect, it is a penguin-counter's nightmare—more penguins than one's thumb can possibly tally-whack. A previously unsurveyed location and absolute, total overload. Adélies in all directions. The groups are too large and cover too much territory. I'll have to estimate, counting fistfuls upon fistfuls of penguins. There's no way precisely to tally every single nest. But no complaints: It's a chance to add to *The Penguin Bible.*

Steve will proceed with his mapping exercise, and estimate numbers by noting nest densities and the amount of area covered by the Adélies. We'll compare results later, see how close or far removed our respective estimates may be. Assuming our fingers and faces don't freeze. The northwestern slope gave us a nice lee on our ascent, but now it's total exposure and the wind's still gusting hard. As Steve departs, a trailing group of about ten sheathbills saunters after him. He tells me later that they followed him everywhere, vainly hoping that he'd somehow produce some nibbles and snacks.

One curiosity is the lack of skuas. We see a couple of them swirling over the edges, but for the entire morning we encounter only a handful. Forty miles southwest, at Paulet, there's a similar dearth. While Antarctic brown skuas opportunistically will take eggs and small penguin chicks, they spend most of their lives as fishers. So, one suspicion is that Heroína's surrounding waters are poor fishing grounds, and not the best place to be when penguin eggs and chicks are no longer available.

From this high perch, there's a complete, 360-degree view of neighboring islands and the vast and endless Weddell Sea. The island's flat-top plateau is gouged by tall fjords, with insanely steep edges—not the best access for ingressing and egressing penguins. Heading to the far end of the plateau, an eerie, cinemascope panorama encompasses my sight lines. A strange orange glow fills the gap between the low, dark ceiling and the dark blue, ice-pocked ocean. The orange blush extends forever. I stretch my arms and pretend I hold these little cubes between my fingers. I can touch sea and sky. The combination of cubes and fingers and otherworldly color are speckles in my hands.

Just a little warm-up for counting these guys. It won't be easy. There is a major surprise: a smattering of gentoo nests. They have never been documented this far east in the Peninsula. It totes to a few more than two hundred nests, all past peak, the incubators sitting on two eggs. If the pattern of other locations holds, their breeding schedule lags behind that of the Adélies. The gentoo nests are mixed among the Adélies, with no aggressiveness between the two species.

The gentoo nests can be clicked and tallied individually, but not the Adélies. They'll have to be estimated. Where the Adélie groups can be walked and I can see all of the nests, they can be estimated by fistfuls—figuring out approximately how many nests fall within a closed fist, stretched at length in front of my eyes. At the edges, looking down at totally inaccessible and distant patches of penguins I can't reach safely, I go for fingerfuls, approximating how many penguins fit a finger-length, stretched and extended. There are two keys to this: trying to maintain a similar distance from each group you're estimating, and knowing in advance the range of values for fistfuls or fingerfuls. The first order of business is determining whether it's fifty to seventy-five nests for each fist, or perhaps seventy-five to a hundred. Same with the fingers. If you can't maintain the same distance, you have to adjust the range of values accordingly. It's a painstaking process, proceeding from Point A to Point B and constantly tracking what you've estimated and what you haven't. Tedious, but it works.

Our counting and mapping proceeds for two hours and twenty minutes. Steve and I meet on the northwestern slope and slowly descend to the landing beach. It's excellent to catch the lee again.

We scramble quickly downslope, fearing lurking berserkers. My thoughts run to whether I'll ever return here. It could very well be a one-off. Heroína is so far out of the way. Robert's right on time, as usual, and he whisks us back. I race to the bridge to thank Oliver, and we're off to the south, aiming for a Paulet Island landing in early afternoon. The barometer's rising.

Steve and I dump our gear and start processing the numbers. My estimates range from 285,115 to 305,165 Adélie nests. Steve comes in between 248,710 and 300,000. All tolled, the mean is 284,748. Not too shabby. And as it plays out over the rest of the day, this was only the beginning.

Steaming southwest, the skies clear. It is virtually cloudless when we reach Paulet Island. Robert agrees to take us by Zodiac to the Eden Rocks, located about five miles north. These two adjacent islets lie off the eastern end of Dundee Island and are surrounded by shallow, uncharted water. Neither seems longer than a half mile from one end to the other. *The Penguin Bible* doesn't list Eden Rocks among the Adélie sites. They've never been censused. In fact, they've hardly been noticed. Not even a *B* designation. I'd scouted them from the air the previous January with *Endurance*'s Lynx helicopters, and they're loaded with Adélies. The seas are totally slack, so it's another opportunity to seize new fodder for the database.

Robert drops us at the southern end of the western islet, and we clamber out. He or Carsten will return in about ninety minutes. Not a lot of time, but we'll do what we can. There's no clear path to the main part of the rookery, and it takes twenty minutes to scramble over the jagged rocks and reach the interior. The Adélies are spaced over three or four levels and they're just about to hatch—

the same situation as at Heroína. When we reach the highest point, there's a clear view of the eastern islet, another half mile distant. In sum, the Eden Rocks present another situation where fistfuls are de rigueur: On the western rock, there are an estimated 19,649 to 20,785 nests. On the eastern islet, there are an estimated 24,600 to 28,905 nests. Carsten finds a more convenient retrieval point on the eastern flank of the islet, and we climb aboard, heading back to Paulet.

The day has flipped to full sunshine. Sculpted bergs line the route, with porpoising Adélies scattering from the Zodiac's path. The northern end of Paulet is surrounded by slopes rising to 175 feet above sea level, all speckled with black dots of penguins against a guano-pink backdrop. This is where all visitors tend to land. The island's volcanic cone, at 1,150 feet, lurks in the background. It is a relatively well known and often visited site, and the recent estimates of sixty to a hundred thousand breeding pairs jangle in my head. Karl Andreas Andersson, a zoologist who visited Paulet with Nordenskjöld's Swedish Antarctic Expedition in 1901–3, described the island as the largest Adélie rookery he saw—containing "several hundred thousand" penguins.

When I flew over Paulet the previous January in one of the *Endurance* Lynxes, there was an excellent view—my first—of the huge canyon on Paulet's southeastern side, which is never visited by tourists and which appears to be as jam-packed with Adélies as the crowded and regularly visited northern part of the island. Thus, my penguin barometer senses an estimated Adélie breeding population that is closer to two hundred thousand pairs. What it means is that today Steve and I have encountered somewhere between three hundred thousand and a half a million Adélie pairs. For the moment, *The Penguin Bible* lists a Peninsula- and South Shetlands-wide Adélie population of 692,536 pairs, 294,169 in the Weddell Sea subregion. Today's estimates from Heroína Island and Eden Rocks are totally new—and essentially advance the number of Adélies in the subregion by an entire order of magnitude.

As always, this austral breeding season has produced myriad numbers of penguins, tons of guano, and innumerable reflections. Yes, the promise of science is substantial. And yes, these penguins may indicate quite a bit about life on the planet. But there is so much we *don't* know—so many colonies we haven't yet investigated. So much work still to be done, assuming we don't crash first—either populations or helos. When you work on *Endurance*, for example, one of the first orders of business, especially if you're flying, is a bit of mandatory helicopter orientation. You're trotted down to the hangar on the flight deck, where the birds are normally housed with rotors folded and tucked. You are shown how to get into—and then zip up—the bulky, orange-red flight suits, which must be worn at all times when flying. On top of that goes a life vest, which you slip your arms through, and which has a long strap that goes between your legs and clips to the front end. Snug as a bug in a rug—a very hot rug. You literally roast until you figure out how to extricate yourself from this conglomeration of straps, zippers, and buttons. The assumption may be that, when airborne, your accumulating interior heat balances the frigid air flowing through the unheated cabin. We try the bulky flight helmets, which have thick rubber ear cups, supposedly to contain the excessive noise—but are, as we later learn, insufficient to stifle totally the rotors' high-decibel whirrs.

These birds are dangerous and they are exceedingly noisy. There are earphones in the helmet and a small, drop-down microphone to swing before your lips, thus allowing direct contact with the pilot and flight commander riding forward. If you're visiting the hangar but not actually flying, you must wear hard plastic and rubber hearing protectors when the helos are running.

The orientation then continues with a tour of the cabin in one of the helos—through the sliding door and into a small space that seems no greater than nine or twelve feet square. Seats can be placed inside and there are belts to secure yourself safely. Or, if the doors are open and you're banging photos, there are dispatcher harnesses to strap to your waist, which connect to a stanchion inside the helo, and which assist the flight commander in retrieving you if you tumble out. Perish the thought. My vertigo's already kicking in. And of course, if you need to be slung down to a particular location, they'll reposition the winch that lies to the side in the cabin, tie you to its metal cord, and drop you down.

I was about to sign the mandatory waiver sheet, indicating I understood the safety precautions, when I hear this last dose of advice: "When you *crash*, remember to push the window panel *out*—and *do* get out, as fast as you can."

"What do you mean—*when* we crash?" I quickly asked. "Don't you mean *if*?"

No. I'd heard it correctly the first time. Flying helos is totally parlous—much, much worse than a gazillion nipping and screaming chinstraps. I heard that *Endurance*'s new commanding officer, Captain Barry Bryant, had been flight commander on a Lynx that had crashed—and that he'd fortunately survived, albeit with serious injuries. So when *when* arrives, you do have some chance of pulling through. Whew.

The fear quotient is intentional. Better to know the worst that can happen and go uphill from there. Thus, I find it totally comforting that *Endurance* employs two crack maintenance teams, which tend constantly to the two helos—like caterpillars swarming a juicy bush. Foam canisters are within easy reach if there's an accident or a fire. My colleague Brent Houston and I watch a few training sorties and we are very impressed. The maintainers don't quite rebuild the machine every time it flies, but little is left to chance. To the limits of the maintainers' abilities, the helos are kept in top running order. They know every rivet and bolt and when it was installed. All the wear and tear is closely monitored and parts are routinely replaced— even if they seem to be doing well. There is no fooling around. I hear of a recent Lynx incident, when one of the strong, ninety-pound titanium blades simply flew off. Only about eighty flying hours a month are allowed, and there are frequent flight maintenance days when the helos shut down completely, so adjustments may proceed at a less frenzied pace.

Counting down to flight time, one of the helos will be pushed and wheeled out, strapped to the deck, and the rotors unfolded and extended. A complicated warm-up phase begins. The railings on the deck are lowered so there's absolutely no interference with the whirring helo rotors. The pilot and observer—the bird's two-person crew—emerge to begin the raft of preflight procedures. A flight coordinator orchestrates these routines from on deck. If you're flying, you need to get to flight deck well ahead of your scheduled departure because the flying exercises track a strict schedule.

There are other rules, all of which will be reiterated and rein-
forced in succeeding days. Once the helos are fueled, the pilot checks
the compression, tests the rotors, and the helo is unstrapped by
the maintainers. The intended human cargo—whether penguin-
counters, hydrographers, other scientists, or the captain and officers
going off to make a base inspection—stand fully suited behind a
white line at the hangar entrance. The blades are spinning furiously
and you can't move forward and load until the pilot gives the high
sign. The thumbs-up signal comes and you proceed quickly, head
lowered, get in the cabin, shut the door, connect the audio cord to
your helmet, strap in, and wait for liftoff. If you make mistakes
with any of these rules, packs of biscuits—cookies—have to be
brought to the flight crew. Transgressions include crossing the white
line without a life jacket. Or inflating a life jacket erroneously. Or
forgetting to wear ear protectors.

When you reach your target, the standard procedure is to attach
the dispatcher harness, slide the door open, kneel on the edge, and
begin your shooting—constantly talking with the pilot and observer
to position the helo as necessary. It's an undeniable rush to be
hovering in place, right where you need to be. The photography is
accomplished at an elevation of at least 850 feet, to keep disturbances to a minimum. Flying close to the penguins is avoided as a
matter of routine, emergencies excepted. If you're being dropped for
some ground-counting, the helo will land, with rotors spinning; you
slide the door open, hop out, and as quickly as possible offload
your gear. The important aspect, before the helo departs, is to lie
prone and cover your gear completely. This prevents any *gash*—
garbage or stray material of any kind—from getting sucked into the

rotors, potentially causing the helo to crash. We note a mark on the side of one of the helos: An outline of a skua with a big black X through it. The reality is that, sometimes, live gash maneuvers into the rotors—and is splattered in all directions. A decidedly unhappy fate for this particular skua, but fortunately, there was no serious damage to the helo.

The first season with *Endurance* added substantially to the Antarctic Site Inventory. We achieved oblique aerial photodocumentation of fifteen previously censused sites and added five new ones to the catalog—including Brown Bluff on the Tabarin Peninsula and Devil Island. In addition, we were able to reconnaissance sixteen sites, like Eden Rocks, which were candidates for regular censusing in years to come. The helos became the means to explore areas where, literally, few had previously tread. Encountering these locations from the air proved a totally different experience, like entering another dimension—awesome in the true sense of the word. From sea level, the perspective is earthly—of being tied to and grounded on the skin of the planet. From above, that perspective expands limitlessly. You spy vast space that seems impossible to fill.

Anne Kershaw, who operates the expedition company Adventure Network, once told me a story about this vast space. Her late husband, the renowned Antarctic pilot Giles Kershaw, loved clouds. He loved to fly near the clouds, parse the clouds, go around the clouds—but especially, he liked to see them. He gleaned peace from the clouds and the sky. He was in his special element. He was *one* with this enormous, undefined arena. Flying much higher than shags and skuas. Those dreams started to coalesce as my flying time drew near. And it would be just a matter of time. After a slow start, with hurricane winds delaying our crossing of the Drake Passage, we'd made it south to the South Shetlands. The good weather was holding.

I'm invited to attend the Captain's Operations Meetings each evening on the bridge. The *ops meetings* are a chance to make last-minute alterations, depending on weather and other objectives. The agenda is managed by Richard Taylor, the navigator, who seriatim asks each department head to bring the captain up to speed on the day's developments and detail prospects for tomorrow—the engineer, Danny Payne, and how the ship's handling; the supply officer, Peter Tyler—affectionately, the *pusser*—and matters dealing with the ship's provisioning; the flight commander, Nick Dukes, and flying prospects and plans. The lead hydrographer during this work period, Mike Pounder, briefs the captain on where the trisponders need to be placed for the charting exercise near Vega Island. Adam Peters, the first lieutenant and the captain's principal liaison to all the departments, fills in with sundry details. I'm asked to keep everyone abreast of our progress on Inventory photodocumentation.

The Antarctic is totally demilitarized under the Antarctic Treaty and *Endurance*'s mission is a conglomeration of politics, hydrography, science, and logistics. She enables the captain and British Foreign and Commonwealth Office personnel to make regular inspections of other nations' activities, as provided under the Treaty. Substantial mapping work is intended, as navigational charts are constantly being updated and revised, and new routes charted for the first time. On the port end of the bridge, a massive computerized chart recorder is the guts of this hydrographic work. It marries readings from the ship's sophisticated sonar system to signals received from

solar-powered trisponders that the helos and the hydrographers—
the *drogies*—have placed at key ground positions surrounding the
route being surveyed. When everything is up and running, the ship
follows specific track lines, moving off course only if ice gets in the
way. The chart recorder bangs away constantly, accurately marking
and pinpointing the depths at precise locations on the chart.

Endurance is the former *Polar Circle*, a Norwegian-built vessel that
once worked in the Antarctic tourism trade, and which is officially
classed as an icebreaker. I'd worked with Frank Todd on the old
Endurance, which ultimately was scrapped and replaced by this spiffy,
modern vessel for the 1991–92 austral summer season. She's painted
red and bears the official Royal Navy designation, *A171*. She is 58
feet abeam, 299 feet long, displaces 6,500 tons, and has twin diesel
engines with a top speed of 16 knots. The normal complement is
18 officers and a crew of 102 men and women. The ship is thoroughly up-to-date, with women in all departments—from the officers on the bridge and in the wardroom to the maintainers on the
flight deck.

The ship has bow and stern thrusters for extra maneuverability.
She can break half-meter-thick ice if necessary and has a maximum
ramming speed of eight knots. The bridge spans abeam for almost
the entire length of the top deck, and is fifty-nine feet above the
waterline. There is excellent visibility fore and aft, and video monitors on the main console allow the captain and officers to keep
close track of the flight deck and other parts of the ship. There is
a passive-roll-reduction tank located high in the ship, but with the
vessel's somewhat rounded bottom, all of the high-seas rolling is
hard to eliminate totally. The officers have a wardroom and dining

area one deck down from the bridge, and a few decks below that the senior and junior ratings have separate dining facilities and messes.

Being from the *colonies,* I couldn't initially grasp the constant stream of messages pouring from the bridge. In navy parlance, they're called *pipes*—and usually begin with: *Are you listening there?* Or: *Do you hear that?* It took me days to understand some of these announcements: The morning wake-up pipe consists of a piercing boatswain's whistle and an even more jarring *Call the hands, call the hands, CALL THE HANDS.* There were pipes for morning *phizzies*— phys ed, also called *huffers and puffers.* I also was baffled by some of the signs and notices. The door to the doctor's office announced the various times for *sick parade*—when you had to queue to see the doc. And when the helos finished for the day, it was LOSDFS— *land on, shut down, fold and store.* We had to select our meals in advance—a mystifying selection of bangers, jumbos, and onions, and that rare treat, chicken mad-ass. I think the steward meant *madras.* Thankfully, *Jackspeak: The Pussers' Guide* to British naval lingo, sponsored by the makers of Lamb's Navy rum, helped me wade the morass. No—those aren't kelp gulls or skuas out there. They're Antarctic *shite-hawks.* And if the wind is really gusting furiously, it's of course, *blowin' a hoolie.*

When we were on the flying docket, one pipe was sweet, sweet music: *Do you hear there? Do you hear there? Hands to flying stations. Hands to flying stations. No gash is to be ditched. No smoking on the upper deck abaft the mainmast. Hands keep clear of the hangar and hangar roof.*

It was time to fly.

Our first morning of flying was a real rush. We had a flying brief at 5:45 A.M. The met officer's weather report was for low stratus but no precipitation, the barometer holding for most of the day, and with some risk of katabatic winds, icing, gusts, turbulence, and patches of sea fog. After a slew of these briefings, I realized that the exact same risks were always present. The guts was whether *hoolies* were blowing, and the extent of the ceiling and visibility. If trouble developed, the helos needed to get back without much ado. Today, with low stratus predominating, the helos wouldn't be doing any vertical photography missions—vernacularly, *vert phot*, which requires clear sky up to about ten thousand feet. Using a huge camera mounted on one side of the helo, the goal is to fly direct lines at a substantial height, with the photographic results ultimately used to adjust and align nautical charts the ship is preparing or amending.

The navigator closes the meeting, and off we go. First, a quick swill of orange juice in the officers mess, then down to our bunks to dress and grab cameras and notebooks. We enter the hangar from the rear, grab hearing protectors, and load into the flying suits. In full flying gear, already sweating to the gills, we wait at the hangar opening, back of the line, as the maintainers complete the preparations. Today we'll fly with Matt Shrimpton and his observer, Mark Young. The other team consists of the flight commander, Nick Dukes, who observes for the senior pilot, Iain Banks. We're given the high sign and march forward. One of the maintainers slides the door open, and in we go. The beginning of many great adventures.

That first morning was Penguin Island and King George Island—right over Copa Beach, then on to Nelson Island, Robert Island, the Aitcho Islands, Greenwich and Half Moon Islands, and back to mother. Another day, we had a full-scale overflight of Deception

Island, providing excellent views of the immense numbers of chinstraps at the Baily Head and Vapour colonies. From Deception we flew to Livingston Island, doing some reconnaissance at seven thousand feet. The sky is mine and this territory below has never been touched, never examined. Perhaps it will stay that way.

The slowest speed the helo can maintain is about seventy knots, and she maxes out at 120, but the preference is to keep her cruising at approximately a hundred knots. I lean forward and Matt gives me a rundown of the controls and dials. While nodding comprehension, I don't fully understand the aerodynamics.

At one point, Matt asks: "Ron, can you tell what's happening?"

"No."

"Well, look at the altimeter. We're in a free fall."

"What do you mean *free fall*," I blurt, as we drop radically, plunging hundreds of feet, straight down.

Matt explains that it's a safety maneuver—a *controlled* fall, like going down a quiet elevator, practicing what to do if the engine fails. If you maintain an upright position, the blades will continue spinning. Of course, *controlled* or uncontrolled, there's still the problem of somehow ejecting *when* you hit the water. The flight briefing rings in my head—and my ears begin popping, painfully. At a thousand feet, Matt cranks the engine, successfully. No problem. Cool as cucumbers. These guys definitely aren't charismatically challenged.

Our return to Deception features a close look at Hannah Point on Livingston, and an overhead view of two blowing humpbacks. We return to Whaler's Bay, just inside Deception's caldera, by flying right through Neptune's Bellows, the narrow passage to the sunken interior caldera. I've done the Bellows innumerable times by ship, a few times by Zodiac, and now, by helo.

One new location that we visit is a small island at the head of Antarctic Sound—Jonassen Island. It is named for the Ole Jonassen who accompanied Otto Nordenskjöld on one of his major sledge journeys in 1902–3. The island is difficult to access from the sea. Banksie balances the helo on two wheels, and we offload. In the Sound, there is a roiling mass of penguins—perhaps eight to ten thousand or more, spread in huge dark rafts over the water. There must be swarms of krill massing in the narrow channel. It is an eerie sight—penguin heads bobbing constantly, lots of audible penguin chatter, which carries a far distance in the calm, cold air. Two minke whales pass near the rafts, with crabeater and leopard seals cavorting close to the island. I wonder if this is the prime feeding area for the Paulet Adélies, perhaps for the Copa Adélies who cross the Bransfield Strait to find their meals.

We raise Matt and Mark via radio, who tell us to get ready. They're on their way back from Hope Bay and will retrieve us in about five minutes. The twenty-minute return flight is a fantastic ride—zooming twenty feet over the waterline, slipping between tabs, with wingovers and twists left and right, rising only to go over bergs. All that's missing are the Wagner overtures.

The flight team members keep their eyes peeled for new penguin locations. Another day, Nick and Banksie report huge numbers of penguins at Brown Bluff, which they'd reconnoitered while flying drogie teams into Hope Bay. It was one more site that hadn't been previously censused. An amazing location. Mike Pounder recalls having rejected the site for a boat camp because of too many penguins. The day Brent and I visit is glorious: A cloudless blue sky. Scenery reminiscent of the Utah canyonlands. It is the only exposed turf on the northeastern side of the Tabarin Peninsula glacier, with an exposed beach running about four thousand feet from east to west. The surreal aspect is a dominant ocher bluff, rising to an elevation of twenty-three hundred feet. There are long strings of Adélie nests broken in a few locations by rock slides, which appear to have wiped out a large number of nesting territories. The highest Adélie group lies at an elevation of six hundred feet. We can hear the rush of a glacial melt stream running below. There are numerous dead chicks from previous seasons. I note footprints in some of the snow patches, wondering who else may have visited. Then I realize these are prints from rocks that have tumbled from above. The estimate is about twenty thousand Adélie chicks, including a blondie that's lost its pigmentation. There are more than three hundred gentoo chicks. But all of the chicks are past the peak of crèching and some have already hit the beach. In other words, our chick estimates may be off, and they really don't tell us enough. We still need nest counts. More gaps to fill.

But isn't that the point of all this penguin-counting? Ultimately, the censuses will suggest trends and possibilities: Are penguin populations stable, increasing, or decreasing? If there are changes, why? But all in all, I stand silent—awed and daunted by the incomprehensibility of this continent. There are more penguins than I ever imagined and at times I feel I'm accomplishing nothing. Brown Bluff, Eden Rocks, the southern canyon at Paulet—there are so many new colonies to add to the data bank, convincing me that we're just scratching the surface. It is the humility of recognizing "holes"—forcing us to dig even harder for explanations.

I ride with the door wide open—the blazing sun glistening on the tabulars below, which shimmer like trapezoidal cubes on an endless, dark blue pond. We climb higher and higher, discover canyons and plains we've never noticed, replete with dots and specks of penguins—uncounted penguins.

They fill my viewfinder and I snap the shot.

I am *one* with this enormous, unsolved mystery.

The penguins are mine, if I can reach them. And if not, I'll spread the news.

The picture will fuel dreams.

And others will follow.

FOUR

....

Circumcision Bay

I don't go for fancy cars
For diamond rings
Or movie stars
I go for penguins
Oh Lord I go for penguins.

Penguins are so sensitive
Penguins are so sensitive
Penguins are so sensitive to my needs.
                                        —LYLE LOVETT

Gentoos. Charcot.

Always, there is this mix of penguins and history.

The eminent French explorer—dubbed the polar gentleman by

Commander Robert Falcon Scott. And the gentle gentoo—the most placid of Antarctic penguins.

In less than an hour, if not thwarted by multiyear ice south of the Lemaire Channel, we'll arrive at Petermann Island—in Charcot country. The swath of 110 miles between the Lemaire Channel and the Antarctic Circle was the locus of Charcot's years of exploration. In 1903–5, during the First French Antarctic Expedition aboard *Français*, Charcot wintered at Booth Island, around the corner from the north end of the Lemaire Channel and about ten miles above Petermann. In 1909 Charcot wintered over once more, icing his vessel *Pourquoi-pas?* into a small bay at Petermann called Port Circumcision. Petermann also happens to be the most southerly outpost of gentoos on the planet. And it is where, through the efforts of Louis Gain, Charcot's lead zoologist and botanist on the second expedition, we first learned snippets about the intimate lives of Antarctic Peninsula penguins.

Right now, at the head of Lemaire Channel, sheltered in the lee of Booth Island, the visibility has become almost nonexistent. For long seconds, the snow hangs in the heavy air, then makes a feathered free fall to the surface. Limitless dark gray gloom pervades in all directions—like a dusky Peninsula night. The quiet is interrupted softly by the *zwip, zwip, zwip* of gentoo penguins intently whisking south. A few small growlers—ice chunks a few feet thick—very occasionally rattle the hull. The ship weaves slowly through the annual ice, which lies broken and spread in all directions. The current and winds have done their trick, moving this ice around sufficiently, and the odds are excellent for breaking free to the south. Our course through the Channel spurts west and southwest. If this were sunset and the sky clear, the great ball of red would be sinking right into the channel, with colored streaks of lavender, orange, yellow, and crimson strafing the sky.

Still, there is some spectacle to enjoy: The channel's high walls give respite from the blow and, in the calm, assist the panorama of flakes floating hither and thither, from the water's surface to the upper limits of visibility. The entire scope of vision shimmers with flecks and crystals. Every so often, the newly fallen snow swirls and lifts and pulsates over the cracking ice, reminding me of the autumn leaves tumbling over my backyard. Boreal autumn, austral spring— my contradictory October advances to the month of birth, November—to life renewed. *Zwip, zwip*—on to gentoodom.

The slopes towering above the channel have never borne the footsteps of human intruders. I've been through the Lemaire when avalanches dropped from high cornices on Booth Island, obliterating the watercourse, producing a nuclear explosion of white dust erupting from the water. Or when leopard and crabeater seals were crammed on every third or fifth floe. There are always surprises: Perhaps a British Antarctic Survey twin-otter airplane buzzing to starboard and heading north. Or a prowling orca—a killer whale— showing its six-foot-tall dorsal fin. Maybe a fast-moving minke whale huffing quickly south. It is today or it could be aeons ago, when the cliffs parted and gave the sea its narrow inroad.

There have been occasions when thicker, multiyear ice provided some exciting navigation, sometimes blocking the journey and thwarting a passage, but not today. Thin annual sea ice, less than a meter thick, covers about 60 percent of the channel and the rest is open or consists of easy-to-push brash ice, which leaves plenty of maneuvering room. Ice slabs that can't be avoided are easily pushed aside by the ship's forward progress, creating further, triangular leads extending to the horizon.

We proceed slowly. All drowns in this vibrant stillness, even the drone of the ship's engine. The captain barks directions to the helmsman and the helmsman responds in kind, once the rudder has shifted to the intended position: Port easy. *Port easy, sir.* Midships. *Rudder midships, sir.* Steady as she goes. *Steady, sir.* Starboard ten. *Starboard ten, sir.* Ease to five. Midships. *Rudder, midships, sir.* Steady, steady as she goes.

Today, one regret is that seals are few, though one floe has a newborn leopard pup nuzzled next to mom. Snow petrels, dark-phased south polar skuas, kelp gulls, and blue-eyed shags provide some avian entertainment, coursing through the flakes. The snow petrels, which are totally white save for a black eye and black feet, move like ghosts through the powdery realm, above the ice and into the far distance.

During the First French Antarctic Expedition, Charcot examined and charted more than six hundred miles of new coastline. In 1908–10, *Pourquoi-pas?* explored an additional 1,240 miles of unfamiliar coastline. French connections—indeed, Charcot connections—abound. The history and the penguins foment my Parisian illusions: The nattily dressed, meticulously groomed, orange-billed 'toos strolling over the ice foot could be crossing Pont Neuf to the Left Bank. Or heading down the Champs Élysées. Or sitting at outdoor cafés gulping krill and fish hors' d'oeuvres, watching humanity gambol past. Or just *zwipping* enthusiastically from one side of the Seine to the other.

One awesome aspect of working in Antarctica is feeling connected to the world at large. Working in The Ice necessarily means collaborating, day in, day out, with people from so many different countries. It's the only place on earth without national boundaries. There have been seven territorial claims, but all are now, under the Antarctic Treaty, essentially held in a foggy room, in abeyance—not discussed and not pushed. At annual Treaty meetings, the kiss of death attaches immediately to any issue exuding even a whiff of sovereignty—of one country trying to exert itself at the expense of another. Though the pace is sluggish in these international meetings—requiring a consensus of all twenty-seven *voting* countries for anything to happen—it has somehow worked.

The Treaty germinated in the stretched-out International Geophysical Year, which lasted from July 1957 to December 1958. During IGY, a barrage of scientists descended upon Antarctica to examine anything and everything scientific—from atmospheric physics to zoology. Twelve countries established science bases to assist the effort, then kept the goodwill flowing. In the following year the simple, fourteen-article Treaty agreement was signed. It went into effect two years later. Larry Gould, the eminent US geologist and Antarcticist, who was Admiral Richard Byrd's chief scientist and a chief proponent of the Treaty, called it a Magna Carta of modern times. Indeed. It is so simple and to the point—a testament to humankind's best instincts, which turns 10 percent of the planet, *forever*, into an unowned, unoccupied zone of peace, science, and environmental consciousness. I've often wondered how they expelled the lawyers from the negotiating table. Such an agreement wouldn't see the light of day today.

Most important, the Treaty preserves a special heritage: It gives free access to all, irrespective of nationality—assuming, of course, they can somehow safely get across the Drake Passage. I believe the free-access aspect is the most fitting tribute of all, one that respects the continent's rich exploration history. Antarctica is the only place on earth where you don't need to be dead to have something named for you. The map jumps alive with names of those, current and past, whose exploits and achievements stoke our imagination and dreams. Not only my study area—but the whole continent—is dotted with names either honoring an individual who worked in Antarctica or a noteworthy event, or that serve as tributes to benefactors or sponsors who assisted efforts to bring various expeditions and explorers south. More than forty countries now participate in a system that was forged because hearty bands of explorers and scientists from many nations had the gall and guts to pursue dreams. They sought the planet's last geographical goals, tested the limits of human endurance, and tried unmasking secrets of how the multitudinous strands of life intertwine.

The internationalization of the Peninsula can't be missed. Placenames everywhere spew history, adding layers and complexities to whatever reasons one had for coming south. I was chasing penguins—not realizing that this history would inform and infiltrate so many of my own choices and adventures. The southwestern end of my study area—between the Lemaire Channel and the Antarctic Circle—is a fair example. The narrow Lemaire Channel is about seven miles long and runs in a northeast-to-southwest-and-west direction. It separates Booth Island, formerly known as Wandel Island, from the more substantial land of the Antarctic Peninsula.

The channel was first discovered by Dallman's German Expedition of 1873–74 and later navigated by the Belgian expedition of Baron Adrien Victor Joseph De Gerlache De Gomery in December 1898. Gerlache named it for Charles Lemaire, who was a Belgian explorer in the Congo. Petermann Island was another Gerlache discovery during the 1873–74 expedition, which Gerlache named for the German geographer August Petermann. And if the Antarctic is a place for dedicated dreamers to pass the torch from generation to generation, Gerlache was one of Antarctica's most notable donors. In 1897–99 he led a highly successful scientific expedition aboard *Belgica*. Both Roald Amundsen, who later led the first expedition to reach the South Pole, and Frederick Cook, who later spuriously claimed reaching the North Pole, served under Gerlache. North of the Lemaire Channel, the main route connecting the Bransfield Strait with Anvers and Brabant Islands, just north of Lemaire Channel, is named for Gerlache.

Gerlache was part of the tradition—sharing secrets and ideas with others similarly inclined. He played godfather to many succeeding expeditions, including advising the 1903–5 French Antarctic Expedition of Jean-Baptiste Étienne Auguste Charcot. Gerlache actually had planned to go all the way south with Charcot, but, anxious about his new bride, Gerlache got off at Buenos Aires. Charcot was left to his own devices—and he succeeded. He was the son of the prominent and famous physician Jean-Martin Charcot, who was considered the father of neurology. The elder Charcot performed seminal work on hypnosis and hysteria, and was one of Sigmund Freud's teachers. When Dr. Charcot died, Charcot the younger, a physician in his own right, traded his inheritance for the vessel

Français and polar exploration. When funds ran short, a national subscription campaign buoyed the coffers. Initially, Charcot planned to rescue Otto Nordenskjöld, whose Swedish national expedition had disappeared in the northwest Weddell Sea, beyond the northeastern tip of the Peninsula.

In Buenos Aires, after Gerlache left the expedition, Charcot also learned that the Argentines, on the vessel *Uruguay,* had successfully rescued Nordenskjöld's party. So he shifted plans and aimed farther south. During that first expedition, in 1904, Charcot's winter quarters were on the western side of Booth Island, at a site now called Port Charcot. Four-mile-long Booth Island forms the west wall of the Lemaire Channel and provides the lee we're now enjoying.

Charcot took exceedingly good care of his men. As on a modern tourism expedition, there were lectures and discussions, wooden slats that could be drawn to allow a little privacy in the individual bunks, and rather good food. Even a regular supply of freshly baked bread and croissants. The pet pig, Toby, was an entertaining diversion until it choked to death, pigging out on some freshly caught fish *before* the hooks could be removed. Then there was Charcot's onshore Christmas picnic, during which he wound up the portable gramophone to play music to the penguins.

Charcot returned in 1905 as a hero to his entire country, but not to his wife, a granddaughter of Victor Hugo, who divorced him for desertion. Before going to the trough and remarrying in 1907, Charcot secured a prenuptial agreement from his new wife, Marguerite. The deal was simple—that she'd acquiesce in any of his future polar exploits. It was a future that quickly arrived, one year later. *Pourquoi-pas?* left Le Havre on August 15, 1908, and Marguerite—affectionately called Meg—joined for a while, disembarking in Punta Arenas. Charcot reached Deception Island in mid-December and returned to Booth Island on December 29. On visiting his prior winter digs at Port Charcot on the northwest side of Booth, he remarked that it hadn't changed at all.

I know the feeling. The glue throughout these waters is that most of the scenery doesn't change or move—hasn't, and likely won't, during our brief tenure of years. To port, a few waddling gentoos can be seen climbing upward over the snow, their black backs puttering uphill from the base channel to the heights at Glandaz Point and Loubat Point. They resemble small, dark escargots. The highest reaches are a few hundred feet above the waterline. Astern, the north end of Booth Island is barely visible. The snow is deep this season and I suspect the gentoos won't have too easy a time setting up their nests.

Another thought is that Gerlache, Amundsen, Cook, and Charcot, while venturing in this area, likely observed the same gentoo colonies and encountered ancestors of these gentoos *zwiping* onward to Petermann—these ballerinas of snow and freezing water who dance the same steps they've danced endlessly from year to decade to century.

Scores of gentoos are porpoising through the open leads, in groups of three to fifteen animals. They easily outpace our careful meandering. They slice the air, then plunge briefly below the surface, before their next upward push. It is a very clean routine, with the water parting and gently breaking the day's last, solemn breaths. The white patches on the gentoos' heads are visible as they peak out of the water, head stretched forward and slightly upraised, feet relaxed behind, chubby bellies barely inches above and parallel to the water's surface. A closer inspection shows beaks agape, sucking gasps of air. Almost instantaneously they submerge again, emerging just a few yards beyond.

We pass through the Channel and only loose brash looms ahead. Despite the snow returning to horizontal and a radar screen splattered with white patches of ice, touching down at Petermann is going to happen. The endless bundles of first-year ice are easily plowed, more an annoyance than hazardous. To port, where the channel's movement is minimal, perhaps nil in spots, the leads are starting to freeze.

The first signs are small crystals—called *spicules,* or *frazil*—suspended in the topmost inches of the water. The surface begins to appear oily. As this consolidates, the sea assumes a matte-like appearance that is decidedly soupy—*grease ice.* With further hardening, the greasy soup lumps together into an elastic crust, inches across, called *nilas.* As the crust is further jostled by the wind and sea currents, it clumps into characteristic *pancake* shapes, often rounded and upturned at the edges, and perhaps many feet in diameter. The freezing process leaches salt out from the ice. The pancakes may freeze together to form continuous sheets—floes, merging to an even greater whole—the *pack.* With a day or two of freezing, sea ice may grow to a thickness of greater than half a foot, and over the course of winter to a thickness of nine or ten feet. Sea ice that survives one summer of melting is called *second-year ice,* and it will rise higher in the water. Sea ice that survives at least two summers of melting is called *multiyear ice* and will be practically salt free. The older ice may be tinged blue, first-year ice, green.

Charcot discovered Port Circumcision on January 1, 1909. He named the island in honor of Bouvet de Lozier's discovery of Cape Circoncision, the northwestern cape of Bouvetøya, which lies well north of the Antarctic. Charcot's New Year's Day discovery also links to the holy circumcision day on the church calendar, when Christ first shed blood for humankind. From this outpost on Petermann, Charcot used the launch from *Pourquoi-pas?* to examine the uncharted coastline to the south. Many oceanographic, seismographic, and magnetic studies were accomplished, but there was a crashing stop when the boat ran aground on Cape Tuxen. The men managed to refloat the launch and they limped back to Petermann for repairs. The charting efforts resumed, continued through January, and ultimately reached below the Antarctic Circle to include the whole length of Adelaide Island. *Pourquoi-pas?* spent that winter at Circumcision, with Charcot employing a unique line of hawsers across the entrance to protect the ship from incoming ice.

This entire stretch teems with Charcot's discoveries. Below Petermann and the Argentine Islands, down the two-mile-wide Penola Strait, is the French Passage, named by the British Graham Land Expedition of 1934–37 to commemorate Charcot's navigating and charting this route for the first time. The passage skirts between the Argentine Islands and a complex series of potential hazards farther south—Anagram, Roca, and Cruls Islands—providing a safe route west from the Peninsula to the open ocean. And well south of the Circle there is Marguerite Bay, which Charcot discovered and named for his patient, loving Meg.

It's calm along the Petermann shoreline and easy to follow the gentoos proceeding into the small, protected cove at Port Circumcision. The hawsers protecting *Pourquoi-pas?* in its winter shelter were slung across the huge boulders lining the cove. Today, most of the boulders are still covered with snow, merging with the ice foot that extends seaward. The tide is down about a foot and a half, which leaves many yards of the ice foot unhinged and overslung—and dangerous. This will crack, loosen, and disintegrate as spring advances. The trick is finding the landing spot where a boulder still supports the ice, offering some firm, safe footing for getting onto the island. During the winter, it would have been possible to walk across the cove safely. I leave the Zodiac, hustle over the ice foot, and settle next to one of the boulders. Gentoos mill about the exposed areas, starting to rummage around for last season's pebbles and nests. A few Adélies are present, too. They breed on the northeastern point and I'll have a chance to check on their breeding progress later.

The temperature hovers around 26°F, and the wind continues blowing at about thirty knots from the northeast. The gray gloom continues, but fortunately, the snow slackens. A fine, four-inch-thick powder hides the deeper pack that's accumulated over the winter. Reaching the abandoned Argentine hut a few hundred feet beyond the landing site won't be hard, but tramping three hundred or more yards to the Adélies at the northeastern tip will be more of an ordeal. Petermann is a one-mile-long island that rises moderately steeply to a rocky summit, more than 650 feet above sea level. Its snow dome may linger well into summer and nurture a bloom of red and green snow algae, but none is in evidence today. Beyond the hut and uphill to the west, many 'toos have begun trudging up to the higher reaches. Shortly, all of Petermann's penguin pathways, high and low, will resemble the best of ski slopes, with well-worn, sinuous "runs"—both downhill and cross-country—extending from the Port Circumcision hut uphill and west and downhill clear to the northeast Adélie colonies. Lift tickets and day passes, however, aren't required. Only long toenails. South of the hut, a cross has been erected in memory of British Antarctic Survey personnel who perished nearby.

In all directions, gentoo heads pop above the waterline. From the ice foot on the west side of the small bay, I see gentoos everywhere rolling on their sides, splashing playfully, seemingly preparing for the next water ballet. There are backstrokes, sidestrokes, and much porpoising to and fro—the latter in one sense being a penguin version of the butterfly stroke. All brushtaileds are fussy bathers, cleaners, and preeners. On outbound trips, the gentoos spend oodles of time flushing their feathers, doing their Esther Williams routines, and exuding a buzz of electricity, as if they're really excited about heading out to feed. My suspicion is that they're cleaning the residue they've amassed during their shore visit—a potpourri of guano, mud, crud, and dirt—so their feathers and their bodies are duly primed for fishing. So nothing slows them down if they have to escape a leopard seal. These cleaning sessions are protracted affairs. While floating on their backs, many scratch their bodies vigorously with their feet and claws. Others shake their short legs vigorously, as if they're trying to get the lead out. It's akin to making sure the bait's properly pinned on the hook. You wouldn't drive unless your car was in working order. Gentoos always look natty and properly coifed—no doubt making sure they leave no hints to lurking leopard seals. Appearance is important. Their basic coloration—black topside, white below—is a countershading that presumably makes them less obvious to predators. On returning from feeding runs offshore, the routines are repeated, though, it seems to me, for shorter periods of time.

A gaggle of 'toos now swims under the lip of the ice-foot where I'm perched, trying to determine a route for exiting. They're going to have to work today to get ashore. In the bay's clear water, I see them *zwipping* about underwater, trying to build enough speed to pop a few feet out of the water and on top of the ice. They are flying missiles who've taken their skills to a denser medium. They use their broad, flattened wings as flippers and oars to paddle through the water, with their short legs tucked tight to the sides of their fat bellies, and their feet left behind and used only for steering. They are highly maneuverable—flying through the water with the greatest of ease—and it's easy to see why they're successful krill and fish rustlers.

While gentoos normally fish closer to home, Adélies undertake long searches for food during the breeding season—round-trips that may exceed four hundred miles. And while chinstraps and Adélies normally are shallow divers, gentoos effectively exploit nearshore fishing grounds by diving to greater depths—500 feet or more. Gentoos also have more catholic tastes, adding a healthy dose of fish to their basic krill diet. Adélies and chinstraps are more exclusively krill fishers. When the chicks erupt, all three must return home with bellies full of half-digested and not-so-digested protein—and they can succeed even when the krill trawlers' nets are running bare. They can reach fast traveling speeds of up to eight feet per second. Prey is scattered and capture rates vary. Not all dives are successful.

One chinstrap was recorded capturing 112 individual krill on a single dive, in this case tantamount to a rate of one individual krill per second. In terms of weight consumed, Adélies may take twenty-five grams of krill per minute, which calculates out as an individual krill every 1.3 seconds.

Their contour—whether one describes it as ovoid or fusiform, bullet-shaped or egg-shaped—is critical, reducing drag from the water to a minimum. Their watery expertise is further assisted by sturdy, thick, and heavy bones, which reduce excess buoyancy, and a low center of gravity. Flying birds, by contrast, have hollow, much lighter bones. The gentoos' underwater scurrying about, at the moment, seems more playful than intentional. Two gentoos make the jump perfectly—literally squirting vertically from the water and landing directly upright, about fifteen feet away—precise ten-point landings. They miss—but don't disturb—a snoozing gentoo, sleeping erect with its beak tucked under its left flipper.

The penguins aren't *sexually dimorphic,* which means that both sexes appear the same and can't be distinguished by separate field marks. Females are a bit smaller than the males, which allows for some differentiation when a pair is side by side. And often, after copulating, with the female prone and the male standing on top, the male's muddy, grimy feet leave footprints branded on the female's back.

Gentoos, chinstraps, and Adélies don't hop very much. They do walk and run—or what might be called running in a penguin. Basically it's a hobbling along, forced upon them by too-short legs and underslung bellies. You'd waddle too if you lacked knees and elbows. Gentoos do this in a stately motion, without the exaggerated, fast, side-to-side action of a chinstrap pompously moving forward on very short steps, or an Adélie, who's got some swagger to its walk but doesn't seem to bound as quickly and forcibly as the chinstraps do.

The emergent gentoos bow leeringly in all directions, stretching heads forward, confirming their location and the absence of annoyances with which to contend. I have no idea if they can discern the snow depth, but they'll have difficulties finding a lot of pebbles today. I know they can discern colors, but my red anorak is hardly a distraction. Sitting there, at eyeball level, I might resemble just another—albeit, more brightly colored—gentoo. They're just short of three feet tall, and at this pre-breeding moment weigh about twelve or thirteen pounds. It's impressive to see them so closely: The elongated, orange-colored bill with a black tip. Dark greenish eyes with star-shaped pupils. If we stood side by side, the gentoos would rise to somewhere between my knees and hips. All are dressed and ready for an evening on the town, plump and layered—these pseudo-marine mammals. The bill is strong and plated—well enforced for stabbing and pecking. They have a thin white eye ring, with inverse, white-colored isosceles triangles extending from the top of the eye ring to the top of the head, where a narrow white line joins the triangles or ovals together. These white markings, which Murphy elegantly called *fillets*, vary in shape from gentoo to gentoo. Also, there are flecks and splatterings of white color on the gentoo's head, mostly between the fillets and the nape, with just a few dabs forward between the fillets and eyes. There's a clean separation between the black head and throat and white chest and underparts. Black color covers the back, and also surrounds the wings and the paddle-shaped flippers. Later on, after chicks have fledged, gentoos bulk up to eighteen or nineteen pounds for their annual molt, which may last ten days to two weeks.

The fat, webbed, stout feet of gentoos are colored fleshy-orange, with very elongated black claws. Their long, stiff tails—about six inches in length—consist of fourteen to eighteen feathers and are often used as balancing props, much like the strong tail shafts of woodpeckers. These *rectrices*, once molted, lost, or plucked out during a fight, become free-floating fodder that the penguins often use as nesting material. Like my house cats, they swish tails to ascertain what's happening rearward.

These gentoos are very slick. Seawater flows in big globs off of their bodies because they are waterproofed to the hilt. The two returnees, feeling safe and secure, begin preening vigorously and carefully, which continues for incessant minutes. It is truly a sacramental formality. Theirs is the densest feather arrangement of any bird—somewhere between seventy and ninety feathers per square inch—and these short stalks are their prime defense against the cold. They also have internal blubber to aid the insulation, but the feather-packing provides greater than 80 percent of their thermoregulation. It's very efficient. Their feathers don't have quills like those of other birds and lie, intermeshed, extremely close to the skin—the better to trap air close to the body. The interlocking is assisted by fluffy barbs and aftershafts at the skin end of the feathers. We could learn something about layering from them: Feathers. Air. Skin and blubber. They've never needed polyester to keep them snug.

One of the gentoos has begun its preening routine low, near the feet—dipping, shaking, and nibbling its two-inch beak into various patches of feathers, getting them lined up just so. It works higher and higher, occasionally twisting its head and neck almost 180 degrees rearward so it may dip its bill into the feathering at the base of the tail. There is where the penguin's *uropygial*, or oil, gland is located. The process is like waterproofing our leather shoes and boots. After smearing its bill with the magic potion, the gentoo returns frontward to work the oil over and through its feathers. The second gentoo has started higher, preening its chest by stretching its neck up, back, and away from its body, an amazing contortion that enables it to nip, arrange, and tuck the feathers in the upper thoracic area. I'd like to do that kind of stretch, but can't. Their *occipital condyle*, which connects their neck and vertebrae, consists of only one bone. We have two connective bones and, thus, much less flexibility. Every so often, these two stop, peer about, bow, then go quickly back to business. They are extraordinarily fussy.

Toward the hut, where some mates likely have found their old nests, I hear the gentoos' characteristic, slow-paced *hee-HAW, hee-HAW, hee-HAW* calls. The visual version of this trumpeting is a special sight: The gentoos heave their chests many inches forward and back, in and out, with each *hee-HAW*. They really honk with gusto. The calls resemble the brays of annoyed donkeys, an illusion that no doubt explains why they're called *Ezelspinguin* in German. A more regular name in German is *Papua-pinguin*, which refers to their scientific name, *Pygoscelis papua*.

But the etymology surrounding gentoos is an utter and total mess—both the popular and the scientific names. You'd think with such a spiffy bird the naming committee would have done better. The species was named *papua* for the scientific nomenclature in 1791 by Johann Reinhold Forster, who was a naturalist on Cook's world voyage. Forster also happens to be the individual honored with the specific scientific name for emperor penguins, *Aptenodytes forsteri*. But *papua* is an error—gentoos simply aren't resident in PNG. Not even close. *Papua* is a Malay word and reflects Forster's mistaken belief these penguins came from New Guinea. The confusion seems to be that the gentoo bones, from which the type specimen was named, were mixed in with a bag of specimens brought to England from a scientific collecting expedition in the Far East.

The vernacular *gentoo* is another bungle. This name was used by Falkland Islanders in the 1800s, but the origins aren't precisely known. Historian and fellow Antarcticist Alan Gurney notes that the name seems to be an anglicized version of the Portuguese *gentio*— or "gentile"—and is a name that's also been used by Muslims in India to describe Hindus. Gurney even discovered an eighteenth-century English travel book referring to the "Jentoo dancing girls of Madras." To me, this suggests a bit of slander resulting from someone's experiences roaming the British subcontinental empire. Robert Cushman Murphy earlier had suspected a reference to either a Hindu or a Telagu. The eminent paleontologist and penguin paleobiologist George Gaylord Simpson thought this penguin's characteristic white head markings might have reminded someone of a turban. My inklings were confirmed by an acquaintance who is expert in subcontinental linguistics. The Hindi word *jantu*—which would be pronounced "john-too" with a soft "t"—means "creature," "zoo animal," or perhaps "insect." A much older Hindi word, *jhantu*—which would be pronounced "jhahn-thoo" with a harder "t"—means "pubic hair," and is fairly commonly used to curse someone in the most derogatory fashion possible. Confirming foot-prints back to India, it has been common practice since the days of empire to anglicize a Hindi "j" to a "g" and a Hindi "u" to "oo."

By the turn of the twentieth century, the name *Johnny Penguins* had much currency among the sealers in the Falklands. And because this name seems to lack negative or ethnic connotations altogether, I'm sorry it hasn't survived. Murphy, who worked South Georgia in 1912–13, used *Johnny* extensively in his writings. In Spanish, gentoos also are called *Pinguin de Pico Rojo* and *Juanito*.

And whether *Juanito* or *Juanita*, my preening penguins are perfectly comfortable in today's bitter cold. As with the other two stiff-tailed penguins, if it gets too hot, the bare areas at the base of the bill and just above the feet allow excess heat to disperse. One of the preening gentoos extends its left wing, showing a very bright pink undersurface—revealing another means of cooling off. Just below the surface of the underwing, warm blood passes in one direction and cold blood in the other, permitting a very efficient heat exchange to take place. The bright pink flush is typical of penguins returning from offshore swims, where they've been working and fishing hard, expending substantial energy. They often will flap their wings in the cold, ambient air to cool down even further. The bright pink color contrasts strikingly against the white breast and belly. And if the light is right, their glistening white bellies may reflect both the pink from the underwing and the fleshy-orange color from their feet.

With open mandibles, one gentoo grabs its right wing close to the shoulder, then *squeegees* outward to the tip, seemingly trying to remove the last remnants of salt water from the feathers. Then it starts from the outer edge, moving in. It repeats the dexterous procedure, whisking the right wing out and in twice, before starting on the left one. They're really amazing. The salt water isn't even a serious problem, however. They can drink it, something we surely couldn't do—and survive. The trick is a built-in osmosis system in the vicinity of their nasal passages, which processes out any excess salt the penguins accumulate. It is an adaptation that all seabirds have. Species spending the most time at sea have the most well-developed desalinization plants. The filtered drops of salt water run down the penguins' beak, often are shaken from the bill tip—or sometimes just drip to the ground.

For these two gentoos, the preening ambles on with no end in sight, and I've got work to do. It could continue for hours. I set off toward the hut, the perimeter of which generally clears early in the spring. I want to check on the progress of the sixty or so gentoo pairs that normally nest around the hut's edges. Today, they seem perplexed: Snow has drifted to a depth of four to five feet on the eastern, seaward side, and has substantially impeded efforts to find their precious nest stones. The gentoos are waddling about nervously, ready to get on with nest construction and repair, but they can't because the snow is too, too deep. Many scrape furiously, trying to find the rocks—the exact stones—they used last season. Others turn in circles, braying and strutting a palpable, nervous energy. Four of them prance on top of and over my boots, totally unconcerned with my presence. Squabbles break out frequently, but these aren't of the blood-and-guts variety so common among the chinstraps. Gentoos are dubbed "gentle gentoos" for good reasons. It will take considerable work to trample the snow to a more manageable thickness. Disconcerting, perhaps, but they never seem deterred.

On the northwestern and western sides of the hut, which enjoy the lee, it's a rosier picture. There's been less exposure to the winter weather blowing in from the strait, and many gentoos already have pounded the thinner snow cover down to their precious pebbles and rocks. And with some protection from the wind and blow, the tramping and their lying prone have produced considerable mud, which has further mixed with the guano. The apparent result: filthy and happy with a whole lotta courtin' goin' on. This "setting-up" stage may go on for weeks.

At three of the pebble nests, I observe one of the mates wiggling around in its stone-cup nest, with the other mate attending nearby, within inches. No eggs have been laid, as yet, but they're right on sched. It's a few calendar days away from mid-month, and Louis Gain, with Charcot, recorded the earliest gentoo eggs on November 18. The gentoos, remarkably, seem to know each other well—both visually and vocally. Many others are paired off and bowing and walking around each other noisily and purposefully, regularly stopping to raise beaks to the sky and uttering their chest-distending *hee-HAW*s of recognition and announcement. These ecstatic displays aren't as boisterous as those of the Adélies and chinstraps, which partly reflects the gentoos' penchant for smaller rookeries. The present-day breeding population of gentoos over the whole of Petermann is greater than seven hundred pairs. In very early November 1909, before breeding was fully under way, Charcot's biologist, Louis Gain, counted 112 gentoo nests on the northeastern end of Petermann. And while chinnies and Adélies may accumulate in rookeries of hundreds of thousands of animals, the largest gentoo assemblage in the Peninsula is at Cuverville Island, at the intersection of the Errera Channel and the Gerlache Strait, where four to five thousand pairs nest in scattered groups over a wide stretch of territory.

Gentoos are inveterate pebble-merchants—and thieves. Bandits, all. And robberies have begun in earnest. All three brushtaileds want rocks to line their nests, but gentoos are the most accomplished brigands. Consider this one pair on the leeward side: I'll call them Leo and Molly for ease of description. Leo, presumably the male, is hanging around the edges of his pebble nest, arranging stones, bowing constantly to Molly, presumably the female, who's sprawled comfortably in the nest. They seem to be a very experienced pair: lots of random beak-nibbling. And the mutual bowing seems endless. Leo and Molly's nest lies within a body's length of two other nests. Their closest neighbor, whom I'll call Madeleine, lies prone on her nest, and generally keeps her back turned. Occasionally, Madeleine will peer behind to see what Leo and Molly are doing, then quickly turn away. Leo takes a moment to stretch his neck toward Madeleine and the other neighbors, then begins to saunter through the melange. At the northwestern corner of the hut, Leo climbs up the snowbank, which is about four feet high at this point, makes a left turn, and walks the snowbank all the way around to the southwestern corner of the hut, where another stone nest is starting to thaw.

Leo gently descends the snowbank, brushing past Ez and Lis, the putative occupants of this emerging nest, who still are very much into parading around each other, not quite ready to finish the snow removal. But Ez and Lis's pebbles are showing quite nicely, luring Leo like a magnet to metal. In full view of Ez and Lis, Leo plucks one of the emerging pebbles—a two-inch beauty—with his beak. Ez and Lis notice but don't give much of a squawk, returning quickly to their mutual *hee-HAW*-ing. They may be a younger couple, still waving their orange bills at each other, testing their gentoo-ish routines, and seemingly more concerned with debating than with Leo's plundering. Maybe Leo's got it figured that these two are an easy mark. The robbery completed, Leo charges past Ez and Lis, but instead of digging in his claws to climb the bank he decides to stay low and walk through the mud and past other emerging nests to make his return.

It won't be a straight shot home: Leo meanders among a slew of sitting and standing gentoos, a few of whom give him a strong peck and stab, before he reaches a guy wire that reinforces the end of the hut. The wire extends from the northwest tip of the roof down to a cement anchor base on the ground, which is buried in the snow. Leo and Molly's nest is just on the opposite side of this stanchion. Though penguins sometimes learn tricks of avoidance, Leo hasn't quite mastered the art of ducking under this particular wire. He seems rather confused by the barrier and decides to trudge up the snowbank, make a quick U-turn around the wire, then slip down toward Molly, all the while grasping the precious, two-inch-long pebble in his beak. Molly has been dutifully sitting in her nest, guarding stones from the neighbors.

As soon as Leo drops the prize at the base of the nest, Leo and Molly engage in a customary mutual ecstatic display to reinforce their pair bond. Both stand, raise beaks to the sky, and bellow their donkey calls to one another. While the display proceeds, the ever-observant neighbor Madeleine extends her neck as far as she can and immediately swipes the jewel that Leo has just retrieved. Madeleine places it neatly inside her growing stone dome, arranges other paraphernalia in her collection, and keeps her back turned.

When finished with the ecstatics, Leo stares leeringly for his new pebble, which obviously he can't find. His eyes literally bulge from their sockets. *Where has it gone?* Leo looks left, right, then frustratingly—or so it seems—shakes his head vigorously and stares right at Madeleine, the prime suspect. Madeleine sneaks a rearward peek, but in a nanosecond turns away again, totally refusing any eye contact.

Madeleine becomes interested in a very clean gentoo who's approaching the hut, obviously just returned from a feeding run. Might be Madeleine's mate. Madeleine rises, emits a *hee-HAW*, and the returning gentoo responds in kind. Contact. They continue to chatter back and forth. *Come home, look at our nest—look what we've got. Yes, yes, comin' as fast as I can.*

Meanwhile, next door, Leo doesn't seem to think the lost pebble is such a big deal, and the purloined gift doesn't appear to disrupt Leo and Molly's mutual affection one iota. That's how it goes. *No problem, there's more where that one came from.* Leo bows a few more times, then speedily departs. He purposefully claws right back up the snowbank and makes a U-turn, making a beeline across the top of the snowbank toward Ez and Lis. They are obviously today's preference. Ez and Lis are still discussing matters back and forth, as before, and Leo has absolutely no problem taking replacement stones. Leo repeats the long mission twice more in my presence.

It is an exciting time. Along with the pebble-stealing routines, there are regular copulations, which means that gentoo eggs will be popping everywhere at Petermann within a week to ten days. In all penguins, the male assumes the upper position when mating, the female lies prone, and both face forward. The general scheme is for the male to caress the female, who raises her beak upward, to be nibbled constantly by the male. After mounting, and while continuing the beak-caressing, the male slowly moves backward over the female's back. This is often accompanied by the *arms' action*—a rapid vibration or movement of the male's flippers. This can be pronounced, as in gentoos, or rather minimal. But no penises: All penguins mate via cloacal kisses. The cloaca is the all-purpose orifice found underneath the penguin's tail, used also for expelling guano when necessary. The male needs to be ready when the female shifts her tail out of the way, so he can swing and lower his tail, butt, and cloaca into position, then squirt sperm onto and into her cloaca.

I have watched hundreds upon hundreds of chinstrap, Adélie, and gentoo copulations. The chinstraps' affairs are rather perfunctory—a quick going-through-the-motions and, when done, a quick hop away, with hardly any acknowledgment between the two. And while I'm sure there are incompetent males in all three species—all presumably young and inexperienced birds—the ineptitude of some chinstraps is noteworthy. I've seen more than a few chinstraps trying to mate with a female's face—that is, totally backwards, and of course, in very short order, they're jettisoned by the female to the turf. On one of these occasions, the embarrassed chinstrap female ran away rapidly and noisily, weaving in, out, and around a large smattering of nests, squawking loudly all the way—announcing, I'd like to believe, the identity of her immature suitor and telling other females to avoid him like the plague. The Adélie males, by contrast, are a bit more animated and respectful when mounted, very regularly checking, first left, then right, how the female is reacting.

But I'm most impressed with the gentoos, whose males I believe to be the true gentlemen-lovers in this tribe. Their *arms' action* is dramatic and greatly exaggerated, with curved, vibrating wings lowered all the way to the female's back, continually stroking her back feathers. Another hut couple is presently copulating—Marcel and Albertine. Albertine occasionally closes her eyelids, perhaps aroused by Marcel's steady stroking of her back with his wings. She raises her bill in the air, touches his, and Marcel gently rubs his bill on one side of Albertine's, then the other. Slowly, ever so slowly, Marcel nudges backward to get his tail in position. Then, after the crucial kiss, he carefully dismounts to her right side and slowly circles counterclockwise, close to Albertine's head, and she continues to nuzzle slightly upward. At this point Marcel faces her and makes a very deep, slightly prolonged "thank you" bow. She blinks and nods back, shakes her head, then returns to nibbling in her prone vicinity for more pebbles to add to their nest. Adélie males will give passing nods after dismounting, chinstrap males occasionally remember to do so—but gentoos seem to have it ingrained.

So much to see, so little time. The afternoon is racing too quickly—and I still need to count the Adélies on the northeastern end. It's a slow slog through the thigh-deep snow. On the way, with Port Circumcision on my right, I ponder Charcot, Louis Gain, and these amazing penguins. I find it totally mind-boggling that Antarctic penguins live virtually *all the time* in subfreezing seawater. They survive because they've adapted successfully to their circumstance: The right body shape. Heavy bones. Excellent diving and fishing skills—including keen underwater vision, high maneuverability, and the efficient use of oxygen stored in both their lungs and blood. Superb thermoregulation—including a special insulation of feathers, blubber, and oiling. The ability to endure long fasting periods during the breeding season and while molting. The successful recruitment of new members of their respective populations. A high survival of mature adults from season to season. A built-in osmosis system.

But their large populations obscure a high toll: While some penguins may live to eighteen or twenty years in the wild, adults are generally lucky to make it past a decade. Most chicks never survive to a second year and, in some Antarctic Peninsula colonies, one season's cohort of chicks may suffer a 90 percent mortality before some of this group return in their third year to the natal colony. As a matter of population dynamics, the important issue is whether deaths outpace recruits, or vice versa.

The specific, scientific names for Adélies and chinstraps are more straightforward than the gentoo's. And with the Adélie penguin, *Pygoscelis adeliae*, there's another French Connection. They're named for the wife of the eminent French Antarctic explorer Jules Sébastien César Dumont d'Urville. He made coastal surveys of Australia from 1826 to 1829 in the *Astrolabe*, then sailed to Antarctica in 1837 in the *Zélée*, discovering Joinville Island and many other locations in the northern portion of the Antarctic Peninsula, in the northwest Weddell Sea, and in the Erebus and Terror Gulf sectors. Notably, Dumont d'Urville had worked in the Mediterranean and was responsible for discovering and transporting the *Venus de Milo* back to France. So even in the Louvre, this beautiful work of art conjures thoughts of Antarctica, penguins, and the presumably beautiful Adelaide d'Urville. I trust she wasn't accorded this honor because she was low-slung with a chubby belly.

The chinstrap, *Pygoscelis antarctica*, has the most practical vernacular name among the *Pygoscelids*. The common name, of course, focuses directly on the chinstrap's distinct morphological character— the thin black band that extends across the white chin and throat, from ear to ear. The specific, scientific name *antarctica* refers to their narrowly proscribed Antarctic range. Indeed, at the time of the Second French Antarctic Expedition they were called "Antarctic Penguins." By the time of Bagshawe and Lester's Graham Land Expedition of 1920–22, they were often referred to as ringed penguins. The chinstrap moniker is a bit more recent. They also have been called the bearded penguin, the stonecracker—because of their raucous calls and displays—and in Spanish, *Pingüin de Collar* and *Barbijos*. The latter refers to the strap that secures a gaucho's hat. In German, they are the *Stormbandpinguin* and in French, *manchot à jugliare* or *manchot à antarctique*. In vernacular Russian, they are called "police penguins."

Remarkably, nine years into the twentieth century, nothing was known about the annual cycles and breeding proclivities of the brushtailed penguins. But what we do know, we began learning right here, at Petermann, with the Second French Antarctic Expedition. Charcot employed a crack team of scientists on his 1908–10 quest, including Maurice Bongrain, astronomer, hydrographer, and seismographer; Ernest Gourdon, geologist and glaciologist, who had traveled on Charcot's first expedition; René Godfroy, expert on tides and atmospheric chemistry; Jules Rouch, meteorologist and physical oceanographer, also expert on atmospheric electricity, who later headed the Oceanographic Institute of Monaco; and J. Liouville, zoologist, who later became director-in-chief of the French Institute of Science. And of course there was Louis Gain, the zoologist and botanist, who also climbed the ranks when he returned, ultimately becoming the director of the French National Meteorological Office.

Louis Gain was the first penguin-counter on Petermann, censusing 925 Adélie nests on Petermann's northeastern end. Gain's work preceded by three winters the emperor penguin discoveries of Edward Wilson, Birdie Bowers, and Apsley Cherry-Garrard at Cape Crozier, on the other side of the continent. Gain's seminal experiments began on January 12, 1909, when he marked fifty adult and seventy-five young Adélies on their right legs with celluloid rings of differing colors, the colors varying according to the age of the birds. He also marked twenty adult and twenty young gentoos. In October and November, after a long hiatus, the Adélies returned to Petermann and Gain was able to trace twenty-five of the adults he'd marked nine months previously. But no young birds were recovered. From these results, he deduced that the Adélies return to the same rookery year after year, and that young birds don't return until they're at least two years of age.

Gain keenly examined penguin behavior, from their pebble-rustling to their territoriality. He found the Adélie penguin, in particular, to be "a brave animal" who

> rarely flees from danger. If it happens to be tormented it faces its aggressor and ruffles the black feathers which cover its neck. Then it takes a stand for combat, the body straight, the animal erect, the beak in the air, the wings extended, not losing sight of its enemy. It then makes a sort of purring, a muffled grumbling, to prove that it is not satisfied and has not lost a bit of its firm resolution to defend itself. In this guarded position it awaits events. If the enemy beats a retreat, then the penguin abandons its menacing attitude; often it stays on the spot; sometimes it returns and, lying flat on the ground, pushes itself along with all the force of its claws and its wings. Should it be overtaken, instead of trying to increase its speed, it stops, backs up again to face anew the peril, and returns to its position of combat. Sometimes it takes the offensive, throws itself on its aggressor, which it punishes with blows of its beak and wings.

He had great admiration for the Adélies: "This bird is everywhere, watches over everything; it is to him, indeed, that the Antarctic belongs. Curious, unruly, violent, a chatterbox and a blusterer, of an extraordinary liveliness, you should see him dart like an arrow from the water to a height of more than 2 meters, and fall vertically down again on the piece of ice or the rock chosen for his nesting place."

Continuing my tromp uphill, I pass fourteen Adélies tobogganing in the direction of Circumcision Bay, furrowing deep grooves in the snow. They're essentially running forward—but with their bellies right on the snow, propelling themselves primarily with their claws and feet, and occasionally with paddle-strokes of the wings. I should have it so easy. Hiking this thigh-deep snow is more labor-intensive. One of my study stakes lies on a rise just ahead. It marks two adjacent Adélie colonies I've been censusing for my inventory project, which comprise a total of more than two hundred nests. Today, there is a vast majority of one-egg nests, with a single Adélie incubating. Only a few non-incubating mates are present. None of the Adélies are on two eggs and the remaining nests are eggless. With Adélies and chinstraps, the feeding runs can last for days. Gentoos, however, take much shorter shifts and prefer daytime runs—and to have everyone home for a late dinner or rest.

The Adélies are dusted from the recent snow. It's not unusual for spring snows to bury the birds totally. It doesn't affect their incubation, as long as the snow melts or blows away reasonably quickly. There's considerable crabbiness and squabbling, penguin to penguin, nest-holder to nest-holder. Many of the Adélies aim evil-eyed stares my way, flashing the white sclerae of their eyes. A few raise the feathers on their heads. Both are signs of aggression and I back off, sticking to the perimeter of the two colonies.

With my counting finished, I move to a higher outcrop, which provides a much better view north to the Lemaire Channel. Considerable brash and annual ice continue to be pushed by the current. Below and a bit east, on both sides of a conspicuous basaltic dike, there's a much larger concentration of Adélies. The dike cuts into the bedrock at the northeastern point, allowing a drainage for the snowmelt runoff, if and when that might occur later in the season.

There's a thirty- to forty-foot drop to the waterline from the flat platforms and ledges at the top of the dike, occupied by nesting Adélies and blue-eyed shags—the Antarctic cormorant. These Adélie colonies are the same ones Gain worked in 1909.

I rummaged the archives at the Smithsonian Institution in Washington, searching for Gain's paper describing the Antarctic penguins and elaborating some of the accomplishments of the second Charcot expedition. The paper had been translated from the French publication *La Nature* and reprinted in the Smithsonian's 1912 annual report. But I didn't know the article was accompanied by a slew of surprising photos, which sent a chill through me: The pictures were instantly recognizable—Baily Head at Deception Island, the basaltic dike at Petermann, places I'd worked for years. Now, ninety years beyond Gain and Charcot, nothing has changed physically. The penguins look the same, too, but they are a minimum of six—and likely, eight or more—generations removed from the time of the Second French Antarctic Expedition. Like Gain and Charcot, I am possessed. Why are we so enamored of penguins? Why do I feel so very connected to Gain and Charcot as well?

Emile G. Racovitza, a Romanian zoologist and botanist who participated with Gerlache on the *Belgica* expedition in 1897–99, asks us to imagine "a little old man, standing erect, provided with two broad paddles instead of arms, with a head small in comparison with the plump, stout body; imagine this creature with his back covered with a dark coat spotted with blue, tapering behind to a pointed tail that drags on the ground, and adorned in front with a glossy white breastplate. Have this creature walk on his two feet, and give him at the same time a droll little waddle and a continual movement of the head; you have before you something irresistibly attractive and comical." And this, from the man who is generally credited with discovering the Antarctic grass *Deschampsia antarctica* on the mainland of the Peninsula, the Antarctic midge-fly, and Antarctic springtails.

Our attraction to these penguins is in no way diminished because their densely packed rookeries can be smelled miles away, if the wind is right. Up close, the guano odor may be overpowering, but it is a mere distraction, part of the price for studying them. Gain has it right: They *are* irresistible. Too many of us strut around like they do. In German, there's even a verb that specifically describes this kind of waddling: *watscheln.* I'm charmed, tempted, lured, enchanted, captivated, magnetized, attracted, and enticed. It doesn't make a whit of a difference that penguins aren't the most intelligent of animals. Unwittingly, they are so, so sensitive to my needs. Penguins simply don't think, worry, or reason—even for a nanosecond. Their software wouldn't allow them to consider doing something thoughtful for *me.* Nevertheless, we strongly bond to these little black-and-white maître d's wearing spiffy tuxedos.

Gain understood, almost nostalgically:

On beaches accessible to the rookeries, there is usually a host of birds gathered there by the thousand, reminding one of the throngs of human beings that are attracted on fine summer days to our great beaches in France. They chat little; simply a few reflections whispered in a low tone, while in the distance one hears the stir of the noisy city.... What confusion in these cities of the Adélie; how many quarrels over stolen pebbles and property rights; how many battles, too, started by jealous husbands! And all this occurs on ground wet with melting snow, stained with mud the color of wine dregs.

Ah, the wine. There's little question that a hot shower and some good cabernet add a pleasant finish after long hours plowing through the guano. At the end of the day, I'm affected by *them* because they're impressive creatures and because of the impressive explorers and researchers who began unlocking their secrets. And because this knowledge is so recently won, I feel a special closeness to the Gains and Cherry-Garrards and Wilsons who have nourished my curiosity, made my Antarctic days more complete. They are my grandparents.

Penguins have captivated the human imagination. They are used to advertise ginger ale in North America and beer in Brazil. Potato chips in New Zealand and breath mints and mouth fresheners in Italy. Ice cream in Ecuador and, of course, a particular line of paperback books throughout the world. In downtown Prague, in the Czech Republic, a prominent sporting goods store has a penguin on its logo. And in Silver Spring, Maryland, just a short, two and a half miles from my northern home, a huge penguin mural adorns a wall underneath the local metro station. All the penguins are depicted boarding trains, heading for downtown Washington, reading their newspapers like every other commuter. At the vehicular intersection closest to the mural, there are signs advising drivers to be careful, announcing PEDESTRIAN SAFETY WE CARE!, with caricatures of a human adult and child, as well as a penguin, crossing the street. I've encountered Antarctic tourists going ashore wearing tuxedos, trying to look like penguins. But it doesn't quite fit. As a friend of mine says: You can put a tutu on a chimpanzee, but that doesn't mean it's a ballerina.

We can't approximate penguins' skills and adaptations. But we can appreciate them.

In 1907 the French satirist, essayist, social commentator, and novelist Anatole France published a book called *Penguin Island*. The story is about the half-crazy, almost blind, and ancient Saint Maël, who mistakenly baptized a colony of penguins—just another batch of heathens he thought needed reformation and redemption. The baptism brought howls of outrage and concern to the Holy Gates. Maël had departed too far from the sepulchre: This wasn't a gift to bestow on birds. Baptism is to wash away original sin, but penguins weren't conceived in sin. Baptism doesn't remove the penalty of penguin sin because there was no sin to begin with. And if baptism is to produce grace and virtuousness, the problem is that penguins are animals, which, to paraphrase one of the other fictional saints, can't achieve the virtues of confessors, virgins, widows, and the like. To repair Maël's grievous error, the Lord metamorphoses the penguins into humans, the better, then, to take advantage of the blessings baptism should provide—and of course, to become good Christians. Of course, they become just as vain, stupid, power-hungry, and mediocre as other, original humans. And no doubt reminiscent of how France, the author, viewed politicians, the church, the military, and other national institutions.

The book was published between Charcot's first and second expeditions. The fictional preface states: "In spite of the apparent diversity of the amusements that seem to attract me, my life has but one object. It is wholly bent upon the accomplishment of one great scheme. I am writing the history of the Penguins." Robert Cushman Murphy used these exact words—and in the original French—as an introduction to his description of the penguin family in his classic book *Oceanic Birds of South America* in 1936. Brian Roberts used a longer excerpt, also in the original French, in his 1940 report on the breeding behavior of penguins, particularly gentoos, based on findings from the British Graham Land Expedition of 1934–37.

So above the basaltic dike at Petermann, I possess a jumble of thoughts and images: Paris. The Champs Élysées. The penguins listening, curiously, to Charcot's gramophone. But mostly I imagine penguins being penguins, nothing else. The fictional preface to *Penguin Island* nods to the long-standing controversy about naming these animals:

> Dr. J. B. Charcot affirms . . . that the true and only Penguins are those Antarctic birds which we call *manchots,* and he gives for reason that they received from the Dutch, who in 1598 reached Cape Magellan, the name of *pinguinos,* doubtless because of their fat. But if the *manchots* are called penguins what are we in future to call the Penguins themselves. . . . He has acquired the right to name them by discovering them. But let him at least allow the Northern penguins to remain penguins. There will be the penguins of the South and those of the North, the Antarctic and the Arctic, the *alcides* or old penguins, and the *spheniscides* or former *manchots.* This will cause embarrassment to ornithologists who are careful in describing and classing the *palmipedes.* . . . For my part, I adapt easily to this confusion. Whatever be the difference between my penguins and those of M. J. B. Charcot, the resemblances are more numerous and deep-seated . . . their grave and

placid air, their comic dignity, their trustful familiarity, their sly simplicity, their habits at once awkward and solemn, ... pacific, abounding in speech, eager to see anything novel, immersed in public affairs, and perhaps a little jealous of all that is superior to them.

Here, here: Let us adapt.
Let penguins be penguins.

FIVE

Nuzzling with Madonna

Things men have made with wakened hands, and put soft life into
are awake through years with transferred touch, and go on glowing
for long years.
And for this reason, some old things are lovely
warm still with the life of forgotten men who made them.
                                                    —*D. H. LAWRENCE*

Bite and sting.

So fiercely bitter cold.

The late-afternoon sky slumps within a black-gray overcoat, the
temperature endures at 28°F, and the damned wind smacks at twenty
knots from the north-northwest—right into our faces. It may be a
straight shot, but this four-and-a-half-mile Zodiac ride to the north
end of Paradise Bay is profoundly uncomfortable. The relatively

short trip feels like an eternity—and I feel like a package of frozen meat. Hard to believe it's a mid-November springtime. The calendar's glimmers are abjured by winter's last spews and exhalations. I prepared with some extra woollies and fleece, but hunched in an open rubber boat and heading full speed into the wind, I find my extra layering rendered useless. It's not the same as counting 'guins on terra firma, where frequent movement keeps muscles limber and blood flowing. Fortunately, this little jaunt will take a max of ten minutes. My nose runs uncontrollably, the goblets freezing quickly and stiffly in my mustache and beard. The rhythmic thumping of the Zodiac's engine matches the chills that pound my body. I don't want to know how awful the windchill happens to be. The only possible modus operandi is to cover as much skin as possible.

Ahead, the hilly South Island of Waterboat Point emerges, marked by a few red-and-orange buildings of the Chilean Gabriel González Videla station. Just beyond is the so-called Main Island, where there are more—and larger—buildings. The gentoos are everywhere and obvious, lollygagging and puttering over the generous, mid-November snow cover, tobogganing down the east side of the Main Island—all seemingly busy. We'll swing around and hopefully disembark at the small, rotting wooden pier at the topside of the Main Island. The more I try shielding my head and face, the more my glasses fog. The more I try cleaning them, the more the lenses ice. Better to dream. Better to think of Thomas Wyatt Bagshawe and Maxime Charles Lester, who worked this godforsaken location more than seventy-five years ago, shivering their bums for a year and a day—yet, in the end, producing the first ever life-history study of gentoo and chinstrap penguins.

It's strange enough they made it to Waterboat Point in the first place, even more bizarre that they survived. These obscure, Robinson Crusoe–like characters have been practically forgotten by history—but not completely. The Treaty Parties have designated the corner of the Main Island where they lived as an official historical site—specifically, Antarctic Historical Monument No. 56. The area is roped off and an English-language sign commemorates the location, though seven decades of gentoo guano now cover the scant remnants: The base of the waterboat that served as their home. The outline of the hut and extension that the men added. The roots of door posts.

Paradise Bay—sometimes called Paradise Harbor—is a wide embayment that lies northeast of Charcot country, at the lower end of the Gerlache Strait. It lies about seventy-five miles north-northeast of the Lemaire Channel and ninety miles as the shag flies from Petermann Island. Bryde and Lemaire Islands form the western perimeter of the bay, the mainland Peninsula bounds it on the east. Waterboat Point juts out from the mainland at the extreme north end of the bay, where a narrow channel ambles toward Andvord Bay and Rongé Island. I'm happy to be returning: In terms of our knowledge base regarding brushtailed penguins, Waterboat Point is *Pygoscelid* Valhalla. The perpetrators were two unseasoned Britons who worked this site for most of 1921 and into January of 1922. They took the achievements of Louis Gain and the Second French Antarctic Expedition onward and upward—to another plane. Hail, hail to Bagshawe and Lester: the smallest expedition ever to spend the winter in the Antarctic. Penguins became their glory and their results have stood the test of time. But it wasn't intended that way.

I envision these bedraggled, wizened characters immersed in tracking the lives and habits of these curious animals. Shivering-cold scientists in tattered clothes studying immaculately clothed, warm penguins. As Bagshawe and Lester experienced, Waterboat Point offers little room to hike and stretch, is frequently windy, and, as today, is anything but paradisiacal. These two left a wonderful bequest—an affirmation that much can be achieved with hard work, dedication, and perseverance. Again, this mix of penguins and history. I need to do some nest counts and check on how the gentoos and chinstraps are doing. Much has changed since Bagshawe and Lester were the harbormasters of Paradise Bay.

They weren't best friends. They were callow, brazen, enthusiastic poseurs seeking adventure. Without a smidgen of Antarctic exploration experience, they signed on as the most junior members of the four-person British Imperial Expedition to Graham Land in 1920–22—Bagshawe as a geologist, Lester as a surveyor. If nothing else, this was testament to their blatant résumé-puffing: Bagshawe, charitably said, had no university training and was merely nineteen. Lester, with further charitable description, had been second mate on a tramp steamer, and at twenty-four, was slightly riper. Neither was expert in the fields for which they were respectively hired, which with twenty-twenty hindsight is substantial evidence that the expedition was atrociously planned and organized. Goals and logistics shifted from moment to moment and the men shifted from location to location—and at Waterboat Point, the leader and his number two finally bailed out. But to the surprise of the whalers who offered passage to safer quarters and then home, Bagshawe and Lester impulsively decided to stay. They had come to carry out scientific observations, they argued, and that's what they were going to do. Their soon-to-blossom fantasy adventure amounted to 366 days alone—cruelly, primitively exposed to the elements.

In the photographs from the expedition, both have a slightly emaciated appearance. Bagshawe was slenderly built, with an angular facial profile, hair and beard as well cropped as possible given the conditions. A very determined look filled his eyes. Lester was a bit shorter, with a broader face, and woollier, more unkempt head and facial hair. His photographs radiate a rakish ebullience. There were few amenities—dogs, a lifeboat, some books, a gramophone—and an abundance of inconveniences—damp matches that wouldn't light, no communications equipment, and sparse survival gear. The whalers' waterboat and extension in which they lived needed constant repair. The structure leaked and, when the stove got unwieldy, occasionally caught on fire. Initially, survival was the only order of business; then, slowly, meteorology and tidal observations. But ultimately, with little to occupy their moments and no room to roam, their therapy and sanity became the resident gentoos and chinstraps. Penguins became the focus of their lives and work. My friend Wally Herbert, the esteemed polar explorer, describes these two as prime examples of the "keen young men" the United Kingdom has a penchant for sending to the Deep South: Gutsy. Determined. At times, extraordinarily naive and excessively macho. Hell-bent on a rousing good time. And despite the craziness, succeeding at times more wildly than they might have dreamed.

Frank Debenham, veteran of Scott's *Terra Nova* expedition and later a founder and director of the Scott Polar Research Institute, said that Bagshawe and Lester possessed a quality that would have annoyed Napoleon—of not having the good sense to know when they were defeated. Debenham had greatly assisted the expedition, from his base at the Sedgwick Museum in Cambridge, and did his best to untangle the financial and organizational mess that John Cope, the leader of the expedition, had created. In the end, Cope produced nothing. However, Bagshawe and Lester, initially the lowest of possible lights, became stars in the adventurer's galaxy.

Debenham recounts one of the annual dinners of the Antarctic Club in London, when it is customary to go around the room, in chronological order, to recognize and toast the various expeditions that were represented. Boisterous carousing was normal, a chance for crusty Antarctic veterans to tell their stories, reminisce, slap backs, and perhaps, wonder anew about their collective and respective fortunes in returning safely. This particular night, when the British Imperial Expedition of 1920–22 was announced, two shy men rose to roaring applause and the raised glasses of all of the veterans. There was tremendous admiration for these lads.

Bagshawe and Lester were likely aware of Murray Levick's popular penguin book, *Antarctic Penguins,* which was published in 1914, but they'd never before seen penguins in feathers and flesh. They may have had some prior knowledge of Gain's work at Petermann more than a decade earlier. On the way south to Waterboat Point, they'd seen some penguins at Deception Island and other locations, but much of this was cursory and more specifically aimed at collecting food—eggs—than studying the penguins' habits. Yet, from these inexpert beginnings, Bagshawe and Lester gathered a mother lode of new information. No, they didn't reach the Pole, die in the field, struggle to survive with Shackleton, or participate on any of the most famous Antarctic expeditions of this century. Unassumingly, they just *did* the penguin work, under the worst of conditions.

After their return, with Debenham's encouragement, Bagshawe produced an account of their full year alone, *Two Men in the Antarctic,* and a classic report of their penguin discoveries, *Notes on the Habits of the Gentoo and Ringed or Antarctic Penguins.* As with many who've been privileged to go south, Antarctica changed lives and perspectives. Bagshawe wrote that "when life is a rush and freedom from worry is almost unknown, it is good to look back upon a time when the affairs of the world were closed to us and when money had no utility.... Before I left England I was told by an explorer friend that when once I had been to the Antarctic, I should, in spite of the discomforts, dangers and difficulties, fall under the spell of its fascination and all my life wish to return. Many times since I have realized that he was right."

The British Imperial Expedition organizer John Lachlan Cope had been a biologist and surgeon with the Ross Sea party during Shackleton's Transantarctic Expedition of 1914–17. According to Roland Huntford, Cope had left his medical and science training to join the expedition, becoming the surgeon when no other doctor appeared. The idea had been for the Ross Sea party to lay depots for Shackleton and his men, who planned to traverse the continent from the other side. But that crossing never happened, with Shackleton's ship *Endurance* sinking in the Weddell Sea. All under Shackleton's command ultimately survived, but that wasn't the case on the far side. The Ross Sea party suffered various calamities. Cope and others were stranded onshore because the support ship *Aurora* was blown and damaged in a blizzard, then was beset in the pack. Three men lost lives on their way back to Cape Evans, where Cope and others were holed up, wiling away their days, becoming irrational if not crazy. Cope suffered from boils and, as days wore on, inflicted his outbursts of temper on the others.

Cope hoped that his new venture would be more fulfilling. Cope's original plans were to circumnavigate the continent. That could not be financed. Replacement dreams included taking a fleet of aircraft south in order to make the first-ever plane flights in Antarctica, perhaps, even, to fly over the Pole. Cope enlisted a young pilot named Hubert Wilkins as the fourth member of the expedition. But Cope's entrepreneurial skills were less than impressive. Even before the four headed south, it was clear that Cope couldn't secure the aircraft. Wilkins was ready to quit, but Cope managed to convince him to continue with Variation C: The four would go to Hope Bay, barely on the northeastern side of the Peninsula, and extend Nordenskjöld's exploratory work south of Snow Hill Island—on foot. The men headed from different embarkation points, rendez-vousing at Deception Island on December 24, 1920. But Hope Bay was iced in and there was no way the men could be off-loaded. Then Cope moved to Variation D: Head south down the Bransfield Strait and through the Gerlache Strait to Paradise Bay, and from there cross over the Peninsula on foot—170 miles distant, to the approximate spot on the Weddell Sea side where Nordenskjöld had concluded his work.

The four-man party reached the north end of Paradise Bay on January 21, 1921. They camped in an old waterboat that whalers from the catcher *Neko* had beached eight years earlier. But soon, Cope and Wilkins lapsed into major vacillation. Cope saw no point in pursuing what appeared to be an impossible trek over the glacier- and crevasse-laden Peninsula, which would have taxed their energies long before any charting and exploratory work might commence on the Weddell Sea side. Wilkins saw his dreams of making an Antarctic flight fizzle like snow hitting the water. For that fulfillment, Wilkins would have to wait another seven and a half years. On February 26, 1921, Cope, Wilkins, and Lester left in their lifeboat, searching for a whale-factory ship that might take them back to Montevideo. They returned in a week on the catcher *Bjerk.* Cope and Wilkins began packing furiously. Bagshawe and Lester, though, decided to gamble on a little history-making.

Our Zodiac swings to starboard, clears a few small floes, and meanders toward the rotten dock. The ice foot still extends past and over the planks, so disembarkation needs to be a quick jump over the bow of the Zodiac and onto the few exposed rocks. This is the Main Island, or what Bagshawe and Lester simply called the Island. It's apparent that the gentoos' breeding season is moving along. On much of the snow-free space between the station buildings, clusters of breeding territories have already been established, with gentoos intently incubating. A quick check of the nests closest to the disembarkation rock suggests that most nests have one egg. Bryde and Lemaire Islands provide a lee, shut the wind, and I am very happy to be onshore, moving about. My stiffness and chill will abate shortly. There are no distractions from street noise, machinery, radio, TV, planes, trains, or cars. The silence amplifies the gentoos' mutual *hee-HAW* calls. I close my eyes and for long moments Antarctica becomes an aural, not a visual, experience. I'm aroused to what I might easily miss: The scratches of the penguins moving over the snow. The tinkles of brash on brash in the channel. The stretching noise as a gentoo shakes its head, flinging salt drips off its bill. The gentoos' breathy exhalations, sprinkling puffs of warm clouds into the air. The quiet hiss of one nearby gentoo. It's as if my ears have lost aeons of wax buildup. The oft-missed noises complete a picture.

The Main Island has a number of large buildings, but today no personnel are on-site. Snow has drifted two yards above the doorstep at some of the buildings. The station sprang to life during the early 1950s but was not occupied regularly following the 1957–58 International Geophysical Year. It is named in honor of the Chilean president who visited the Antarctic in 1947. Through the 1980s, there was little maintenance, with equipment left to rust and with many doors and windows broken or left open and unshuttered. Just east of the rotting pier are rusting rail tracks, which lead up to an equipment and storage shed. On my first visit here, I recall following the tracks toward the shed door, slightly ajar, expecting to find inside the wheeled vehicle or container that was used to haul supplies from the shoreline. Rather, I was amazed to find five very active gentoo nests and one bustling shag nest—all in full swing, chicks doing fine, thank you. A few cracked panes allowed the guano to vent. In recent years, the Chileans have cleared much of the trash, closed the doors, and repainted the buildings. Surrounded by honking gentoos and station buildings, a signpost indicates directions and the thousands-of-kilometer distances to various cities.

Waterboat Point consists of a small set of islands that are disconnected from the mainland—the Antarctic Peninsula—at high water. The prominent spots of exposed land are arranged in a U shape, with the Main Island comprising the left—or western—end of the U, the South Island the southwestern crook. The smaller South Island has steep sides and is about 370 feet long from top to bottom, and at most two hundred feet wide. It lies more than twenty feet above sea level. The U encloses a small, shallow bay where visiting yachts occasionally anchor. The Main Island and South Island are joined by a narrow rock umbilical. Some additional orientation: The Main Island extends about 700 feet from top to bottom and is about 350 feet wide at its broadest, east-west point. At its highest it is 19 feet above sea level. The remains of Bagshawe and Lester's waterboat and extension are at the extreme lower end of the rocky Main Island, a mere six feet above the high-water mark. The water came close, but never flooded them during their stay.

The Waterboat Point gentoos quickly adjusted to Bagshawe and Lester's modifications. The men established a small meat dump immediately northeast of their quarters, toward the small bay. Eventually, they fixed a tide pole just off the northwestern part of the Main Island. About seventy-five feet north of their quarters, they erected a meteorological screen to protect their instruments. The screen was held in place by many wires, which took a while for the gentoos to negotiate. At first, Bagshawe and Lester report, they would run into the wires, be "boinged" backward, then would continue until giving up. One of their birds was so annoyed at the obstacle it started to attack another gentoo nesting nearby, which the angry penguin presumed was the cause of the obstacle. As Bagshawe and Lester's year progressed, however, the gentoos learned to duck their heads and pass under these guy wires. Or they would spend considerable time inspecting the wires and equipment diligently before returning to their nest.

At the bottom of the U, a 150-foot-long gravel bar connects to the mainland at low tide. The right side of the U is the base of a huge glacier extending down from the higher reaches of the mainland, which in places exceeds a hundred feet in elevation. Topping the right side of the U—about 450 feet north of the gravel bar—is a hilly, exposed area the men called Coal Point. A whale-catcher had mistakenly offloaded a supply of coal here—not exactly in close proximity to the men's waterboat home. If the tide is high, the only access from the Main Island to Coal Point, 400 feet away, is via Zodiac. Coal Point seems to erupt from the foot of the glacier and likely connects to the mainland. Today, most of the ice has melted or receded from the little, interior bay. Bagshawe and Lester had watched the gentoos use the sheltered ice in the small bay as a rest stop early in the nesting season, as they were rushing off to fish, or upon their return. The men used this small bay to launch their operational lifeboat, which otherwise was hauled out and left on the Main Island. Even in the best of circumstances they had precious little room for hiking and walking. It was like being trapped on an ice floe.

Today, gentoos occupy the edges of most of the buildings and the space around and under the oil tanks on the western side of the Main Island. When Bagshawe and Lester were here in 1921–22, there were 12,000 gentoos over the whole of Waterboat Point, with 450 chinstraps on the South Island and another 700 at Coal Point. But, now, their numbers are much reduced, no doubt related to the station's construction and operation. The present-day population around the U is perhaps 1,400 gentoo pairs. Only about 8 chinstrap pairs remain, confined to the slightly elevated area at Coal Point. I want to hustle over and complete my chinstrap nest counts first, assuming the tide is sufficiently low. I hike through the snow, past the first building, and reach the raised area where the oil storage drums are located. The nests are packed very tightly, no more than a foot apart, but there's little antagonism between neighbors. A quiet night in gentoo-town. A brown skua sits patiently on top of one of the tanks, waiting for a gentoo egg to be exposed.

The stone perimeter along the pathway is topped with a small Madonna statue. There's been one on this spot since my first visit in the 1980s, and there always has been one gentoo pair insisting on nesting at or on the Madonna's feet, or sometimes behind the statue. But this year's *Virgen Maria* is glass-enclosed and guano-proofed—no longer an open-air arrangement. With the Madonna's new protection, the only choice for this pair is to nuzzle against the box container. Still, this spot remains an excellent, elevated lookout from which to spy passing intruders. Mr. Madonna bows down to his mate, lying prone in the nest; they touch bills, wheez simultaneously, then both raise beaks to the sky for some mutual *hee-HAW*-ing. Mrs. Madonna rises slowly to reveal a very dirty egg. She bends over and gently turns the egg, rolls it up into its brood pouch, and plummets down again on the nest. The spherical egg is about two and three quarter inches long, and two and a quarter inches wide. Mr. Madonna, just a few inches away, leers outwardly at me, but otherwise he seems most interested in whether the egg's been properly rotated. A second egg is coming—forthwith.

I head down an incline to the roped-off Bagshawe and Lester memorial, situated in a froth of accumulated mud and guano. The gentoos have been very active down here, as advanced as the gentoos at the landing site. Many have one egg down and there are a handful already possessing the expected two-egg complement. Most of the snow around the waterboat's remains has been battened away and melted by gentoo feet and bodies. I'm pleased to see that the tide is down, which means there will be no difficulty reaching the Coal Point chinnies. A few putative gentoo nests lie below the tide line, toward the small inner bay. Why won't they learn? The tide swings here may be as much as six feet and these nests aren't going to make it. The builders must be younger, inexperienced birds.

All three of the brushtailed penguins lay two eggs. Theoretically, two chicks may fledge, but there are all kinds of losses and reasons: Eggs stolen by skuas. Eggs abandoned by a starving parent whose mate doesn't return to take an incubation shift. Exposed eggs chilled and frozen because of freak snows or rains. Chicks plucked away by a skua pair working in tandem, one skua distracting the parent penguin, the other skua snatching the youngster, then both pulling it apart to eat. Chicks starving because the parents can't find food. At best, annual production will be perhaps 1 to 1.25 chicks per active nest. To obtain these productivity numbers, it is necessary to record data at two key times. The first window runs mid-November to early December, when egg-laying is at its peak. *Peak* means a majority of nests having two eggs. If all the nests have one egg or none, peak may be as much as a week to ten days off. If the vast majority of nests have one egg, peak will soon follow because brush-tailed lay their eggs two to three—or at most, four—days apart.

But if the vast majority of nests have two eggs, the peak's been missed.

So how do you tell when peak's been reached? Obviously the penguins aren't interested in showing you their prizes. Much of the time you'll have some luck with the penguins randomly stretching and displaying to one another. But even with all the movement, there are times you're not quite sure whether they're on one or two eggs. The problem is that their vertically placed brood patches are fairly long—a good four to six inches—and a second egg may be so well tucked that it's impossible to see. So in times of doubt, the preferred research technique is to approach the penguin from the rear, distract it by placing your field notebook forward—which it will certainly notice and likely peck—then grab its tail and lift upward. This propels the bird, more or less, right onto its face—a position from which it can't move. It's a technique that Bagshawe first described. The penguin's center of gravity is very low, so a little tip forward is all that's needed. It's like knocking over a bowling pin. Quickly, you note the number of eggs and the butt is gently returned to place. This isn't recommended, obviously, without proper training and the appropriate research permits—and it certainly isn't recommended if you're not wearing eyeglasses and if you're not fully prepared to get whacked. In some cases, that means whacked *intensely*. Penguins can't beat their wings as quickly as hummingbirds, of course, but they can get in more licks and combinations than Muhammad Ali in his prime—with both flippers blazing. The other downside, common to all penguin work, is that you might be lifting right when the penguin unleashes a stream of guano.

Once the eggs are laid, incubation is shared by both parents for just under five weeks. In gentoos, incubation consists of short, two- to five-day shifts. At some locations, there is a changeover every twelve hours. In chinstraps, contrastingly, the female takes the first shift, for up to a week. Then comes the male on eggs for eight to ten days, the female returning for about a week, followed by short changes until hatching. The Adélies have the most rigorous and lengthy schedules. The male takes the first shift, for ten days to two weeks. Then comes the female on eggs for seven to ten days, fol- lowed by short changes until hatching. And think about this: With the Adélies and chinstraps, there are rigorous fasting regimes tied to the pre-laying season. The male Adélie, for example, may have been fasting for over a month to five weeks before the female relieves him for the second shift.

The second, key count for my project comes in late January to early February, when the chicks—now resembling little rotund fluff- balls—reach three to five weeks of age and begin to associate, away from their nests, in large huddles, or crèches. *Peak* in terms of chick- counting means censusing the crèched chicks before they head to the beach. *Productivity* is expressed in terms of the number of fledged chicks per active nest. For the first two to three weeks after hatching, gentoo, chinstrap, and Adélie chicks are brooded by their parents. For the first two of these weeks, there's little problem fitting at least partway into the parent's brood pouch. Then, increasingly, the chicks protrude, at best able to keep their heads covered. It's not uncommon to see a lot of brushtaileds incubating what look like two penguin butts.

Crossing the gravel bar, slipping past the glacier, I emerge upon an old *refugio* that the Chileans erected to honor Gabriel González Videla. There are gentoos mucking about on all sides of the hut. Also, there are a number of snowy sheathbills parading from nest to nest, looking for some excreta to slurp. Bagshawe and Lester may have been the first to record the scuzzy habits of these chicken-faced white scavengers. The sheathbills will scurry in after a penguin's shot some guano, or even try to disrupt a chick-feed, so regurgitated food will end up on the ground for them to lap. Guano and mud are flowing substantially near the hut. That González Videla is honored with all of this is interesting. After being elected president of Chile in 1946, with a wild mélange of support, he instituted judicial proceedings against his former campaign manager, the politician and esteemed poet Pablo Neruda. Neruda was an ardent communist and later would be instrumental in Salvador Allende's rise to the presidency. The 1946 election was a marriage of convenience for both of these men—González Videla being the most acceptable candidate to Neruda and the communists and having no qualms about securing whatever support he needed to win. But the alliance broke dramatically, as the new president shied away from promises made to Neruda's faction. Neruda openly accused González Videla of betrayal. González Videla countered by instituting Neruda's removal from the Chilean Senate and issuing an arrest order. Neruda went into hiding and made a miraculous escape to safety over the Andes.

So in this austral springtime of the present, standing amid guano and gentoos, there's another recollection. These political intrigues were the impetus for Neruda's magnum opus, *Canto General de Chile*, which contains many virulent attacks on González Videla. But this work also contains some beautiful poetry about Antarctica—its "peaceful breast that cleans/the cold like a pure rectangle of quartz,/ ...ice made cities raised/on a crystal spire, the wind/ranged your salty paroxysm/like a jaguar burned by snow.... Your cupolas birthed danger/from the glaciers' vessel,/and in your desolate dorsal, life is/like a vineyard beneath the sea, burning/unconsummated, reserving fire/for the snow's springtime."

On the high end of Coal Point, I find the eight active chinstrap nests, with lots of mutual displaying between the paired-off mates. Though occupying the highest possible nesting locations, the chinnies are surrounded by gentoos. One chinstrap nest bears a single egg. When Bagshawe and Lester came south for their Very Big Adventure, their first stop was at Deception Island—and the first penguins Bagshawe encountered were chinstraps. It happened at Entrance Point on November 23, 1920, the same exact spot where I had my first, definitive penguin encounter, sixty-two years and twenty-three days later. In 1920 Bagshawe had these indelible impressions:

> The first thing that strikes one about a penguin rookery is the fearful noise which goes on the whole time; the second, the odour; in fact, these two characteristics enable one to locate a rookery long before it can be seen. The rookery was reminiscent of a farm-yard on a wet winter's day. The Ringed Penguins, who prefer the higher ground for their nests, had quite a long way to go down the slope to reach the sea. Sometimes they attempted to run, or rather waddle, more quickly, but they found this difficult and usually toppled over and had to continue the rest of the journey toboggan-wise, propelled along by their flippers.

Bagshawe's vertigo made this visit, mostly for egging, a quaking, sweaty affair. But there were more penguins. He visited the Baily Head chinstrap colony on the southeastern side of Deception, near an offshore feature known as the Sewing Machine and Needles. On Boxing Day, he made a return to Baily Head. Later, he and others took a motor boat around the western side of the island, past Entrance Point, to more chinstraps.

Then came gentoos. When Cope, Wilkins, Bagshawe, and Lester reached Waterboat Point on January 12, the gentoos had just hatched chicks and the men felt they were disturbing the penguins' peace. Bagshawe and Lester had to move young gentoos to drop stores, and spent much time crazily trying to persuade chickless gentoos to accept these youngsters. Gentoos already with chicks tried to kill the intruding youngsters. Mixed results, mixed feelings. Some of the barren parents eagerly accepted these chicks, others pecked the newcomers mercilessly. Not denied, the scavenging skuas obtained more than a few meals. The *Neko*'s old waterboat, though a mere six feet above the tide line, provided the best shelter—a godsend compared to the trauma of potentially living in tents. The boat was twenty-seven and a half feet long, ten and a half feet wide at its max, and had a height of just under four feet. It was entirely covered in by a deck, which had an overhead hatch for access to the interior. A short ladder allowed the men to climb upward to the hatch. The boat was too heavy to lift and relocate, and it had a minor tilt of eight degrees. In one end of the boat, the men slept in sleeping bags, separated by small tables, and with bookcases behind and above their heads.

Almost immediately they began extensive remodeling, adding an outer hut that was completed on January 17. The inner section of this addition housed their kitchen, a cooking stove made from an oil drum, and a primus stove. There were seats and an additional table, and a wood hole. It was built to a height of seven feet to allow the men standing room. The outer section of the hut gave access to the coal supply in one corner, and a door to the outside on the opposite wall. To reduce drafts, they nailed sacks around the sides of the waterboat and hung spare eiderdowns on the inner side of the lounge—which Bagshawe conjured as typical decor for a "lunatic asylum."

Cope was consumed with other matters. Prospects for crossing over the top of the Peninsula were muddled. There was no clear route and by February 25 Cope was ready to abandon the expedition. On March 3 both he and Wilkins sailed away, leaving Bagshawe and Lester behind. Two days later, the whalers returned, attempting to talk the men out of their silliness. The whalers knew the inherent risks, but the lads wanted to stay. The whalers promised them that the first factory ship down through the Gerlache next season would send a catcher to retrieve them. The market for whale oil had dropped and it was unclear how many ships would come back. Bagshawe and Lester actually hadn't thought about being stranded.

Could Bagshawe and Lester have imagined what they were getting into—what life on a small frozen spit might involve? Indeed, were they creating their own lunacy? At the instant of their decision, there was considerable and obvious doubt these brazen young men would achieve anything. Wilkins, telegraphing from South America on his way home, informed Debeham:

COPE, LESTER, IRRESPONSIBLE, IGNORANT, DANGEROUSLY INCOMPETENT
EXPEDITIONARY MATTERS. BAGSHAWE CONTENTEDLY INACCURATE PLANS
UNSERIOUSLY ATTEMPTED BAGSHAWE LESTER WINTERING IDLY UNCOM-
FORTABLE. COPE DISHONORABLY ATTEMPTING FURTHER COMPLICATIONS.

It is true they were never really comfortable. The reality hovered
from being not-too-discomfited to being downright miserable. A
crack allowed light to enter and was satisfactory when the wind
wasn't howling. Matches were damp and starting the stove was difficult. They had a lifeboat and sledge boat for short excursions, but
basically stayed close to home. There was an electric torch to assist
their nighttime wanderings and note-taking. They busily tended to
setting up the gramophone. The alarm clock was cranky in the cold,
and was too large to be warmed in the sleeping bags, as Lester often
did with the chronometers. They had dogs and some books—Darwin, Dickens, and Thackeray, but there were no bona fide windows
and the light was minimal and dim. At times the men wished they'd
chosen a more scenic and interesting location. They felt confined to
a small country garden; it was almost like being in prison. Proper
haircuts and baths were unknown.

A first order of business was adding to their larder—winter
would be soon at hand, but it wasn't a pleasant proposition. Perhaps
anticipating future nightmares, Bagshawe recalled a visit to nearby
Shag Point, where he and Lester found bands of chinstraps attacking
them en masse, pecking and flipper-whacking with hostility and rage.
They began killing gentoos—fifty fully or nearly fledged young,
which Bagshawe detested:

It was particularly distasteful to me, for I had begun to study their lives seriously and had become fond of the amusing creatures. We looked on them as our friends and the one redeeming feature of life at Water-Boat Point.

The usual method was to shoot them with a rifle and then, if they were not killed outright, to hit them on the back of the head with a geological hammer. The latter operation was quite sufficient by itself, but the penguins were becoming elusive and seemed to scent danger. . . . Their preparation was soon reduced to a fine art and I could decapitate them, cut them open, cut off the breasts and legs, and take out the hearts and livers very quickly. At my period of maximum efficiency I could butcher them at the rate of fifteen an hour.

At one point, Lester actually broke the butt of his rifle trying to kill a penguin by smashing it over the head. But amid the gory reality of survival, they were intrigued by the penguins—and became committed to learning more about them. Meals became science investigations. The young gentoos would make some fine eating, but the men examined their food source closely. They found stones or pebbles in many stomachs, which no doubt assisted penguins in grinding and digesting their food, and established that these youngsters were eating krill and occasionally fish. The largest pebble was an inch and a half in diameter, and the most stones found in one stomach was fifty-three. One of the fully fledged birds weighed twelve pounds, almost 14 percent of which was krill stuffed into its very full belly. From this point forward, whenever penguins were killed, measurements were taken. Keen observers, they noted that one bird had a three-eighths-inch-thick blubber layer round its neck and heart, which thinned around the stomach, then thickened around the legs. This specimen also produced the remains of 960 krill in its belly.

The gruesome but necessary task became more difficult in mid-March, when penguins became scarce. The men turned to killing seals, which they hated: "We should never have dreamed of such repulsive actions, but here we were callous about it. I suppose that the necessity for food brings out the savage instincts of 'man the hunter.' At home, we politely allow the cloak of civilization to blind us to the slaughter necessary to produce our daintily cooked meals." Warming their hands in the entrails of a seal brought little consolation.

By late March, with snow accumulating and their molt completed, the gentoos began reveling in the snow. To the men's amusement, they would toboggan along on their breasts, propelling forward with beak and flippers, then sliding down with flippers tucked to the side. One gentoo went a distance of thirty-six feet. Bagshawe and Lester were drawn to the gentoos' playfulness and equanimity, but were irked by the chinstraps' irritability. The men found the quiet "continually disturbed by the sound of their blows as they chased each other around the rookery. The old birds had frequently to put the younger generation in its place." Bagshawe and Lester considered the South Island chinstrap rookery a veritable "babel of noise," where the birds "screeched more than ever, and many a time we praised heaven that we lived amid the quieter and lower-keyed Gentoos, and not near their squawking cousins." By mid-April, the weather worsened and all the chinstraps had gone. The gentoos—

a few of which would visit off and on during the winter—were now wallowing in the guano, then spending long moments cleaning themselves at sea, but undoing their clean appearance as soon as they came ashore.

During Bagshawe and Lester's winter, the daily mix was approximately four hours of dusky light and twenty hours of darkness. It was a painfully frigid experience. They shivered for months. From Bagshawe's twentieth birthday on April 18 through the end of August, the wind was constantly at gale force, and temperatures went as low as −16°F. They endured the same tiresome meals: Seal meat stewed, fried, or minced. Boiled penguin breast—their *penguin à l'ordinaire*. Or penguin meat in small chunks boiled with pemmican and pieces of ship's biscuit—dubbed *penguin à la pemmican*. Then minced penguin and more minced seal. Bagshawe vowed mince would never appear on his menu when he returned home—just the memory was enough to satisfy his appetite. Delectables like jam, marmalade, sardines, or beans were in sparing supply. Fried skua breasts and seal brains were rare treats.

Frederick Cook, the United States polar explorer who worked on Gerlache's Belgian Antarctic Expedition of 1897–99, had a particularly unappetizing description of penguin meat: "Imagine a piece of beef, odiferous codfish and a canvasbacked duck roasted together in a pot, with a blood and cod-liver oil for sauce." No wonder Bagshawe and Lester occasionally used Worcestershire sauce, celery seed, and curry powder to disguise the intense taste of penguin flesh. Gerald Cutland, who worked in 1956–57 as a cook at the British station in the Argentine Islands, south of Petermann Island, advised that: "The meat of young shags, seals and penguins makes excellent eating but, in the natural state, it is rather too highly flavoured to be palatable. It should therefore be washed thoroughly and hung in the fresh air for a few days, or in the case of shags for a couple of weeks, before cooking. It is further improved by blanching; this consists of putting the meat in cold water, bringing the water to a boil, then removing the meat and washing it." But Bagshawe and Lester hardly had time for blanching and washing. The penguin meat was always close to spoiling—becoming decidedly "niffy" as they put it, and there was the dilemma of live penguins constantly falling into their meat excavation and fouling the stores.

At Coal Point, I find it curious to see just small numbers of chinstraps amid the hordes of gentoos. For a few seasons at King George Island in Admiralty Bay, well to the north, chinstraps were recorded as aggressively expelling young Adélie penguins who'd dared to appropriate some prime nest sites. The surmise was that the experienced chinstraps had lost nest sites at another island and were absolutely determined to stake a claim elsewhere. Here, the chinstraps are seemingly on the short end, irrespective of experience. They have taken a big hit since the mid-1950s. The base construction was one factor. All chinstraps are now gone from the South Island and the remaining few at Coal Point are surrounded—and perhaps are being ousted—by gentoos.

To make gentoo censuses meaningful, *all* gentoos at a particular location—meaning all gentoos in all colonies—need to be counted. That's because gentoos move around a lot and often change their specific nest sites. They stay in the same general vicinity, but the specific nest site may shift to a subcolony or another colony around the corner, where there may be less disturbance. Chinstraps and

Adélies, by contrast, stick firmly to a particular colony or subcolony, making year-to-year changes in particular colonies or subcolonies easier to detect. If your counts of particular chinstrap and Adélie groups change significantly, you know something is afoot in that site's population. But with gentoos, because of their fragile nest-site tenacity, you've got to count them all. And today at Waterboat Point, that means counting every single nest around the U.

With the small chinstrap contingent logged, I start the gentoo censusing—from Coal Point down past the *refugio*, and clear around to the other side. As a parting shot, the handful of chinstraps tender vociferous, squawking *duh-ARGH'-ARGH'-ARGH', duh-ARGH'-ARGH'-ARGH'* calls in my direction, completely drowning out the more numerous 'toos. Even a few chinnies—if you're close—can blow eardrums.

I slowly tiptoe through the gentoo hordes, tally-whacker—the same metal or plastic counters airplane flight attendants use to determine how many passengers are on board—in hand, clicking all the way. With each click, the scale on the front of the whacker advances toward 9,999. Because I have only an hour to go before the Zodiac returns, today's gentoo census will necessarily be a one-off—no time for repetition.

Initially, it goes well: The gentoos are spread neatly over the rocks and it's easy to keep track of all of the nests. However, the censusing is much harder near the *refugio*. The gentoos are clumped very tightly and surround all sides of the hut. The trick is to pick an obvious point of departure—today I take the corner just left of the door—and to move slowly in one direction or the other, around the periphery of the penguins, until returning to that same starting point.

Because I favor my right eye, I'm a counterclockwise penguin-counter, clicking with the right thumb and using my field notebook—held with the left hand—to block from view what I've not yet counted. Halfway around the *refugio* I encounter a rather strange gentoo—what we call a *blondie,* a penguin whose pigmentation is much reduced. It isn't technically an albino—the eye has its normal color, but the black plumage on the head and back is totally faded. All of its pigmentation genes haven't clicked to the "on" position. The technical term is *leucism.* They're rare items, but over the last three years I've seen blond gentoos, Adélies, and chinstraps. The interesting part is that all of the blondies seem to compete quite well for mates, and to have no difficulty raising chicks.

Blondies are one of the few things Bagshawe and Lester didn't see—but not for an absence of trying. They didn't miss much. These men and their accomplishments are locked into every nook and cranny. I reach the umbilical to the Main Island, and slowly approach the passel of gentoos nesting over the remains of Bagshawe and Lester's waterboat. The few remaining pieces are barely discernible. I guess it's appropriate that what's left is thoroughly guano-fied. I envision the stitched-together panoramic photographs that Bagshawe included in *Two Men in the Antarctic,* taken from approximately the same position where I now stand. Standing over these gentoos, I turn slowly 360 degrees, absorbing how much has changed, how much has not. The glacier front is a bit reduced, but the channel north to Andvord Bay looks the same, and Bryde and Lemaire Islands appear basically the same. But the penguin swarms are gone. The gentoos are down by a whopping 75 percent from Bagshawe and Lester's time, though holding their own—probably increasing a bit—since the base was erected here in the 1950s. The few remaining chinstraps, as long as they last, remain the southern-most chinstraps nesting on this side of the Antarctic.

I back off slightly, admiring one gentoo pair going through a set of loud mutual displays, bowing and *hee-HAW*-ing to each other, totally focused on their gentoo business. This pair—indeed, all of the gentoos displaying over these historic artifacts—may descend from birds Bagshawe and Lester closely watched. No doubt, as time lapsed for the first eight months, the men didn't have a bundle of work to fill their days. Sure, there were regular weather observations, augmented later by tidal measurements, but these kinds of data col-lection are serial—required at certain intervals, say, hourly—and complicated only by extreme weather. When Bagshawe and Lester decided to take on penguins, things changed: They had to be focused at all times because penguins don't perform on a specific hourly sched. The necessity, however, greatly assisted their sanity and I'm grateful they got their fingernails dirty with penguins. Their detailed, almost obsessive-compulsive observations filled in quite a bit of that jigsaw puzzle known as the natural history of gentoos and chin-straps.

As winter receded in August, the returning gentoos were welcome sights for their weary eyes. But with each hopeful glimpse of spring there were crushing reminders of cold moments still to suffer. Bag-shawe's clothes were disintegrating. The accumulated snow had squeezed their limited outdoor space even further. Their life revolved around the plot of guano now below my feet. As Bagshawe put it: "Our kingdom was an uninhabited continent, yet with all its five and a half million square miles we could walk only a few hundred yards!" Frost grew thick on the roof of their living quarters, primarily from their breath freezing above. One night, slabs began falling on Bagshawe. They had looked forward to the moon's eclipse in mid-September, but there were too many clouds. In frustration, Bagshawe wrote: "The man who called this spot Paradise Bay should have the honour of living here!...Even the penguins are short-tempered." The men observed stiff fights among the scrambling, returning gentoos, with "indignation on the faces" of the combatants. Occasionally, gentoos shot across the colony, one in pursuit of the other, wreaking havoc to all.

When they'd arrived the previous January, repairing the waterboat and adding an extension were the immediate priorities. The penguins already had hatched chicks and without nest counts and marked birds early on, any observations regarding their breeding biology would have been less than meaningful. But eight months into this craziness, with the emerging 1921 austral spring, Bagshawe and Lester's curiosity blossomed exponentially. Their previously untainted eyes were more focused.

They noticed immature birds keeping to the inner bay and not occupying nest sites. Having first-year gentoos prior to and during the nesting season suggested that gentoo chicks don't wait for two years or more to return to their natal site. The men's greatest fascination, though, was the huge congregation of gentoos that gathered for feeding runs each night and early morning around 1 A.M. These masses were an extraordinary sight—what the men believed to be the most impressive sight during all their days at Waterboat Point—and they only seemed to occur prior to the breeding season.

At midnight all was quiet, penguins prone on the snow. But an hour later they rose and began marching to the north end of the Main Island. From the South Island, another column of troops marched across the small, inner bay to the top of the Main Island. At Coal Point there was another gentoo accumulation. Bagshawe and Lester called it the Period of Massed Fishing Expeditions. The gentoos waited for that precise moment when, in their minds, it was most propitious to go to sea. Bagshawe noted an urgency: "Several birds were crowing vigorously as if they were issuing commands to the others." The Massed Fishing Expeditions, an organization so strange the men thought they were dreaming, repeated each morning until egg-laying began. They kept still for fear of disturbing the gentoos' organization. Within an hour, just as dusk lightened, the thousands were gone.

As Bagshawe describes, after seeing the birds arrive in the rookery during the day, in no particular order, squabbling and chasing one another about, it was almost incredible that such a "disreputable mob" could be "transformed into a well-disciplined army. If a crowd of as many thousands of human beings were to gather in like manner, packed close together, there would almost be certain disorder. But not so with the penguin. He has his methods of organization and even if his plans are a little upset as they were this morning, owing to the very low tide, he merely finds the next best point from which to take off and leaves from there." The mass movements were precise and powerful, as if all the gentoos contributed to one huge organism—wakening, stretching, looking in all directions, then marching. The gentoos would remain packed at the jumping-off spots for thirty to sixty minutes. Then, in a line, all began diving in. The entire departure process took seven or eight minutes, then again, silence.

At times, when the tide was too low at the north end, the throng would reposition its departure point to the west side of the Main Island. On another occasion, the entire mass rotated and swirled in place, as if no one wanted to go first—that it was best to take up the rear. This was accompanied by lots of pushing, shoving, and vocalizing. At times, it appeared the gentoos wanted to leave in bunches, with a lead penguin determining when the group should go. Those hanging back, remaining on shore, waited until numbers swelled sufficiently before another group departed.

The Mass Fishing Expeditions attracted leopard seals, looking for their own meals. On one floe, Bagshawe and Lester saw one lep sleeping over a dead chinstrap, using it as a pillow. They observed another lep dragging a gentoo from the ice into the water. One day, Bagshawe and Lester recorded that gentoos were late in returning, apparently unhappy to find that fast ice in the small bay had severed from the shorelines of the U, leaving big leads in between. No doubt suspecting more leopards, the gentoos accumulated by the thousands on the severed slab of ice, and took the entire day risking the leads and swimming toward their nests, just a few hundred feet away. Bagshawe and Lester noted that copulations became more frequent as the Massed Fishing Expeditions lessened in intensity. Once the gentoos were actively tending nests or chicks, the fishing excursions seemed to be exclusively individual affairs, taking place in shallower water nearer to home. The chinstraps never massed to fish, always preferring individual feeding runs. Bagshawe and Lester realized that the gentoos were prone to short feeding runs and daily returns to the nest. Even after the mass expeditions ceased, the individual feeding runs seemed to end late in the day, with all fishing stopped until the next dawn's dim light.

Bagshawe and Lester's admiration was considerable: "One looks down on this miniature society in the same way Gulliver looked down on the Lilliputians. Some were respectable, some disreputable. Among them went on all the every-day activities of a 'civilized' community. Bravery, loyalty, determination, immorality, deception, thieving, fighting and love-making; the comedies, the tragedies and the adventures; all the vices (and some of the virtues) of humanity were paralleled in the penguin settlement." This, despite occasional annoyances. In mid-October they had a pair of trespassing gentoos who insisted on using the top of the waterboat to nest. These gentoos loudly paced at night like anxious watchmen above the men's heads: "We requested them with some force to desist, but they took no notice, so we dug a trench in the snow round the bow to prevent them from reaching their prospective home. We were beaten, however, for they avoided the trench and climbed on the roof of the hut and so, *via* the sacks of sennegrass, to the boat-deck."

In early November the bulk of the chinstraps returned, and the men made a number of excursions to Coal Point to track their nesting progression. Differences between the species emerged. The chinstraps were smaller and, they believed, more alert and restless. Bagshawe and Lester thought that the chinstraps had greater concern and determination with respect to protecting and covering their eggs, and that gentoos were more prone to desert their biological heritage. Then a stray Adélie appeared, walking "with steps like a gouty old man.... There is as much difference between the disposition of an Adélie and a Gentoo as between a Frenchman and an Englishman, for the former have a decidedly Gallic restlessness of temperament. Several times he walked to the edge of the ice foot and prepared to jump back into the sea, but a fresh party of gentoo arrivals jumped on and caused him to rush back as hard as he could in a fearful panic. He made several more attempts to leave, but was scared back by new arrivals each time, so he gave it up as a bad job and bustled around with the mob, 'kaaing' a great deal."

With nesting in full swing, the snow-clearing and stone-pilfering rituals became obvious:

The penguins were incorrigible thieves, and the party round the ash-dump dared not leave their nests for fear of robbery. Fighting and high words went on between them in the early morning. The saddest part about it was that they were immediately outside our bedroom and had absolutely no consideration about disturbing us.... Every penguin—it is safe to generalize—is an accomplished and experienced thief. The penguin prefers to steal stones from the nest of a neighbour than to make an arduous journey to the shore for them. The sight of a stone must provoke the same evil feeling in a penguin that a bulging wallet of treasury-notes does in a pickpocket, the only difference being that the pickpocket does his job as secretly as possible, whereas the penguin is quite blatant about his.

Gentoos were regularly observed clearing away snow from the proximity of old nests, often lying on their sides, and propelling the snow away with their feet.

By late November, both gentoos and chinstraps were on eggs, which produced a crisis of conscience. There was initially great delight in discovering eggs—the men really craved a change of diet. But Lester "very considerately and without hesitation put aside any idea of eating the eggs until there were sufficient for observation purposes. We were both anxious to eat them, but we felt that the scientific work should have preference." But eat them, they did. Again, this matter of keen young explorers eating penguins. I've met few Antarctic explorers or researchers who relished the act of taking penguins or their eggs. All of their takings were respectful, never callous—in a fashion honoring the wild game which provided sustenance and survival. Antarctic history is strewn with examples: When the ravaged men of the Swedish Antarctic Expedition, whose ship *Antarctic* had just sunk, finally made it to Paulet Island in the Weddell Sea, it was February 28, 1903. The Adélies were fledged and the crew raced furiously to kill what few remaining penguins they could muster. Wally Herbert tells me that when he and others manned the small British Base D at Hope Bay in 1955–58, they would collect Adélie eggs for food. The eggs were carefully stacked in crates of flour so that none of the eggs were touching. The crates then were marked on each side with numbers—one to six—and stored, with the men turning the crates every three days so that a different number was uppermost. In this way the yolks would settle in the center of the egg and the eggs would stay "fresh" for a longer period of time—up to a maximum of six months.

Bagshawe and Lester preferred boiled gentoo eggs but found the slimy, transparent albumen rather unappetizing. They noted that chinstrap yolks were a pleasing shade of yellow, while gentoo yolks possessed a stranger, bright red-orange color. My favorite story regarding these red-orange yolks derives from Harrison Matthews, another keen young man who worked on the 1925–27 Discovery Investigations at South Georgia. While Matthews sowed oats with the whalers, they goaded him, finally, to partake of a special drink they called the *prairie oyster*. It happened one morning when everyone was lolling about downing drams of whisky and rum. A chap named Esbensen suggested a switch to *prairie oyster* shots: One gentoo yolk, a pinch of salt and pepper, a large tot of gin, and some Worcestershire sauce. Timid Matthews started with gentle sips, but prodded to show his manliness, chugged the whole shebang—at which point, his epiglottis closed down and he nearly choked to death. Bagshawe and Lester stuck to boiling and occasional frying—a "wonderful scrambled-egg-cum-omelette meal." At one point they became more adventurous, blowing eggs for specimens, but were overwrought when some of the chinstrap eggs actually contained chicks in various stages of development.

With eggs popping everywhere, they needed a system for following the progress of specific nests and mates. By strategically painting enamel numbers in particular locations, they began tracking more than forty nests. Bagshawe, inspecting an incubating bird closely, noted: "I committed *lèse-majesté* by lifting her up by the tail while I inspected her new acquisition. A penguin is top-heavy, and if one upsets its equilibrium by raising the tail, the bird lies powerless on its breast. In that way eggs or chicks can be examined with comparative ease."

They did not have celluloid rings, as Gain had utilized at Petermann Island, so they marked gentoos primitively—with dabs of

India ink they brushed on when standing or kneeling next to them, or which they applied from a distance using a bamboo pole with a brush attached to the end. Sometimes they used fountain-pen ink. With the substantial windchill, the ink frequently froze. Once birds had settled on nests, they painted marker stones in front of particular nests they wanted to watch. Then the problem became the guano the penguins frequently sprayed on the marker rocks, which quickly obliterated the enamel. Much repainting was necessary. In addition, they began marking eggs, with India ink proving much better than their pencils. Bagshawe noted how cold his hands got trying to keep pencil notes in the frigid air. But one stock item they did have was celluloid map-holders, which could be slung around their necks. They prepared sketch maps laying out their study territory and indicating where marked nests and birds were located. The map was inserted into the holder and easily carried around by the men while making their met or tidal observations.

The increasing amounts of sunshine that spring caused rapid thawing and turned the rookeries into a state of filthy quagmire. The gentoos nesting in the ash-dump began wallowing in an assortment of old, stinking penguin carcasses and flippers, guano, ashes, food tins, and other assorted muck and rubbish. The cooperative gentoos accepted stones Bagshawe and Lester offered. Their meticulous observation adds credence to the idea that if you just sit and watch—and watch carefully—there is much to see: Gentoos eating snow. Gentoos occasionally vomiting krill as a prelude to going fishing once again. Penguins sleeping either standing with beaks tucked under one of their wings, or while lying prone. Routine dives into shallow water from the edge of the ice foot. More spec-

tacular, six-foot jumps out of the water, returning to the ice foot—
landing either on their feet or breasts. Male gentoos habitually bringing in stones, dropping them, and bowing to their mate. There was
the time when the gentoos had a collective sneezing epidemic.

The men were taken by the gentoos' mutual displays of affection:
The male rubbing its bill on the sides of the female's face, then
both rubbing bills together. The inordinate number of bows when
pebbles were presented. Compared to the more pugnacious chinstraps, they observed: "They are not nearly so plucky as the Ringed,
being, to use a colloquialism, too 'gassy,' making much noise without
a great deal of effect. The Gentoo's fighting display can be compared
with the squabbling of two comic charwomen as against the Albert
Hall fighting of the Ringed." They also observed the gentoos' alleged immoralities: Males often trying to mount females other than
their mate. Once, one of these out-of-wedlock liaisons was proceeding when the rightful female returned home, discovered the immorality proceeding at her nest, and promptly went after both of the
others. In moments, curiously, the wayward male and the lawful
female began attacking the mistress, driving her away. Then, as Bagshawe and Lester noted, he made amends by presenting her with a
cinder to add to the nest, which she accepted with a bow. They
tracked another male who copulated with a strange female after
having intercourse with his proper mate earlier in the day.

Their observation time toted up and the men began to understand
the gentoos' entire cycle. The chick-rearing period lasted through
the end of February, when the chicks' last down molted, and early
March when chicks begin swimming. Some gentoo youngsters returned and still were fed by their parents, though others starved.

The parents molted from early February through most of March. There was a partial migration away from Waterboat Point through mid-May, followed by occasional visits in winter from June through August. The partial reoccupation of the rookery began in August and September, with the rookery reoccupation completed in October. Prior to egg-laying was the Period of Massed Fishing Expeditions, followed by "many desires" from late September on, and frequent copulations in October.

Some of the marked penguins were given names, and were known intimately: Darby and Joan. Bill and Liza, who divorced. The ash-dump pairs. The Sarah couple. And Archie, who was not content with having the best and finest nest in the vicinity. Archie was constantly searching for stones, even from nests that only had a few stones compared to his hundreds. Bagshawe and Lester noted that Archie was almost always observed carrying a cinder to his mate or having an argument with another gentoo about stones in that penguin's collection. They observed another gentoo near the met screen, which continually pilfered stones from a much smaller nearby nest, even when the female of that nest was present. It actually took stones from right underneath this sitting female, even driving away other gentoos who approached with larcenous motives. Then, after driving them off, this thieving gentoo would help itself to as many stones as could be mustered.

There was the "triangle drama" of Horace and Alice, who were "legally married," and Herbert, the intruder. In early October, Herbert tried to interact with Alice and prompted an intense fight between him and Horace. Horace pecked Herbert's head, drawing blood. For many minutes, they swatted each other hard with flippers and beaks, continuing the battle until neither could do more than squawk loudly at the other. Horace still had enough left to bow to Alice. After a short respite, Herbert charged again, but Horace was ready, chasing the intruder across the rookery. Herbert was undaunted. He returned a third time, standing right behind Horace and bowing to Alice. Horace turned suddenly, found Herbert, and chased him again. A day later, Herbert returned with Horace sitting on the nest. Horace immediately spotted him and ran him off. But a toll mounted. Horace was wearing down—to the point of not caring about his precise nesting location. Anywhere within a five-foot radius of the exact spot would do. His bows to Alice became halfhearted, weren't reciprocated, and his dejection seemed to mount. The pairbond dissolved.

Bagshawe and Lester carefully observed the gentleman-gentoos with their exaggerated arms' action stimulating the females' backs during copulation, while simultaneously and audibly beating a tattoo onto their backs. But there were aberrations: One female didn't take kindly to a male's trying to force the copulation, pecking her down and plucking small tufts of feathers. She tossed him forcibly, after which he was chased through the rookery by another penguin. One male tried mating with one of the dead gentoos they'd killed for food, another male with a wounded female. As with all good field researchers, Bagshawe and Lester adjusted their methods as necessary. If intercourse was observed, they could confirm which sex was which, and they remarked males with a horizontal ink mark, females with a vertical mark.

Gentoo nests were found to be much larger and better constructed than those of the chinstraps. Stones and rocks that could be carried in their beaks were preferred, but old bones and tail feathers were commonly used. Some wove in pieces of wood, glass, sennegrass, and miscellaneous junk. One gentoo actually nested on top of a myriad number of discarded food tins and used no other materials. Out of curiosity, the men counted the stones in one medium-sized gentoo nest and tallied a whopping seventeen hundred. The advantage: protection from meltwater or rain that might flood the eggs, or to allow rain to drain rapidly. But there were other nests that were two or three times larger. One gentoo was observed repeatedly bringing in wet stones from the sea, seventy-five feet away, at a rate of eight trips an hour. One nest consisted totally of limpet shells. Another had stones weighing as much as six ounces. They also observed a male gentoo who expected recognition for the stone he'd retrieved. He dropped it at his mate's feet, but she ignored the gift. He then pecked her and bowed—but again, she refused the bow. He picked up the stone and moved it to another part of the nest. Still, no recognition. He pecked her once more and she continued ignoring him. This ballet repeated more than fifty times. Finally, finally, she returned a bow and his *noodging* ceased.

Bagshawe and Lester passed stones to nesting gentoos and, often, they were eagerly accepted. They played with one gentoo who coveted a particularly large, slaty rock. It might have been stolen or retrieved from somewhere across the rookery. As they passed this gentoo on the way to the met screen, it immediately scurried away with the booty in its beak. When the men returned down the path, the same penguin, now on its nest, picked up its large rock and ran away again, waiting until the men had left before returning and once again placing the coveted item in its nest. Lester also examined a gentoo that was obsessively consumed with preening itself. The gentoo's back was turned and Lester slowly approached and began stroking its back with his finger—thirty to forty times before the gentoo realized what was happening.

They saw many three-egg nests, which are not the norm, closely observed the brood pouch, which allows eggs to be tucked next to warm skin, and found they could exchange eggs between nests without objection. Their observations confirmed that the Waterboat Point gentoos averaged thirty-five days of incubation after the second egg, which compares to more recent data indicating a thirty-two- to thirty-four-day period after a completed clutch, for gentoos nesting to the north in Admiralty Bay. With one gentoo pair, they closely observed the spells of duty on the nest. After fourteen days and 336 hours of observation, the female logged 183 hours on duty, the male, 153. The interval between these eggs was 77 hours.

They noted different guano color around the nests—red, green, or green-yellow. What we know now, decades later, is that guano color indicates what the penguin's been eating: Red for krill. White for fish. And green or off shades of green for stomach bile, meaning that the bird is starving. Bagshawe and Lester realized that prey distribution greatly affected and determined the lives of these animals. Chick-raising was a shared activity, so the loss of one mate ultimately meant eggs would be abandoned, or if chicks were present, that they would be lost. As the bird twists in its nest the guano spews in all directions, often leaving colorful and beautiful patterns in a circle around the central nest core. And because of the close proximity, there's always the problem of guano whizzing by your face. It's very common, indeed, to see a sitting bird get sprayed right

A pair of chinstrap penguins displaying at their nest site, which in this case is an excellent "room with a view" of the grandeur of the Baily Head colony and the eerie Deception Island landscape

Chinstrap penguins performing their ecstatic displays at Waterboat Point. Sometimes the noise and din from a plethora of concomitantly displaying chinstraps can be deafening.

Chinstrap penguins sparring at Waterboat Point. Breeding territories in a crowded colony may be no more than a wing's length apart, and they are fiercely guarded. Early on, chicks learn to gape and stab at neighbors—a warning to keep out of "their space."

A group of clean chinstrap penguins returning to their nests by ascending the steep slopes on the Needles Bay side of the Baily Head colony

A parent chinstrap at Waterboat Point "showing off" this season's complement of chicks, which are growing quickly and, at more than three weeks of age, are too large to be completely brooded.

A small group of breeding chinstraps on the Orne Islands, against a backdrop of the snow-capped peaks rimming the Gerlache Strait

Part of the magnificent Baily Head chinstrap penguin colony on Deception Island. Up to 100,000 pairs of chinstraps nest in this colony.

A bobbing, two-stepping chinstrap penguin prancing around the *Prasiola crispa*-laden slopes at Baily Head. Penguins don't have knees, but still they manage to walk and trot along quite nicely.

A gentoo penguin tobogganing over the snow pack on Petermann Island. Gentoos can swim—some say, "fly"—in water, walk and prance over ground, and when the situation warrants, drop to their bellies, pedal with their feet, steer with their wings, and maneuver well over snow.

A glaring, staring Adélie penguin on Devil Island in the Weddell Sea. Of the three *Pygoscelid* penguins, the Adélie most resembles a small human clad in a tuxedo.

A small group of gentoo penguin chicks at Copacabana Beach, Admiralty Bay. Past four weeks of age, gentoo chicks—and to a greater or lesser extent, Adélie and chinstrap chicks—leave the strict confines of the nest site where they were born and gather in larger assemblages called *crèches.*

An Adélie penguin parent and its days-old chick—naked, helpless, and needing the warmth and protection of the adult's brood pouch

Adélie penguins on the ice edge on Paulet Island. In the early, austral spring (October to early December) there may be considerable ice rimming the penguins' breeding locations, which must be negotiated successfully if the penguins are going to set up their territories and, ultimately, find sufficient food for their young.

Adélie penguins riding an ice floe in the vicinity of Hope Bay. Adélie and chinstrap penguins often utilize floating ice as "excursion boats"—rest stops—to enable them to do a bit of preening or relaxing before moving on.

An adult gentoo penguin at Waterboat Point, against the background of one of the buildings now erected on this site. Gentoos are the largest of the three *Pygoscelid*, or brush-tailed penguins, and have orange-red bills and white patches on both sides of their heads.

My friend—an inquisitive gentoo penguin chick—about to hop into my lap, on the beach on the Aitcho Islands. This encounter lasted for many minutes— a very special Antarctic thrill. When you get down to "penguin size," there is a chance for some close encounters with these very curious creatures.

An Adélie penguin, sitting on its eggs, buried in the snow after a freak spring storm on Paulet Island. The penguin, built to endure the cold, is quite snug and content, and with a little sun and melt, it will soon be freed from this position.

An adult gentoo penguin in the midst of one of its *"hee-HAW"* calls and displays, with its chest heaving in and out

Adélie penguins on an ice floe offshore Paulet Island. This season the island was ringed with considerable ice, and this floe was one stop as the penguins threaded their way back to their particular nest sites.

A gentoo penguin chick emitting a squeaky call and revealing its bristly, spiny tongue which will help it catch fish and krill

A gentoo penguin family at Copacabana Beach, with one of the chicks doing a bit of shuffling and dancing—stretching its wings and showing some typical chick energy

A pair of chinstraps in the midst of an ecstatic display on the Orne Islands. The black stripe is characteristic of this species, which also has been called ringed penguins.

The "Madonna" gentoos at the Chilean Gabriel González Videla station, Waterboat Point. After many continuous years of gentoos breeding at the base of the Madonna statue, station personnel erected a glass-enclosed case. Now, there is protection from the elements as well as from the excessive guano generated by the gentoos nesting right at Madonna's feet.

VIRGEN MARIA
BAHIA PARAISO
BASE G.G.V. 1996

Too big to brood. Gentoo penguin chicks in the midst of dabbing bills with one of their parents.

Nesting penguins are constantly shifting position, to adjust to the ever-changing wind direction. The many shiftings of this gentoo are recorded by the guano stains flung in a circle around the nest.

Adélie penguins staring out to sea in Arthur Harbor. Antarctic penguins are "built" for the cold—having the densest feather arrangement in the bird kingdom, the ability to trap air between their short feathers and their body, a plethora of oil to waterproof their feathers, and a bit of blubber.

...again, my gentoo chick friend on the Aitcho Islands. "For a few seconds, I stroke its back up and down, with no adverse reaction. . . . My lapmate relaxes further, squats on its haunches, and fills my lap with its very fat belly. We continue perusing the surf beyond. I feel its heart rapping, and remain as still as I possibly can. . . . What, if anything, parses this penguin's consciousness? I can hardly describe what's going through mine."

Molting chinstrap penguins in the stream gullies at Baily Head. At the end of each breeding season, chinstrap adults endure a complete, painful body molt before heading off to sea for a long winter season away from their breeding grounds.

in the face by its neighbor, the splattered gentoo then shaking its head vigorously to remove the excrement.

At times they sat for hours before a group of nests. They ascertained that each gentoo recognized its mate's voice rather well. One bird would "crow"—as they put it—then the penguin's mate would rush up, sometimes from twenty-five feet or more. Another well-known couple was Lionel and Lame Lizzie. She had a bum leg and was easy to spot. They nested near the meat-dump, in close proximity to the men's living quarters. One day, Lame Lizzie was out in the bay, while Lionel was busy trolling around the meat-dump. Lionel plodded down to the bay, while Lizzie went exploring on South Island and began climbing uphill. When Lionel returned to his nest, he started *hee-HAW*-ing, at which point Lizzie immediately turned back and hurried to him as fast as she could limp. The distance involved was more than a hundred feet.

Though they logged fewer hours with the chinstraps, enough was gleaned to compare the two species' respective life history cycles. The main difference was the chinstraps' total migration from Waterboat Point, which they desert completely from mid-April to early November. The chinstraps did not feed in large groups prior to egg-laying. Where the two brushtaileds mixed, the chinstraps took the higher locations and seemed to have some kind of arrangement, as if the gentoos at Coal Point and South Island would leave nesting spaces open for the chinstraps who hadn't yet returned. The chinstraps' copulation pattern was similar but lacked the gentoos' exaggerated arms' action—the flippers were used more for balance and keeping steady, kept to the side. Chinstrap nests were not as well constructed or substantial, averaging about 350 stones and filled occasionally with bones and molted tail feathers. The chinstraps' incubation period also averaged out to thirty-five days after the second egg, compared to data indicating a thirty-two-day period for chinstraps in Admiralty Bay. Bagshawe and Lester thought the chinstraps weren't quite as cunning as the gentoos in terms of their stone-pilfering but were much braver and more willing to protect their nest than the timid gentoos, who'd run as soon as trouble neared. Bagshawe and Lester noted the chinstraps' flipper tremor when the men approached, *displacement behavior*—akin to biting fingernails when one doesn't know what to do.

In Bagshawe's *Notes on the Habits of the Gentoo and Ringed or Antarctic Penguins* he made comparisons to Gain's discoveries in 1909 at Petermann Island and Levick's observations of Adélie penguins from 1910–13 at Cape Adare on the far side of the continent, south of Australia and New Zealand. Bagshawe and Lester didn't see male penguins fighting for females as Levick had suggested with respect to Adélies. The men also disputed Levick's notion of females taking up nests and waiting for returning mates to come to them. Bagshawe and Lester wondered whether the gentoos arrive mated, anticipating future results suggesting that gentoo mates may stay together in the winter. Levick had found adult Adélies fasting until eggs are laid. Bagshawe and Lester didn't believe that gentoos had this habit— though we now know a short fast may occur. However, they suspected that chinstraps engaged in a prolonged fast before laying. Whereas Levick described Adélies riding ice floes for amusement, Bagshawe and Lester thought that amusement wasn't the goal and that the penguins rode Levick's so-called "excursion boats" to sleep or rest, or when they'd mistaken the ice for terra firma. Contrary to

Levick's observations of Adélies, Bagshawe and Lester did not find "hooligan" male gentoos or chinstraps attacking stray chicks.

The men truly appreciated the cold realities of penguin life: "That the young of the penguins ever see the light of day is somewhat remarkable, for what with one adversity and another a good proportion of the eggs are never hatched. If neglect and bad management were not compensated for by an egg which can, with its fatty contents, withstand an enormous amount of misuse, the race of penguins would fast become extinct. If a young bird is tenacious enough to reach the adult stage it deserves to live." But their amusement and intrigue was drawing to a close.

On December 18, 1921, the whalers returned—Captain O. Andersen aboard the *Svend Foyn I,* which also carried Arthur G. Bennett, the Falkland Islands Dependencies magistrate, a keen penguin observer in his own right, and the master of fresh egg sandwiches at Deception. There was much worry about the men. Bagshawe's parents had been in regular touch with Debenham, pleading for any available news.

Bagshawe and Lester wanted to stay a bit longer. Andersen told them that Shackleton, then beginning a new expedition on the vessel *Quest,* also had offered to retrieve them. Bagshawe and Lester asked if Andersen could return in a few additional weeks, allowing them to pack properly and, of course, to complete more penguin observations.

The remaining days were memorable: Chinstraps about to hatch on January 4. Sarah, the gentoo near the met screen, hatching her chicks on January 8. The men had constant reminders that gentoos "spend more time talking about their eggs than sitting on them and keeping them warm." Lester cooked potato chips. Andersen's willingness to arrange another retrieval, as it happened, was a godsend. No one was aware that farther north, at South Georgia, Shackleton had suffered a fatal heart attack on January 5.

On January 13, the catcher *Graham* arrived to take them out, a year and a day after they'd begun:

> Much as we had upbraided the climate, we felt lumps rising in our throats, for we had grown strangely fond of the old hut and the inhospitable island. We had a special affection for the hut, for we had built the greater part of it ourselves. It seemed like desertion to leave it to its loneliness.... We wondered if Sarah and the other penguins would miss us. They had been our friends and we knew that we should miss them. Who would be the next visitor to this place, the picture of which would forever remain imprinted on our minds? It had been an experience which, though I would not particularly care to repeat, yet I would not have missed for worlds.

If they had regrets, they were an inability to tackle certain questions that logically arose: Would gentoos raise chinstrap chicks, or vice versa? How long do penguins fast when molting? If young birds do not return the next season, where do they go? When do they return? What is the lifespan of a gentoo or chinstrap?

I can hear my Zodiac returning, so I hustle upslope from the waterboat's remains, round the corner, and gaze once more at the Madonna gentoos. There's a stirring on the nest and Mrs. Madonna gives me a strange look—an invitation to check her closely, one more time. I nudge forward and I have a vision of Bagshawe and

Lester's meteorological screen, their tide pole, the converted water-boat, and these gentoos they knew so well. The Madonna gentoos easily could be direct descendants of Lionel and Lame Lizzie, Darby and Joan, the Sarah couple, or the ash-dump gentoos.

Mrs. Madonna lifts, flaps her wings, and there it is—a bright white, brand-new egg with a few bloodstains, laid just within the last few minutes. It gleams like the untouched snow at my feet, a fitting tribute to Bagshawe and Lester—a legacy of penguins going on and on and on. She bows to both of her eggs, emits a low hiss of recognition, gives the new egg a full rotation, then gazes to her mate standing nearby. Mr. Madonna returns the bow, walks around the nest, and hops in, changing over and taking custody. She wedges between the lip of the nest and the Madonna box, nuzzling the side of the enclosure with her neck and body, raising her beak skyward. She turns to her mate and the two begin a typical mutual display, with heaving chests and loud *hee-HAW*s.

Bagshawe and Lester were as opportunistic as these gentoos. They carved a special niche for those who learn by determination, hands-on experience, and *not* being afraid to dirty themselves with some crucial, local details. They'd be pleased to know that gentoos still rule at Waterboat Point, albeit in considerably fewer numbers.

Bounding away in the Zodiac, another photograph fills my screen: A view of Lester sitting on the rigging of the catcher *Graham*, which has just taken the men away from Waterboat Point—forever. It's a poignant moment. He stares ahead, fixed on a peaceful, endless sea—on gentoos and chinstraps that would inhabit his and Bag-shawe's remaining days. What began as a crazy impulse grew to keeping meteorological, ice, and tidal logs, then evolved to the first study of the breeding biology of gentoos and chinstraps. The work was pursued passionately. Indeed, one commentator credits Bagshawe and Lester with collecting more data per man-hour than any Antarctic expedition until the advent of satellites and computers. It is a substantial bequest.

Others will carry on their work and explain further mysteries, following large and indelible footprints.

SIX

....

Hardwired

How is it these quilled milk-bottle
doorstops, straitjacketed in blubber,
without either knees or elbows, that
have to sleep standing, still seem
so hilarious a reflection of *us*, the
spoiled rich kids of natural history,
that notwithstanding our scant fondness
for others of our kind, we do love penguins?
—*AMY CLAMPITT*

Whizz. Bang. Pop.

With each roller, chinstraps explode over the black beach. Missiles past my face. Somersaults. Nosedives. Sideswipes. Some are slammed to the beach with backs *down*, white bellies and pink-flushed underwings *up*. Many eject onto their pink feet. All scoot immediately above the tide line. Behind me, extending a mile inland, the amphitheater is packed.

So many penguins, never enough time.

I'm always elated to return to the glories and multitudes of Baily Head. It is located on the outside, eastern end of donut-shaped Deception Island. The geology and volcanic scenery are mind-boggling. So, too, are the teeming mobs of chinstraps. The real truth is that I'm simply wild for chinnies—and this staggering cathedral is the *mother* of all chinstrap landing sites.

Don't get me wrong: In their respective fashions, all three *Pygoscelid* penguins are a rewarding experience—curious, interesting to study, and at times, a real hoot. Personality-wise and otherwise, they resemble us too much. But the three species exhibit vastly different temperaments, drawing us perhaps to relate to one species over the other two. Many prefer the placid, laid-back gentoos. They're really gentle creatures, a bit skittish, and rather tender in behavior to one another. Others are jazzed by Adélies. They're the penguin most depicted in advertisements and publicity campaigns, all decked out in little tuxedos, and a tad spunkier than gentoos. But chinstraps are my undeniable *crème de la crème*, my *pièce de résistance*. I've been mad about chinnies since I first encountered them at Entrance Point, a mere three miles from Baily Head, just around the corner to the south and west.

Why chinstraps? Well, put it this way: They're not exactly wall-flowers. I am fully seduced by their breathless pace of life—pudgy krill-balls who pompously saunter close, jump over your feet, and peck you with every ounce of verve and conviction they possess.

They conjure a variety of adjectives and descriptions: Pugnacious. Highly animated. Full of life. Outrageous. Frenetic. Overly zealous. They have piercing yellow eyes that lock tightly to yours, or look right through you. How can you resist high-climbing penguins who seem so totally cocky and full of themselves? It's all or nothing with chinstraps: There are no halfway measures. They possess a nifty black-and-white coloration. The black on the head held fast by a thin black strip running across the chin, they resemble palace guards, and they have the loudest voices in penguindom—absolutely, fundamentally jarring. They look you up and down with gusto oozing from each feather tract, indefatigably braying back and forth with boundless energy. They may be the smallest of the brushtaileds— about the same height as Adélies, just over two feet tall, yet lighter, between eight and eleven pounds—but they make up for their slightly trimmer profile with this tenacious *attitude:* Heads bopping. Shoulders swaying. If you remember the movie *Stir Crazy*, you'll know what I mean—Gene Wilder and Richard Pryor prancing around the jail, pompously chanting: "That's right, we're *bad*. Oh yeah. That's right, we're *bad*."

In another sense, they're a precious commodity: Because of their proclivity for heights—and by choosing some truly out-of-the-way places to breed—they're the most difficult of the brushtaileds to study and examine. Many of these sites present otherworldly vistas. In other words, chinstraps clearly pick rooms with a view. You might say they're penguins with *attitude* and *altitude*. Baily Head is representative—a paradise of more chinstraps than can possibly be imagined. Stories about Baily Head are legend.

The rookery is staggeringly large: an estimated 75,000 to

100,000 breeding pairs, which means, of course, 150,000 to
200,000 actual, individual animals. If the average productivity is one
chick per active nest, that raises the numbers further, an immense
225,000 to 300,000 individuals. Think of the amount of guano
flowing at the height of summer. Or how much krill is necessary to
keep the protein flowing. The French biologist Louis Gain visited
Baily Head en route to Petermann Island on December 7, 1909,
estimating 50,000 pairs. In 1926–27, Arthur G. Bennett roughly
estimated 40,000 nesting pairs. Brian Roberts in January 1937
counted 72,660 pairs. Estimates from 1957 through 1989 ranged
from 37,500 to 100,000 pairs, though data in the early 1990s
suggest a decline. The paucity of visits to Baily Head directly ties
to the weather—some of the worst the Peninsula can offer. In the
prevailing stiff wind, the beach rises in fury and is frothed in a white
foam that crushes the cobble to a fine brown pebble many feet deep.
Blue sky is unusual. Hard pellets of snow, sleet, and rain often mix
with the loose ash that swirls, tornado-like on the landing beach or
at higher reaches of the rookery, scraping and searing any exposed
skin. The flying cinders also may affect one's tear ducts, and there's
no protection from the numbing chill.

The logistics are an utter nightmare. The entrance beach presents
some of the roughest landing circumstances in the Peninsula. More
often than not, visits have to be scrubbed. Many attempts are made
in early morning before breakfast, when seas and swell are somewhat
calmer. It is the wettest of wet landings. Part of the difficulty is
that the four-and-a-half-mile-long, ruler-straight, black and red ash
landing beach is totally exposed to the Bransfield Strait. The beach
essentially runs north to south along Deception's right flank. If the

visibility's good, Livingston Island can be spied, fifteen miles distant. The glacier cap on this side of the island, hidden in a mask of ash, abuts the black beach. The ice cap, offshore current, and wave action conspire to change the shape of the beach constantly. Further, because the beach drops quickly to depth, large swells and a pounding surf are de rigueur. Without experienced drivers, Zodiacs are easily overturned in the breakers. Once ashore on the south end of the beach, the rookery is accessed by heading southwest and inland. But even if mishaps are avoided and you arrive fairly dry and in one piece, there's still a long tromp to the higher reaches. To examine this place closely, one needs hours.

The ash beach isn't the only entrée to the cathedral. It also may be reached by hiking over the top from Whaler's Bay and the island's inner caldera, but this route has its own particular vicissitudes: five miles of volcanic slag, usually damp weather, and, generally, not much time to savor the penguin feast on the other side. Over the top, there are the twin risks of whiteouts and hidden crevasses. Good visibility is an oddity. Thomas Bagshawe used this overland route to Baily Head in 1920. Another choice is to hike up and into the rookery from the small bay underneath Baily Head's highest rim. But this narrow path, involving a steep climb of a couple of hundred feet, doubles as a major chinstrap ingress-egress point that winds through a large number of slope-nesting penguins. I've done both—and they're interesting alternatives—yet the most breathtaking access point remains the long black beach on Deception's eastern side.

A beach landing is never a picnic, even in the best of circumstances. Today's surf is more horrendous than usual, but we make it in relatively unscathed. Never deterred, the chinstraps keep coming—all the time. They're going right for the beach, without hesitation. A wave breaks and as the white crest begins to topple, they *surf* the crest—adjusting quickly with flippers and feet to maintain their momentum. But try as they might, the landings are a hodgepodge of splatters and rolling tumbleweeds. As quickly as possible, they vault upright, scurry forward, away from the breakers. Their eyes are wide with determination.

Aside from crashing Zodiacs, the only additional arrival hazards are Antarctic fur seals. As the spring and summer progress, Antarctic fur seals increase in numbers along this black beach and occasionally climb into the rookery. It's a reminder that these carnivores were almost wiped out in the early nineteenth century. They have teeth as sharp as razors and, seemingly, as long as pencils. In their midst, the notion of personal space—yours—takes on new meaning. These fierce competitors easily outrun juicy human prey, so you've got to watch your backside. You don't dally on this beach without some means of poking away the gnarly Antarctic Terminators. Male fur seals have a particularly bad perfume, which is easily noticed downwind. I vividly remember one unnerving moment at Baily Head when, totally engrossed in the chinstraps plunging on chests and bellies through the roaring surf, I and my entire, square-foot space on the beach suddenly were enveloped by a fetid, permeating cloud. Mr. Macho was approaching at full tilt, head reared and cocked, huffing and puffing for a quick snack. Thankfully, his precedent smell offered a brief moment to jump clear of harm's way.

But the worst fur seal incident occurred in the late 1980s when I was an expedition leader. It was a rough landing and we'd just managed to get about eighty people ashore, a testament to the inordinate skill of my Zodiac team—David Kaplan, René Preller, Julio Preller, and Mike Messick. The ABs—the able-bodied seamen on shore—were soaked to their chins pulling in the Zodiacs, then shoving them away, preparing to receive another load. It can be a harrowing disembarkation, with passengers streaming off both sides of the Zodiac, which has come to the beach in reverse, thus flattening the swell. Jumping out, passengers need to avoid the boat's transom, where the outboard engine is clamped, and race quickly to higher ground. Some are soaked. But anxious for their chinstrap moments, they usually peel life jackets and rain gear immediately, eager to begin.

There was an elderly gentleman in this crowd who was an ardent videographer. He eschewed the routine of lightening his load and went right to work, desperately wanting video of the hundreds and hundreds of chinstraps barreling, pounding through the surf and exploding like pop-up dolls on the beach. I'll never forget the incident. I was patrolling up and down, assuring myself that no one had gotten injured, all the while carrying a long pole to fend off any fur seals that might be an annoyance. The man sat no more than two or three yards from the edge of the surf, totally absorbed in the crashing chinstraps. I decided to give him a few minutes before encouraging a safer filming location. I poised behind him, pole in hand, worrying whether one of the seals from the corner of the beach might wander over and cause a problem. What I didn't expect was a fur seal lunging at him, right through the surf. I saw him fall backwards as a really large wave hit the beach, with an enormous male fur seal, jaws agape, bounding directly at this red-parka target.

I was quickly between the man and the seal, shooing the seal away with my pole. The seal headed away and I turned back to this gentleman, who remained frozen with his back planted firmly on the beach, knees and legs raised. It took many minutes to ease his fear and get him to stand. He kept describing what he saw through the viewfinder: Chinstraps bolting left and right and then, one huge set of teeth filling the frame. It's not a pretty circumstance, for sure, but this place is theirs more than ours.

Upbeach, all the way to the northeastern tip, Macaroni Point, waves are crashing and chinstraps are pouring onto the black sand. The clear sky is an unexpected treat, adding an azure backdrop to this already imposing, awe-inspiring craterful of penguins. Since to-day's schedule is relaxed, there will be more than enough time to burn and I imagine some defining chinstrap encounters about to materialize. The southern end of the beach is dominated by a con-spicuous ocher and brown rock headland called Rancho Point—or *Punta Rancho*, the camp point. It is a 560-foot-tall bluff that marks the broad entrance to the Baily Head rookery. The alternate name derives from Francis Baily, an early-nineteenth-century English as-tronomer who reported on Henry Forster's pendulum observations inside the Deception caldera. From the entrance beach, the amphi-theater stretches southwest for more than a mile, elevating across a vast terrain of pink, green, black, and white color, finally culminating on a long, sinewy ridge flooded with chinstraps. On the high eastern side of the rim, to the left as you march uphill, orange, crusty *Xanthoria* lichens adorn the rocks. A meltstream with swiftly flowing water drains the large, elongated, bowl-shaped valley, which is pock-marked with hummocky topography.

The grandeur of Baily Head isn't apparent from the beach. You need to get above the tideline and follow the ample meltstream to the higher reaches of this aptly described "Hollywood Bowl of Penguins." The higher you hike, the more impressive the view. Ovals of nesting chinstraps extend to the high ridge backing the colony, which dominates the landscape. In early November the entire area may be covered with snow, deep in the lower parts of the valley but relatively thin on the upper slopes. By December, all the snow may be gone, and the amphitheater of penguins becomes flush with pink penguin guano and green swatches of a common weed—actually, an algae—named *Prasiola crispa*. But whether snow or algae or barren volcanic rock, the common thread is chinstraps—everywhere. From the high rim, a mile inland, there's a spectacular view of the nearby sea stacks—the Sewing Machine and Needles, which rise to almost a hundred feet above the water. These appear to be the eroded remnants of an offshore, eruptive center and cone.

Baily Head visits always seem memorable, especially when the chinstrap breeding season is in full swing. The unfolding spectacle is fairly described as *sensory overload* or *biological overload*—there simply is too much to see. Baily Head is so hard to reach, and it's rare to be able to visit at length, without time pressure. Today, I want to see my chinnies going through all the motions—to see them in full breeding regalia, in all their glory. But just as important as studying chinstrap breeding biology up close and personally, I want to address one lingering difficulty head-on: My never-ending *penguin-cognition delusion.* PCD is a natural phenomenon—a cognitive fallacy that afflicts everyone who comes to the Antarctic Peninsula. It begins when you initially encounter penguins in relatively *small* numbers—say twenty here, thirty there, perhaps a few hundred over the course of a particular visit. You're having such a great experience with these ten, twenty, or a hundred penguins, enjoying their antics so much, you can't possibly imagine seeing *more* intriguing behaviors and happenings. *But there always will be something new. And there always will be many, many more of them.*

I've countered some of this delusion by returning again and again to the Peninsula between early November and late February. This frame encompasses all of the action—the entire brushtailed life cycle. I've seen much: Chinstraps and Adélies returning in the austral springtime, joining the gentoos who have stuck around at favorite fishing spots during the winter. Courtship and copulation. Chick-rearing and -fledging. Chicks heading to sea. Adults molting. And then I've observed all of these penguin venues lapse back to their stark, naked autumn calm. Therefore, I feel bonded with the relatively small cohort of penguin researchers like Gain, Bagshawe, and Lester who were able to witness the entire show.

But there always *is* something new, always *more* to see. Experience can't assuage one significant aspect of this pleasant malady—a completely natural misapprehension of *size*. Even now, after all of my field time, I continue straining at times to comprehend and absorb the *whole* show: Eyes dilate and swell, as my field of vision attempts to capture the full grandeur of a jam-packed rookery like Baily Head. Nostrils inflate with the most horrid, nitrogenous perfume imaginable. Ears ache and shake from the noise. At Baily Head the sensory overload translates palpably to thousands—actually, tens of thousands—of screaming, volatile krill-balls, spread over a vast landscape, in multitudes of colonies and groups that are virtually impossible to count one by one.

I keep pinching myself, remembering I'm a small-town kid who once thought that going to the big city was a big deal. Baily Head is a really big deal—my synapses overwhelmed not by traffic or people, but by penguins. During my first significant penguin encounter—the few hundred chinstraps at Entrance Point—I had no idea what was unlocking in the inner and not-so-deep recesses of my consciousness.

They're unusually curious and willingly interested in examining us, face-to-face, without inhibition. But wild penguins aren't used to hand-feeding, so their close approach has nothing to do with looking for food handouts. Penguins are a bit nearsighted, so if you get down to *their* level and avoid any sharp or quick movements you create a safety zone, and it's not uncommon to have one prancing all over you, checking you closely with its beak. I thought my initial hundred animals were a terrific experience, but truth be told, this wasn't definitive. Sure, it was my initial, face-to-face, toenail-to-boot meeting—and there's no question I loved those chinnies at first sight. But something was missing. I was tasting some of the icing, without any bloody idea regarding the size of the cake. I remember Frank Todd telling me that first day about the hordes at Baily Head, bemoaning that we wouldn't be visiting it on our intended rotation of sites. It was something to tuck in the memory bank for the future, though Frank added, inimitably, that it was *a bitch to visit*.

The next season, working on another ship, the *Lindblad Explorer*, I got closer. Mike McDowell, the expedition leader, had considered landing at Baily Head, but conditions were substantially less than ideal. As a sidelight, after the passengers were safely ashore at Whaler's Bay, inside Deception's flooded caldera, Mike copped a Zodiac and took me over to the small bay near the Sewing Machine and Needles, directly beneath Baily Head's towering rim. In the rain and fog, we climbed to the top, for Ron's Little Preview. My jaw dropped, the Big PCD in full bloom. It was wall-to-wall penguins, with activity everywhere. Spread below were what I conjured to be a *gazillion* chinstraps. Who can count that high? Under the rim—in the direction we'd just climbed, two hundred feet below—streams of chinstraps raced to a ledge above the rolling sea, nervously waiting a chance to jump in. Their demeanor suggested prowling leopard seals roaming the shoreline. A dream was fueled, a magic and magnetic attraction—a promise to return again and again and again.

So this early December day is a rekindling. I feel a chaotic, life-affirming thrill watching the scrappy chinstraps rushing back to mates, high in the hills. Ineluctably, powerfully, I'm drawn to large penguin colonies in the breeding season. Penguins' lives are normally fast-paced and riotous, but the calamity seems heightened during this particular stretch of time. Drama, pathos, and high comedy weave inextricably over the penguin landscape—all to be enjoyed, assuming I can trudge uphill successfully and savor the action from a front-row seat.

They rumble on the entrance beach and assault the crushed stones with explosive energy, surfing beachward on muscle-tight chests, resembling millions of energized lemmings. Perched on a slight rise of beach, just short of the surf, I have a stage-center seat in an IMAX theater of chinstraps, who spew and smash, 3-D fashion, right into my lap and just past my eyes. More whams, bangs, and pops. All are sparkling clean from their feeding runs offshore, their narrow black chin stripes glistening against the pearly white and wet neck feathers. Their immaculate appearance is negated in only one respect: After these healthy krill runs, their feathery cummerbund barely contains a newly acquired yet temporary plumpness. They are rather spiffy-looking, and all that seems to be missing is a top hat and chauffeur. Beady yellow eyes slit my countenance, trying to shrink my towering height. Shaking and trimming quickly finished, they anxiously prance inland and upward toward the colony's center. Hungry, incubating spouses await them. Call it herding behavior or troops on a mission, these hardwired chinstraps lust ahead with little delay. I note few deviations from the preordained plan. They can't be denied, and nothing stops the onslaught.

There is a constant flow of chinstraps up and down along the stream—hordes leaving or returning en masse. The chinstraps' orientation today is British: The uphill throng moves left of the stream, with the downhill throng to the right. Many of the chinstraps don't have the patience to walk the edges and ford straight through the stream, irrespective of the water's pace and depth. All of them make it, though some are better than others at finding stepping-stones in the middle. Some sink in the gushing water to their bellies, some to their throats, a few even swim across. None of this effort seems a bother. They're troops on a mission—with an important job to do, and nothing, certainly not some swift-flowing meltwater, is going to interrupt them. They emerge quickly and continue waddling forward, wherever they're going. The shape of the melt stream changes each season. The ash surface is easily gouged. Much depends on the amount of winter snow and how quickly it melts. But the stream never stops flowing. Even when the year's snowfall has gone, the stream will be fed by Deception's glaciers and ice cap.

Baily Head's mold represents aeons of volcano-altered rock. Ultimately, on its higher reaches, as it transforms into a holy synagogue of chinstraps, the colony becomes a striking amalgam of green mosses, orange lichens, and pink penguin guano set against the volcanic motif of gray, black, and white. It is a perfect place to study or, as some would say, endure penguins. The landscape is characteristic of Deception's violent past, substantially littered with explosive remnants and huge, pockmarked bombs. The guano smell takes some time to ignore. The guano also has a way of invading one's gear and pores, where it remains and defies both strong detergent and extended aeration.

The protein explosion is another indication of the chinstraps' short window of opportunity—a tight, two- to three-month frame to quickly find their mates, court, copulate, lay, incubate, and fledge this season's young. If a chinstrap winds up with the same mate from last year, the result is more circumstantial, as opposed to true love. The pair bond depends on the female's return to last year's nest site and how soon it follows that of the male, the pair not being together during the off-season. The male chinstrap will return as early as possible to set up shop, the more experienced breeders accessing the taller, more rugged nesting sites that have been blown free of snow by the howling spring Antarctic winds. The male claims his turf, unfurls his rousing ecstatic display, and expects that she'll be there, shortly.

Chinnies normally lay two eggs, with incubation and feeding

shared by both parents. After returning to their nest sites, the chinstraps are in a hard fast, trying to find their mates and get the season
rolling. Some are well along: The oval communities are throbbing
with noise. Experienced breeders presumably take the inside territories, less experienced chinstraps filling the edges. There's much
tangling from nest to nest—beak-stabs, parries, and thrusts—and
many eggs have already been laid. After laying, the female takes the
first incubation shift, for up to a week, then the male returns—
fattened a bit from feeding—for up to ten days. Then the female
returns for about a week, and short shifts proceed to hatching—
after approximately a little more than a month of incubation. After
eggs are dropped, the couple quickly transforms to a model sharing
arrangement. Both incubate. Both gather food. Both chase skuas.
Until the chicks leave their loose crèche, about two months after
clutch completion, parent chinstraps are saddled with more work
than I'm sure they can imagine. It's part of the evolutionary deal.
And if they weren't selected for this routine, chinstraps surely would
vanish as a species.

After hatching, chicks are brooded for two to three weeks and
fed for a total of six to seven weeks. Krill, that "power lunch" of
the Antarctic, is the chinstraps' main grocery item. Demands, demands. Tending to penguin children is extraordinarily stressful. The
chicks *always* want more food and the parents feel constant pressure
to retrieve more and more krill. At three to four weeks, the large
chicks begin to form loose crèches, not as tight and large as the
crèches of Adélie chicks, before heading to sea at about seven weeks
of age. The chicks presumably migrate northward as self-sufficient
birds, never again to be fed by their parents—in fact, not likely to

interact ever again with their parents. Young chinstraps may return to their natal grounds in their second year of life but won't attempt breeding until the age of three. Most never make it.

Ahead of me, the Baily Head colony rises gloriously. The meager stone nests are laid out, at flipper lengths, over a vast expanse of guano-stained black ash. Circles and ellipses of chinstraps extend all the way to Baily Head's high rim, with each group containing at least twenty to forty pairs, some as many as five hundred. The higher locations are favored because they are free of snow early in the spring. But they do require a mile-or-greater hike from the entrance beach, or a steep climb of more than a hundred feet from the small bay under the high rim. Those streaming downhill, heading for feeding runs, bear the marks of home—bodies packed with mud and slime and, in some cases, thoroughly krill-stained. Those who are returning, heading uphill next to me, bear fat and clean, pearly white countenances of diners who've just enjoyed a long, filling re-past. There is a massive traffic jam to my left, among the clean returnees. I examine one dead chinstrap in the meltstream, its pin feathers scattered, like litter, in the downflow. Skuas have worked much of the guts, but the wings and head are still intact, completely submerged.

Generally speaking, penguin sex is a short, sweet, and routinized affair—and it is hardly done in private. For the researcher immersed in the day-to-day lives of these frenetic animals, this important ritual sets the table for an eight-week stretch of concentrated activity—both for the penguins, who are about to be consumed with the task of raising chicks, and for the researcher trying to ascertain breeding prosperity in a particular colony. Opus, the magnificent cartoon penguin so brilliantly conceived and drawn by Berke Breathed, often ruminates about the lust in his heart. Amen. But to be accurate about chinstraps, they have both lust *and* territory in their hearts. Once the male reclaims his territory after a long winter away from Baily Head, the mates need to find each other and get on with necessary business.

I, too, am feeling a bit lustful—a bona fide voyeur wanting to absorb these animated routines. Now halfway to the rim, I approach one oval with approximately three hundred nests. Three quarters of the perimeter of this group is easily walked. The fourth side is totally eroded and drops sharply to the meltstream. The urgencies of the short breeding season are apparent. The chinstraps are short-tempered and combustible. A vigorous fight erupts, with one bloody, enraged chinstrap forcing another bird over the edge, the loser plummeting fifty feet downhill. The chinnies have copped the best-drained locations to breed, occupying many hummocks and bumps that haven't yet eroded or blown away. The steeper hillsides rising to the rim are similarly claimed.

I move upward another sixty feet to the next oval, with perhaps two hundred nests. Only half of this perimeter can be walked, with two sides of the oval dropping sharply downhill. Again, I sit—wanting to take in as much as possible. Greeting-parties of ten to fifteen penguins hustle toward me, chattering loudly—*duh-ARGH'-ARGH'-ARGH', duh-ARGH'-ARGH'-ARGH'*, with their heads pompously swaying back and forth—as always, checking passports and taking names. Nearby, one potbellied chinstrap falls flat on its face, then stares down the stones that presumably caused its inelegant missteps. The nests are packed very closely and the adults are incredibly edgy. The fierce behavior continues. It seems that any intruder—even a neighbor chinstrap trying to get home—is a candidate for merciless pecking and pummeling. In the narrow pathway between nests, one chinstrap bites another's neck, then pushes its face into the guano and pulls the offender out of the colony—all the while beating it relentlessly with its hard-edged wings. And it's not done silently.

On the far side, there's a bloodied penguin who's barely survived a leopard seal attack. Its mate incubates a single egg, with a second presumably on the way. But if the bloodied mate dies, the other can't do the job by itself, and the season may be lost. Fasting is part of the deal—from the time they hit the beach in the spring, up to and through the end of the first incubation shift. But excessive fasting won't be accommodated, especially when the adult becomes so depleted its own survival is an issue. If no relief, the adult leaves and marauding skuas have a feast. The widow or widower will return next season, find another mate, and go on.

Across the oval I observe another of those totally incompetent, inexperienced chinstrap males. He's mounted his presumed mate backward, his cloaca to her face. He starts wiggling his tail and she immediately rises and knocks him over. She gives him a sharp beak-stab and he scampers away, being quickly replaced by another suitor who begins to circle her. This goes on for long minutes. They stop, face each other, and begin displaying chest-to-chest, heads waving left and right, both squawking at each other with beaks open. If these two establish a pair bond, they will use a slightly less raucous version of this display as a mutual greeting, whenever a nest-relief occurs. In Adélies, males do considerable ecstatic displaying on their own, both to claim territory and to advertise that fact to prospective females.

Penguin sex is critically important. And because Antarctic penguins do so well at reproducing themselves, they have survived extraordinarily well as species. Darwin would be proud. They are prime examples of successful evolution in action. We humans seem to ponder our value in starkly individual terms, often critiquing our individual prowess intellectually, physically, sexually, or according to some other narcissistic measure. And while some of us contemplate whether we're headed for heaven, hell, or something in between, some of us too easily ignore that the true test of successful evolution actually ties to our collective success as a *species*. Our one-on-one successes are rather irrelevant.

Examining penguin reproduction, therefore, casts a slightly different light on our slight niche in earth's scheme of things. They take a pounding and keep on ticking, so to speak, and I'm rather confident they have no appreciation of individual worth. They're too programmed, too hardwired. Nothing seems to divert them from their mission. There's no time for kissing and foreplay—they proceed virtually straightaway to copulations, assuming mates successfully find each other when the breeding season commences. There is no rest and they undoubtedly get weary from meeting the chicks' endless demands. Their window of opportunity is so, so short.

That's why I've come. To witness them, firsthand, tackling the obstacles—spreading the genes to another generation. To see the chaos—a potpourri of courtship in full flower—it's best to get to Baily Head in early December, and to get to as high a vantage point as possible. I'm right on time.

Two nests away, I see another variation of this mutual greeting. It's a low bow-and-hiss affair, with the two chinstraps dropping their heads forward with extended necks, then slowly twining their heads and snaking them skyward, showing the sides of their heads to one another. With beaks closed, they each emit a low, guttural *awwhhhhhh.* In the middle of the oval, one chinnie starts a vigorous ecstatic display, its beak to the sky, and is loudly and swiftly joined by eight to ten others. It's hard to quell the anthropomorphism, but the higher reaches of Baily Head present a wild scene—a veritable soap opera of growls, snubs, charges, stark jealousies, and fights.

These are the concerns: Have the males made it back to the little pebble nests that served as home last season? Has the female in the pair survived the winter? I want to see more males loudly croaking for their mates and sweating out the wait. Will they divorce? Do chinstraps have affairs? Well, it all depends.

The clock ticks.

Next to me, another stand-up fight has reached the knockout and knockdown stage. Both combatants are bloodied. The stronger of the two forces its chest at the other, whacking it with a stream of flipper blows. One of the punches mashes the other penguin's face and knocks it to the ground. Going for the kill, the victor stomps on the loser's belly, then boldly stabs and grabs the other's neck with its beak and pushes it downhill. The blow's momentum and the steep incline cause the losing bird to tumble unimpeded until it disappears over the edge of the hummock. The victor raises its beak to the sky, erupts into another ecstatic, with wings outstretched, screaming wild and repetitive *duh-ARGH'-ARGH'-ARGH', duh-ARGH'-ARGH'-ARGH'* calls as it jaunts over to its nest, which I hadn't initially noticed. The two mates exchange some *quiet mutuals,* again this low bowing followed by raising their twisting necks slowly, growling their low, orgiastic moans. Blood still flows from the combatant's face, but these are superficial wounds that will disappear, washed by the sea, during the next feeding run.

What's happened is this: Mr. Chinstrap returned a few days ago to his previous year's nest site, awaiting his mate's return from her off-season jolly. Where is she? Will she make it back with reasonable dispatch? He waits. A few days overdue—no problem. But now, almost a week has passed. His hormones are escalated to fever pitch. The coming season is all too short and there's no time to diddle. He's also starving. Patience has evaporated. In utter frustration, he's courted and mated with an unattached female who happens by.

The denouement arrives with the original Mrs. Chinstrap, who finally returns and finds a young intruder in her nest. And Ms. Wrong, after a veritable heavyweight championship bout, is the one who, presumably, just got pummeled mercilessly and tossed downhill. Mr. Chinstrap, no doubt, has lots of *'splaining* to do. But Mrs. Chinstrap doesn't hold much of a grudge. She can't. Time's too short. The now reunited mates again twist their heads to the ground, then in unison raise their necks and beaks skyward, accompanied by more low, groaning *awwhhhhhhhs.* Shortly they will copulate, repeating the act two or three times, and within two weeks their two eggs will be laid, two to three days apart.

Above me, saucer-shaped lenticular clouds birthed by strong katabatic winds over the Bransfield indicate foul weather arriving imminently. But this scene must be savored, at least briefly. I've reached Baily Head's highest ridge. At this level, the peak of mating has passed. A number of clutches are complete, one mate incubating, the other away, feeding. The panorama is extraordinary. Toward the island's interior, for mile after mile, specks of chinstraps gleam like jewels against the volcanic landscape.

The ridge line undulates up and down like a vast curtain. The nitrogenous perfume and increasing wind rustle various thoughts. Among these chinstraps, I sense a powerful freedom and an immense privilege. I've come to witness a particular spectacle and I haven't been cheated. Darwin marches on.

On the high rim, I stretch prone, lying quietly, simply taking in as much as I can—still dealing with my PCD. One returning chinnie is pounded and pecked along the route back to its nest. Another holds in its beak a rock that's twice the size of its head. Three pairs erupt into mutual ecstatics, their hot breaths spiraling upward. Below, an endless stream of chinnies rises through the fog now enveloping the meltstream. A few are fast asleep with beaks tucked under wings. Do they have REM sleep?

Seeing chinstraps firsthand—having this eyeball-to-eyeball experience—is special. Six chinstraps scurry forward, skipping closer and closer. A few bend over in their characteristic, snake-necked posture, slowly raising their heads to engage my stare. Their deep and darting yellow eyes articulate a new path—a contemporary yellow brick road, inviting me to appreciate their lives and to connect with them.

Which brings Albert Einstein to mind. Despite his own revolution of quantum mechanics, he never wavered from believing that the universe is governed by discoverable laws in which a God-like mystery inheres. In his words: "God does not play dice." But, having tackled such mysteries and having integrated their concomitant complexities into his everyday life, he reportedly viewed preachers and their preaching as blasphemous. It was in this sense: Einstein had seen more majesty than they had ever imagined, and he felt that their sermons weren't the result of firsthand sweat and experience, that they simply weren't talking about the real thing.

I hunker closer to the ground, my head poised at chinstrap eye level. My reduced size surely entices their penguinesque curiosity. My legs stretch across the outside edge of this high pink and green breeding oval, left elbow propped on the ash, head lowered to *Pygoscelid* height. There are ecstatic displays and raucous *duh-ARGH'-ARGH'-ARGH'*, *duh-ARGH'-ARGH'-ARGH'* calls from two birds barely beyond my boots' reach. Other chinnies stride over, dipping beaks into my parka's folds and crevices, inspecting my nooks and crannies. One gives my face a close going-over, and jumps back when I exhale. Within five minutes, a few have crawled around my back, and one prances on my hip and on the side of my chest. It stops, raises beak to sky, and begins an ecstatic roar from my highest point. I feel like I'm part of the scene, a bona fide part of them. Or, in Walt Whitman's words:

I think I could turn and live with animals, they are so placid and self-contain'd,
I stand and look at them long and long.

They do not sweat and whine about their condition,
They do not lie awake in the dark and weep for their sins,
They do not make me sick discussing their duty to God,

Not one is dissatisfied, not one is demented with the mania of owning things,
Not one kneels to another, nor to his kind that lived thousands of years ago,
Not one is respectable or unhappy over the whole earth.

So they show me their relations to me, and I accept them,
They bring me tokens of myself, they evince them plainly in their possession.
I wonder where they get those tokens,
Did I pass that way huge times ago and negligently drop them?

They have no fear. As Robert Cushman Murphy suggests, a chinstrap has a special "kind of *bon camaraderie* if he meets you where he has no reason to resent your presence." Murphy recounts Arthur G. Bennett's story of croaking to chinstraps and having one respond by popping into his boat and soon falling into a doze—apparently planning to stay and sleep unless evicted. Yes, knowing them is life-affirming, the profuse reward for those lucky few of us who've gazed into the eyes of chinstraps.

They are hard to fathom: They have a relatively short longevity, survive an environment I can't tolerate, and continually humble me with routines that effortlessly get them through their frenzied lives. Can't fly—but they are remarkable swimmers, migrating as much as two thousand miles if necessary. How do I relate to a creature that's succeeded so well, whose numbers have blossomed into the millions? No doubt, with awe and respect—and some curiosity about still-unexplored ties between them and us.

I pick up a few unclaimed stones and offer them to the chinstrap who now ambles inquisitively at eye level. It grabs one token with gusto, as if it's stolen a great prize, and scampers quickly toward its mate and chicks on the far side of this pink guano lek. But abruptly, as if it's hit a solid wall, it stops, turns completely to catch my eye, then bows deeply. I return the homage with a nod of the head and a wave of my right hand. It croaks, raise the stone to the sky, shakes its bill, then runs away frantically, no glances back.

I want to be free, like them. They simply are. Never planned, hardly contemplated, and not asked. I don't want to be an actor locked in a role that others dictate. My short time needs to be its own legacy. I dream a new paradigm, conjuring hazy views of unexplored territory, an unending quest for a better understanding of penguins, and recognizing, humbly, our biological ordinariness.

So give stones to chinstraps. And dream of humans risking greater connections. Imagine our résumé evolving from uncontrolled consumer to enlightened participant in the scheme.

SEVEN

....

Slick Chicks at the Copa

Penguins are beautiful, interesting, and funny. They are a pleasure to watch even though they do smell and their voices are not melodious.

—GEORGE GAYLORD SIMPSON

There's excitement at Copacabana.

The season's first Adélie chicks just hatched out—and in all the Adélie colonies, there's a whole lot of pipping going on. The little guys are breaking through their shells and lots of peeps and chirps can be heard. But the actual sources of noise aren't immediately obvious—or easily located—because parents have the chicks well covered. In two weeks the gentoo youngsters will show, with chinstrap chicks popping two weeks beyond that. Shortly, the guano and protein spewing forth will reach a seasonal peak.

I'm very happy to be back at this isolated bit of turf in Admiralty Bay, where I've enjoyed so many consequential penguin encounters. The memories flow in droves. It is the site of the longest-running penguin study in the world, fast approaching the twenty-five-year marker. The project's investigators, Wayne and Sue Trivelpiece, have influentially mentored my penguin education—and for more than a decade have spun me to myriad nuances regarding the breeding biology and feeding ecology of chinstraps, gentoos, and Adélies. As a consequence, I have a strong attachment to the work done here, as well as to the select, few researchers who've carried these data forward. My penguin bona fides have blossomed at Copa, and this abundance of prime penguin moments has also nurtured an attitude: I believe penguins are key to understanding more about the interconnections of life in Antarctica and, more broadly, regarding our changing global climate. Antarctica is the engine that drives the world's weather and penguins are integral aspects of the system. The questions may be complex and the answers difficult, obscure, or impossible—but that's hardly the point. These complications have bred a humility and respect I'd otherwise lack. Perhaps I'm just reflecting Wayne and Sue's influence—tacking to a different plane— but I'm grateful for the direction.

Why work on penguins? And why here? As Wayne describes:

Copa is a microcosm. By and large, penguins are among several predators that rely almost entirely on krill during summer. Of all the predators, they're clearly the easiest to study because they're flightless, present in large numbers, not particularly afraid of humans, colonial, and site-tenacious—all of which allows you to study a discrete population through time. The young that are born here return here to breed when they reach adulthood and begin breeding. Adélies and chinstraps go away and spend the winter in two completely different habitats. Gentoos won't migrate if the bay stays open. When they return in numbers during the Antarctic spring, we can look at certain factors like overwinter survival, percent of young that breed, and weight of arriving birds to get some indication of the food resources in these very different wintering habitats.

From a slightly different perspective, Sue notes how captivating it's been—how Copa and how Antarctica have taken over:

It's been a real constant in our life, coming each October and staying five months each season. The Ice never really leaves us. It's never far away. Even for all of the time we're home, [we are] constantly going over the data, looking for patterns, trying to understand more and more about what we've been observing. We can't wait to get back the next season. And on those long days—when the work's difficult, disgusting, dirty, and we're simply frozen to the bone, there may be wild thoughts of hot fudge sundaes, pizza, and good cheeseburgers, but I still wouldn't trade. Like everyone who's spent lots of time down here, it's rather hard to describe the feelings. All of us get this Antarctic fever into the blood. On a day-to-day basis, the focus—always—is on what really needs to get done at that moment, wondering where some of our birds might be, what new data might come rolling in. Copa is a privilege. There are few who have had the special chance to make Antarctica an important part of their lives, and it would be very upsetting if we wouldn't be coming back. I'd miss the whole interaction of so many life-forms—leopards hanging out in the bay, humpbacks blowing offshore, penguins rushing about, and getting to meet so many wonderful people from so many nationalities.

The line to Wayne and Sue Trivelpiece and their long-running Copa project literally begins with Louis Gain, of the Second French Antarctic Expedition, who visited Admiralty Bay in 1909 before accomplishing his seminal penguin work at Petermann Island. Next comes Thomas Bagshawe and Maxime Lester at Waterboat Point in 1921–22. Wayne and Sue have confirmed many of Bagshawe and Lester's observations, and tackled questions Bagshawe raised when leaving Waterboat Point. Work on Peninsula *Pygoscelid* penguins continued in 1934–37 with Brian Roberts's study of gentoo breeding behavior. Then came a two-decade hiatus. The next chapters were Bill Sladen's bird-banding program in the South Orkneys in the late 1950s, David Parmalee's investigations at Arthur Harbor on the southern end of Anvers Island in the 1970s—and the mother of all penguin studies, Wayne and Sue's ongoing work in Admiralty Bay, which began in the mid-1970s.

I've visited Copa a number of times in recent years, in the process of transferring from ship to ship, pursuing my inventorying of Antarctic Peninsula visitor sites. During these layovers of a few days, I've had a chance to participate with and assist the Copa team in various aspects of their work—from egg weights and measurements to krill sorting, nest and chick counts, and chick banding. I always anticipate new field experiences that will add to my penguin data bank.

Earlier this afternoon, the trip over took much longer than expected. Copa is located just south of the Polish Arctowski research station—normally, a ten- to fifteen-minute Zodiac ride. Today it took thirty-five. Robert Parthe, chief mate on the *World Discoverer*, was slowed to long, puttering moments weaving through the ice. The chunks packed the Admiralty Bay shoreline, extending in places for more than three hundred yards offshore. While he worked in and out, moving through the leads, we had exceptionally close looks at three leopard seals riding the floes, including one within fifteen feet, which turned its head, gaped, then bared its nasty incisors.

The usual modus operandi is to line up the Zodiac for a straight shot at the front door of the Copa hut, running a course between the two huge boulders on the cobble shoreline, which lie about a hundred yards apart. This avoids most of the submerged rocks. Today, however, the usual straight shot is out of the question. Too much ice. We struggle in, watching carefully for rocks in the shallows, then, on our closest approach, off-load our bags. Robert is away in a rush. The wind stirs and dark clouds close from the northwest. Snow is coming.

I'm quickly into the thick of penguins. They are everywhere, up and down the beach. A semblance of Copa normalcy. North of the hut toward Copa Rock and Ecology Glacier, the gentoo and Adélie colonies look packed, as usual. Despite the offshore ice, many penguins are *zwipping* back and forth, charting their passage to the beach. A few bolt directly upward out of the water, plopping feet-first onto convenient floes. Flustered—looking left, looking right—they seem to be squawking with annoyance: *Wait a sec. This isn't the beach. Damn, another forty yards to go.* Gentoos, Adélies, and a very few chinstraps preen on the cobble just up from the surf. The slopes above and behind the hut are still snow-packed, with only three weeks to go until summer solstice.

Above and past the raised beach, a small wooden footbridge crosses a narrow melt pond, which is still frozen. The hut lies about a hundred yards beyond, way above tide line, nestled on level ground. The grass and turf are covered in white. Obviously, there hasn't been much sun and thaw thus far this spring. In some years, when the researchers return in late September or early October, drifts cover the door, the snow seeps in, and the field season starts as an extraction operation. The front porch of the fifty-foot-long hut is stacked with polystyrene cases and coolers full of drinking water, veggies, and other supplies. All food is brought in, with the bulk of frozen meat, chicken, and fish stored in a locker at Arctowski. Four gentoos scurry past, returning to mates lying upbeach. The snow showers begin. The gentoos fall prone and turn their backs to the gusts, covering eggs, shielding their treasures from the nascent storm.

My colleague Steve Forrest and I are on a short layover between ships and site counts. We drop our load inside the hut, grab binoculars and notebooks, and head out to assist with end-of-the-day rounds. In the ensuing two hours, the weather turns to a full-fledged horizontal blow. Returning to the hut around 8 P.M., cold and numb, we're ready to unwind and catch the details. Beyond and behind the hut, Wilson's storm petrels are performing their courtship dances on the snowy, eighty- to a hundred-foot-tall slopes. Copa's slick chicks are popping.

In another four to five weeks, at crèche stage, these chicks will be slick matte balls of damp down and general filth—and the dedicated Copa corps will be trying to band them for future reference. I can see it now, clear as the days I've assisted with this banding foray. It's called the *roundup*—and it isn't a pretty sight. It is a time of flying slop and guano, when the researchers resemble mud creatures from another planet. And when the smell—our smell—is totally off-putting. The upside, for science, is important. Wayne and Sue have gathered a wealth of cutting-edge information, in part because all three of these closely related penguins happen to nest in close proximity at Copa. It is unusual to have all three so close at hand, so there is a unique opportunity to study and compare their respective breeding and feeding ecologies.

Specifically, the roundup is an integral part of the Trivelpieces' investigations—banding an annual cohort of chicks of the three brushtailed penguins, which theoretically may be tracked in seasons to come, providing insights into everything from what they eat and whether they'll survive to their choices for partners and whether they stay paired or separate. Each season they band a thousand Adélie chicks, a thousand gentoo chicks, and as many chinstrap chicks as they can muster—chinstraps being somewhat less numerous than the other two species in the vicinity of the hut. The timing for the roundup is keyed to the chicks' crèching routine—when they move away from their nests, gather in groups, and begin to shed the last of their down feathering. Once the down is tossed they'll resemble spiffy, almost identical versions of their parents, and head to sea. At roundup time in late January and early February, Copa's snow melt is generally complete, so the research team faces a plethora of mud ponds and guano pools. Boots and plastic-coated clothing provide only so much protection. It's a messy job that someone's got to do.

You pray for a relatively windless and sunny day. The technique is for two or more of the team to gently corral the young birds with a wide-mesh, loose-rope net. The other researchers climb inside the loop, then slowly and carefully pick up one after another chick for banding. The old "ring and fling" technique, as it's sometimes called. You grab one of the fluffy chicks' wings at the shoulder, near the body, your thumb below, the rest of your hand on top of the wing. With your other hand grabbing the second wing in a similar fashion, you draw the chick to you, placing it between your legs, head up and belly down, and with beak forward and tail aft. This theoretically ensures that excretions from either end of the penguin travel in the proper direction—that is, far away from your face. You hold the chick in place by drawing your thighs and knees together, then dip into your parka or jacket pocket, grab a metal band, spread its leaves, and manipulate the band around the left wing. The numbered band fits in the narrow crook of the wing close to the body and will float freely. The bands are specially tailored—wide enough so the wing can be easily maneuvered, even allow room for growth and molting, but secure enough not to slip off.

All of this sounds great in theory, ignoring the reality that the wind never really stops in Antarctica. And whenever I've assisted with the roundups, it's been gusty as hell. Thus, if the chicks scatter too much in and through the mud and guano, you'll come away looking tarred and feathered, with penguin down splattered and pasted over your face, hands, and clothes. The worst part, perhaps, is that the banding needs to be done with bare hands, to ensure that the tags are properly placed. Without gloves, however, the cold and wind usually conspire to produce fiercely numbed fingers. And if the chicks start flailing and whipping their flippers, more than likely you're going to get nailed on the bare hands and fingers, which stings terribly. But, as Sue describes it, the hands-on experience handling these penguins-of-the-year is amazing, veritably uplifting: "Sometimes, if you've got a real fighter, you can hear yourself saying, *You're gonna make it, fella. Go get 'em, we want to see you back in a couple years.* On the other hand, when you're banding a thousand or more chicks, it can be hard thinking about individuals. No doubt, you get very attached to banded adults and known-age birds that you've worked with for a while." Some are totally skittish, others more relaxed.

All in all, a connection is made—one develops an unyielding respect for these animals, which are so fragile, so unaware. Of course, who knows if there is any penguin awareness? The world out there is surely a big fog. You feel their hearts pumping against your palm. They are amazing specimens—taut chest muscles, splotches of down still obscuring their juvenile plumage, enormous feet, strong wings. These youngsters have never seen a leopard seal, but they'll soon encounter one. Perhaps to die, to be shaken right out of skin and feathers by this predator. When the chicks' down is totally shed, they're presumably able to thermoregulate properly. But many will succumb to the cold. Some will never learn to find food on their own.

A couple of standard, human routines follow the roundup. First off, everyone gathers on a promontory, letting the wind remove—as much as possible—the down clinging to clothes, extremities, and bare skin. If it's been a really muddy, awful, disgusting roundup, the only choice will be to destroy your clothes, even after a thorough rinsing in the surf. To avoid this hassle, Wayne and Sue keep a large supply of totally grotty, old roundup gear in the outer shed. Nonetheless, some of this relic clothing can't be salvaged. Fresh air and glorious scenery are substantial antidotes to three hours of finger-numbing, mud-laden, nitrogen-rich chick banding. But even better is taking the two- to three-mile hike to Arctowski for a well-deserved shower.

Roundups will come soon enough—but tonight, the hatching chicks are the big news. One of this season's researchers, Laina Shill, attempts the daily radio sched, fitfully, frustratingly, trying to pass the good news on to the boss: "Chickens, Wayne. Can you hear me? Copa, *Abel Jay*, do you copy? Wayne, we've got chickens." No response. Presumably, hopefully, he's on the other end. Wayne's presently on the vessel *Abel Jay*, steaming toward Cape Shirreff on the northern end of Livingston Island. There, Wayne will assist the US National Marine Fisheries Service in establishing a new predator-prey project. Wayne's wife, Sue, who normally co-leads the work with Wayne, is monitoring details from a distance, having just given birth to the couple's second child. Matt Becker, managing Copa in their absence, jiggles the receiver buttons, trying to better the reception. The high-frequency connections can be nightmarish, even with Copa's new—and much taller—aerial. The nearby hillside and the interior of King George Island block a direct line-of-sight transmission toward Livingston, which lies seventy-five miles southwest with many peaks and a variety of terrain in between. There's considerable interference, and for the moment all we're getting are crackles and nonspecific noise.

Again, Laina booms the news into the handheld mike: "Copa, *Abel Jay*, do you copy? Can you hear me? We've got chickens, Wayne." Finally, there are a few garbles, faintly reminiscent of Wayne's voice. Laina, Matt, and another colleague, Tim Bennett, lean close to the receiver. She transmits one more time and unexpectedly Wayne booms through, rather clearly: "That's great, you guys. Excellent. Now the fun really begins." All around, smiles erupt.

"Yeah, Wayne. As usual, up at Big Foot in the Point Thomas rookery. And there's pipping and squeaking everywhere. We're going to be early this year. Hope all is going fine with you." Matt takes the mike to check a few project details with Wayne, passes along a hello from me and Steve, and signs off until tomorrow night. Now, with the radio sched completed, we can turn to mealtime—and more penguin buzz. Which is Standard Operating Procedure at Copa. No matter the day or time, it's always penguins, penguins, penguins.

All of us assume different, food-oriented tasks and begin sorting through what we've seen—or what we hope to see in the days ahead. Tim and Laina note what's been happening at their *repro sites*—who's still with whom, which nests have failed or lost eggs, which nests have been buried by the snow, and whether fights for mates are still occurring among the late nesters. There remains considerable snow on some of the access routes up to the higher Adélie colonies, with the penguins still needing to claw their way uphill when returning to their nests but having an easier time in the other direction, being able to toboggan and slide downhill when heading off to feed. Tim talks about his gentoo triad, with two males and one female tending a single nest. Two eggs were laid, but the nest then failed, inexplicably. Matt mentions that he, like Steve and I, has noted the large number of leopard seals riding ice in the bay, though no one's observed any penguin kills. He muses further about the whales. The humpbacks haven't returned to the bay as yet, which in turn suggests that the krill haven't returned either. High summer hasn't actually erupted.

The chatter reverts repeatedly to the chicks: How hard it is to see the new hatches. How deceptively far the chirps carry—either through the holes the chicks pip in their shells or from the protection of the parent's brood pouch. How fragile and naked they appear when first out of the shell—with just a slim down covering, needing to stay tucked in the brood pouch for warmth. How the parent leans backward, showing its helpless chick, lets the chick inhale some fresh air, then lowers its beak so the chick can nibble some regurgitated krill. How the resident skuas have begun patrolling the edges of the colonies looking for penguin snacks—eggs or juicy little chicks.

Our food gradually emerges, we grab plates and chairs and drinks, huddle around the small table, and continue to chat and reminisce. It's terrific to be back. The weather begins to clear, which means we'll have a chance, over one of the next few days, to check the chinstraps at the southern end of the study area. Working with the Trivelpieces and their colleagues is a hoot—from chick roundups to stomach pumping to egg weights to nest censuses to long, unbelievably filthy days in the field—moments when you'd die for a prolonged six-month retreat at an idyllic, warm spa. But not until the penguin action abates. The project has a long and storied history. To visit Copa is to jump onto the cutting edge of penguin science— to check out the latest news, views, and theories. Are populations up or down? What effects might global climate change and the ozone layer diminishment have on the Southern Ocean ecosystem? Are these penguins feeding in the same locations? What more do we know about their diving patterns and feeding ranges? Day-to-day penguin work is hard, tedious, dirty, and nonstop—but all who do it gain a renewed sense of purpose and achievement. Simply put, it's the joy of being a biologist—chasing the planet's secrets, getting fingernails soiled with myriad details.

Chicks are the passkey—the *ne plus ultra* of penguin life. To understand the intricacies of the brushtaileds' breeding biology and feeding ecology, penguin researchers must focus on the perquisites of chick production. After more than a month of incubating their annual investment, the Adélie breeders now move to a seven-week period of constant child care and feeding, all the while shrinking and depleting their own energy stores. Four weeks down the line, the gentoo and chinstrap parents will be similarly engaged—equally stressed and busy. Being married with penguin children is the definition of *hectic*. And for the Copa team—Matt, Laina, Tim, and Kasia Salwicka—their professional lives, too, will become comparably crazed. For both penguins and those who study them, the most crucial part of the season has arrived.

The imperative for penguins is evolutionary success or failure, a balance of lives and deaths, the numbers recruited to their respective populations versus those subtracted. The imperative for researchers is to obtain as much information as possible, and the time of maximum data flow is *now*. I marvel, every time I visit, how much information is tracked, recorded, and then entered into the computer. Their pencils are sharpened, field notebooks ruled and lined to record their findings. Work vests are packed, tally-whackers, spring-loaded weighing scales, and nylon weighing bags ready to go. Months of anticipation have led to these coming moments—and the team is ready.

A bit of orientation: Copacabana Beach lies on the western side of Admiralty Bay on King George Island, which is part of the South Shetland Island group. It is smack-dab in the middle of this Antarctic Banana Belt, with a profusion of penguins, colorful lichens, grasses, and moss—tucked near a considerable human presence. The hut is unofficially called the Pietr J. Lenie Field Station, named in honor of the captain of the *Hero*, the US research vessel that for many years brought the Trivelpieces or their supplies into Admiralty Bay at the start of each field season. Lenie Station was dedicated on February 12, 1985. The long Copa beach extends for a kilometer south of a prominent rock jutting into the bay—officially called Llano Rock and, unofficially, Copa Rock. When Wayne and colleagues first worked this long beach, with lots of upright animals prancing back and forth, its resemblance to the storied beach in Rio de Janeiro seemed obvious. After all, being the Banana Belt, why not a vernacular name to espouse the connections? In a similar fashion, the shorter beach north of Copa Rock was unofficially dubbed Ipanema. The Brazilians across the bay at Ferraz Station still tease Wayne and Sue that the *real* Copacabana Beach is a little shorter and the *real* Ipanema a little longer—and that both are *much, much* prettier. But no matter. Beauty lies in the eye of the beholder.

Admiralty Bay is an irregular indentation, ten miles long, on the southern coast of the island. It is about five miles wide at its entrance, between Demay Point on the west and Martins Head to the east. The name Admiralty Bay first appears on the charts prepared by the early-nineteenth-century sealers. The bay has a constantly changing profile: Today, the edges are packed with ice. Bergs float regularly in and out of the bay, pushed by currents in the outlying Bransfield Strait. At night, as the sun sets slowly and late over the western hills, the skies above the bay exude a purple and blue sheen, which reflects off of the water and ice surfaces. A bit to the southwest, Maxwell Bay has such a dense concentration of active research stations, the human presence seems to have obliterated the nonhuman possibilities. In Admiralty Bay there are full-time Polish and Brazilian stations, an occasionally manned Peruvian base, and a rarely used Ecuadorian refuge, but the human hustle and bustle is much less pronounced.

Copa is about a mile south of the Ecology Glacier and about two miles south of Point Thomas, the headland that forms the entrance to Ezcurra Inlet, the western arm of Admiralty Bay. Point Thomas and Ezcurra Inlet were first charted by Charcot and the Second French Antarctic Expedition. Louis Gain, the chief zoologist and botanist on that expedition, made the first penguin counts at Point Thomas on December 26, 1909. The Trivelpieces, therefore, carry on a bit of history. Wayne may be the oldest denizen, human or penguin, in terms of years spent in the bay. En route to a doctorate in ornithology, he first worked here in 1976 with Nick Volkman and Ed Waltz, living in a tent at Point Thomas. The precise spot where they camped is now occupied by the fuel tanks for the Polish Arctowski Station, which was dedicated on February 26, 1977. When Wayne first arrived the bay was empty, but alas the calm and total absence of humans was relatively short-lived.

He recalls:

There have been dramatic changes since I arrived in 1976. Then, Admiralty Bay was totally unoccupied. The old British Station across the bay opened in 1946 and closed in 1961. We established our tent site on what we thought was totally unexplored land. We had visions of people never having set foot here since the days of the sealers. In the intervening years, we've seen four bases built in this bay, two of them being big, full-time, all-winter operations. We used to see one tour ship, now there is constant traffic. This has some positive aspects. A lot more people are seeing Antarctica and it's becoming more well known. There's a growing constituency caring about saving it. The science side of things—like expansion in the suburbs—has just gone wild. Perhaps this island, King George, isn't a fair indication of the whole. It's so close to South America and has grown considerably. No matter how good the intentions, we find, nonetheless, that some of our flying birds—the skuas and gulls particularly—learn to subsist on station handouts and feeding off of some of the garbage. The Copa penguins, fortunately, remain relatively undisturbed.

Copa was a perfect location for a long-term penguin study. Wayne's original locus, Arctowski, lies on the northwestern edge of a mossy and grassy plain, which often becomes soggy and wet from the spring and summer snowmelt. Initially, the station afforded Wayne and his colleagues sturdier shelter and a more practical base of operations. The first large assemblages of Adélies and gentoos were a few hundred yards south of the station, on a hillside rising above the soggy Arctowski plain. During Wayne's initial investigations it became obvious that the site as a whole had immense scientific value. Continuing to the southwestern end of the bay, there were numbers of all three of the brushtailed penguins—fourteen to eighteen thousand Adélie pairs, two to three thousand gentoo pairs, and up to two thousand chinstrap pairs—located in pockets all the way to the Bransfield Strait. There was a unique opportunity to investigate the penguins' habits and lifestyles intimately and comparatively.

With Wayne's encouragement, the Poles proposed to the other Treaty Parties that the study site be designated as a Site of Special Scientific Interest, which would keep nonpermitted, casual visitors away, and help conserve the fragile areas of moss and grass near to the station. The Treaty Parties, via consensus recommendation, consequently established the "Point Thomas Site of Special Scientific Interest" at their tenth consultative meeting in Washington in 1979. The official Treaty designation notes that the "purpose of the investigations is to gain insight into the dynamics of a typical, but particularly rich, Antarctic coastal ecosystem. Studies of the functioning of the inshore and coastal zone in relation to the ecosystem will include quantitative studies of the circulation of matter and energy between the coastal and marine environments."

From the penguin colonies in relatively close proximity to Point Thomas, Wayne and his team kept advancing toward the Bransfield, over the Ecology Glacier to Copa Beach, two miles from Arctowski. The largest concentrations of chinstraps are at Demay Point, Uchatka, and Patelnia at the southern end of the study site, another five to seven miles hiking beyond Copa. In 1978 and 1979, the censusing and mapping were continued by Boleslaw Jablonski, who worked out of the Arctowski Station. Wayne, Nick Volkman, and Rob Butler returned in 1980. Sue joined the project in 1981, shortly after completing her master's degree in ornithology.

Copa Beach offered many advantages. There would be easier access to the southern end of the study site. Even better, the mass of penguins in the vicinity of Copa were far removed from the tumult of human activity—protected to the north by the glacier, to the east by the bay, and south and west by the King George Island terrain. In other words, the Copa penguins were undisturbed and likely to stay that way—an ideal circumstance for an investigation that would take years, perhaps decades. A refuge hut at Copa would obviate the need to walk continually over or around Ecology Glacier to make daily observations. Concomitantly, a central location on Copa Beach also meant that the studies could continue in foul weather. Data wouldn't be missed if researchers couldn't safely traverse the large glacier and make it south.

The first refuge hut Wayne, Nick, and Ed used at Point Thomas was nothing more than a darkened box—dubbed the Cave. It was alternatively wet, cold, uncomfortable, drafty, and clearly not the most ideal of nerve centers. The next season, it was moved to Copa with the help of the Poles. This structure evolved into the Lenie hut, a twelve- by sixteen-foot wooden shed erected during the 1984–85 season, and initially occupied by Wayne and Sue's colleagues Geoff Geupel and Janet Kjelmyr. This larger room, serving both as kitchen and bedroom, was eminently more comfortable. The Cave transmogrified further with the addition of a small entry hall and storage room for the researchers. In 1987, the facility expanded by another room, the Gates Annex, which was an additional bedroom and work area added on the north side and connected to the kitchen area by the refurbished storage area. In 1992, the PTS Annex, named for the amphibious vehicle at the Arctowski station, added a main storage room and a small bedroom on the southern end of the hut, so two of the researchers wouldn't have to live in the kitchen.

Through more than fifteen years, there have been a few constants at the Lenie Field Station. Remember: This is outback Antarctica. There are no pipes, no running water. A gutter-and-tube system connects the sloping roof and a jug below, allowing some meltwater to be collected for kitchen use. Once the snow goes, water may be collected from some of the meltstreams for purification—and this needs emphasis: Meltstreams *without* penguins and penguin guano exist only at the higher reaches. Electrical lines and power plants? None, of course. Copa has fuel-fired generators to keep the computers and radios going, as well as to power a few space heaters. Showers? Forget it. That usually requires a trip up to the Polish station. Occasionally, if there's been constant sunshine, the glory rays are sufficient to warm the water in the researchers' sun-shower device. Bathrooms: No way, José. Again, there is no indoor plumbing.

Until recently, the last order of business each season was to dig a new pit a hundred yards south of the hut, to be covered by the little wooden throne and toilet seat that Geoff Geupel designed and built from driftwood. The throne is not enclosed like a proper outhouse and there's absolutely no protection from the elements. Recent practice has the human waste collected in large polystyrene buckets slung into the hole, and removed when full—which also eliminates the need to dig new waste pits.

The Box aims southeast, affording a clear view of the Bay entrance and the Bransfield Strait beyond. When using this facility there is additional entertainment from the nearby skua pair, affectionately known as the Box Skuas. Whether by original intention or chance, the Box abuts one end of these skuas' territory, so throne sitters necessarily become inured to the brown-colored marauders pecking at shoes, or noisily pumping cackling *long calls* at maximum volume and displaying their extended wings at close range. Immobile on the throne, I've occasionally had the Box Skuas fly right at my face, veering off at the last moment as I raised my fist in the air. Privacy vis-à-vis your co-workers is achieved more systematically. This is managed by the heavy red "Box coat" hanging on the inside of the hut door, replete with paper and other necessities. If someone's using the Box, the coat will be gone. Just wait until they return.

Once on the throne, you can drape yourself with the huge coat and try to shield yourself as much as possible from the wind—the constant wind—but no matter how you cut it, it's an endurance test. As Janet Kjelmyr recalls, the Box affords "an unparalleled view, but the raw truth is that visits to it in subfreezing weather with icy gray gusts blasting everywhere can be quite unpleasant." From personal experience, I think her view understates the misery. It is *totally* unpleasant attempting your business when your entire being shakes uncontrollably. Ah, part of understanding penguins better. It just has to be done.

Between the hut and the Box, there are a few long wooden boards molded into the grass. The shape is a long, narrow rectangle. Rumor has it that they are the outline and remains of a whaler's grave from the nineteenth century. It's a reminder of the ebbs and flows of the human presence in the bay, which also expanded just before Lenie Station was dedicated. The Brazilian Ferraz Station officially opened on February 6, 1984, and is located across the Bay at Martel Inlet close to the site of the old British Base G.

Through the years, Wayne and Sue have logged substantial ice-time, up to six months a season. For Wayne, this adds to more than eight full years in Antarctica with the penguins. For Sue, it's been more than six—an amount of ice-time perhaps unmatched by any other female scientist to date. The Copa project has produced a series of remarkable and unparalleled data sets—some of the best penguin information ever collected. The legacy is substantial: When the project began, only the Adélie penguin, among the brushtaileds, was known to any extent, through extensive work that Bill Sladen undertook in the South Orkneys in the late 1950s and that David Ainley had conducted on the far side of the continent, at Cape Crozier, in the 1970s. As Wayne describes it: "The other brushtailed were an unknown *black box*." But no longer. The Trivelpieces patched together a complex picture of how the gentoos, Adélies, and chinstraps sort out what, at first blush, seems to be the same landscape and feeding territory.

The starting point was the Adélie and its well-documented life history: It is a penguin that spends eight months of the year in the pack ice that surrounds the continent each winter. As the ice breaks in September and October, the Adélies stream back to their preferred breeding territories, males arriving first, ecstatically displaying for mates, with females returning, on average at Copa, within a day or two. Pair bonds are renewed—or if the female doesn't return quickly, new ones formed—then it is quickly on to copulations, gathering pebbles for nests, egg-laying. During this two-to-three-week process, both mates are starving. The eggs are laid three days apart. Once the eggs are laid, the female immediately heads to sea and the male takes the first incubation shift, which lasts about two weeks. By the time his mate returns to relieve him, he'll have been fasting for five to six weeks. He then takes a feeding run of about ten days, then the shifts alternate, for shorter time frames until the eggs hatch at thirty-two to thirty-five days after laying. Just before hatch, the mates are changing over every twenty-four hours—and, hopefully, finding sufficient food to replenish their depleted energy stores and stock up for the food demands of the soon-to-emerge chicks.

The two- to three-ounce newborns are totally dependent on their parents for warmth and protection for their first three weeks of life. The food demands are constant. One parent broods and protects the chick while the other goes off to feed. It is a rigorous back-

and-forth routine, the mates changing over daily. On returning to the nest, the Adélie approaches its mate with a *loud mutual* call, its mate responds specifically, and after this recognition the changeover takes place. The chicks soon recognize the individual calls of their parents. These calls also signal that the food truck has arrived: The chick starts begging with raised and quivering beak, the parent opens its mouth wide, then the chick dips in to enjoy a tasty meal of regurgitated penguin pabulum. At times, the chick dips in so far it looks like the parent is consuming its offspring's head.

During these first three weeks, the chicks grow exponentially and quickly become much larger than a parent's brood pouch can handle. And past three weeks, they will eat considerably more food than a single parent can provide on a single feeding run. Fortunately, at this point, the chicks can fend for themselves. They've grown a thicker down coat, enabling them to thermoregulate on their own, and by assembling in groups—crèches—they can defend themselves more effectively against predators. A new difficulty arises: Parents returning from feeding runs need to sort their chicks from the crèche. They announce their presence with a *loud mutual* call the chick recognizes, and which spurs the chicks to race toward the parent. But other, unrelated chicks are equally inspired, and a crazy feeding chase ensues. Many chicks join the chase, causing the parent to race down the beach until, presumably, only its own, very determined chicks continue the effort. At seven weeks of age and about to fledge, the chicks will have grown to seven or more pounds.

Wayne and Sue wanted to know how closely the Adélies' known pattern and routine was followed by the chinstraps and gentoos—or not. From the project's inception, they established a protocol for collecting mounds of information about key biological parameters. The procedures have been followed unswervingly every season, thus allowing comparisons of key variables between and among the three species. Fecundity: How many nests are established and how many eggs are laid? Survival: How many penguins come back from year to year? Production and recruitment: How many chicks fledge each season and, ultimately, how many are added to the population?

When the Copa team returns each spring—in late September and early October—the first order of business is to survey the entire rookery, map where the penguins are setting up, and make reference to last year's arrangement. There are two objectives. The first is to find all *known-age* penguins. Some of these penguins will have bred successfully or attempted breeding in the past, others will be inexperienced penguins trying to breed for the first time. All will bear characteristic flipper bands on their left wings. The bands are specially manufactured. Originally, these alloy bands were black or silver in color. Now, a heavier composition metal of dark gray color is used. The bands are an inch and a half long when snapped shut and about an inch wide, ovoid-shaped and bulged at one end— corresponding to the upper, thicker part of the penguin's flipper— and tapered to a quarter-inch width at the other end—conforming to the wing's narrower, trailing edge. Where penguin wing meets penguin body, the wing narrows slightly. The circumference of the ovoid-shaped band is intended to be large enough to float in this confined area. Theoretically, the band won't rub tightly against the penguin's feathers or impede the wing's movement.

The band is cut laterally about three eighths of an inch from its narrow end. The researcher properly places it by opening and spreading the leaves at the cut, slipping the two leaves over the wing, then pressing the split ends toward one another until the shorter end slightly overlaps the longer. The researcher snaps the band shut and tight by pulling the long end upward slightly, locking the two leaves against one another. Each band bears a five-digit number—for example, 34001, an Adélie born in the 1990–91 season. When the banded penguin stands erect with wings held at the side, the five-digit number on the band can be easily read from a distance using eight- to ten-power binoculars. Because of the long-term banding effort at Copa, many penguins are known individually and have long histories. In the 1997–98 field season, for example, six known-age Adélies, all sixteen years old, were paired and breeding. And when one mate fails to return and the survivor chooses a new partner the next season, does he or she prefer someone the same age? The banding suggests that age isn't a crucial factor: To use romance vernacular, both *May-December* and *December-May* re-pairings have been identified.

During the early-season mapping and scouting operation, the location of all known-agers is logged, including the precise colony, nest site, landing beach, or other areas where they are seen. It also is noted whether the penguin is alone on a nest, paired and attached to a nest, or simply wandering about unattached to any nest. If a known-ager pairs off, it is important to discover whether the paired birds stay together and form a bond or separate and attempt to mate with others. The known-agers will be followed daily, their sexes verified, their mates banded, and the progress of their nesting attempts recorded. At Copa, chinstraps generally are found on higher ground, gentoos at the lowest levels, and Adélies both low and high.

The researchers' daily observations fill a complicated matrix. Through daily observations and accurate data recording, it will be known when a known-age penguin arrives, pairs, lays, hatches eggs, and fledges chicks. From all data collected on clutch size and number of chicks hatched and fledged—meaning survival to crèche stage—breeding success of the colony can be determined. The researcher also notes the time spent by individual penguins on eggs or chicks and the time that bird's mate is at sea feeding. This gives a measure of nest attendance. If a nest fails, the timing of that loss and probable causes are noted. Failed breeders continue to be followed, if possible, should the penguin return later that season to the rookery. From the Copa database, it is possible to determine whether the known-age bird returned to the colony at which it was born, how tenacious it is to a particular nest site, how faithful it is to its mate, the precise age at which it first visited the colony and when it first attempted to breed, whether it survived from the previous season, and whether there is any emigration or immigration between the various colonies in the study area.

The second major objective each spring is to establish a new series of *repro sites* throughout the rookery—a random sampling of a hundred pairs of both gentoos and Adélies, and as many chinstrap pairs as possible, none of which has been previously banded. Five nests are chosen in each of twenty different areas. Colored rocks and other landmarks are used to triangulate the location of the nests. The five pairs in each area receive characteristic flipper bands. The male or the female will receive a black band, the other will have a silver band, and both bands are coded with color tape so the precise nest is readily identified: say, red for nest I, blue for nest 2, green for nest 3, yellow for nest 4, and brown for nest 5. With this arrangement, it is easy for the researcher making daily observations to record the sex of the penguin on each and every nest. Sex is best confirmed by copulation position—male above, female below. The next best method is looking for "treadmarks" or muddy marks on the back of the female, or the male's larger head and bill when the two are side by side. In Adélies, behavior also may assist: The male's loud ecstatic display is often followed by the female's quiet mutual display, and the male normally takes the first incubation shift. But a quick proviso: They often make mistakes, or better said, they stray from expected behaviors—females sometimes displaying more loudly and ecstatically than males, or curiously, insisting on taking the initial incubation shift.

The researchers set up a daily attendance calendar in their field books. All repro sites are visited and the researchers collect the same data as they do with respect to known-age penguins—egg dates, who's on the nest incubating, chick-hatching dates, and egg or chick failures. Even after failures, the nests continue to be checked, and crucial insights may emerge. For example, if a male Adélie deserts after its long initial two-week incubation shift, it is important to record whether the female ever returns to the nest or happens to be seen elsewhere in the rookery. With young breeders, the failure could simply be a matter of bad timing—the female just doesn't get back on time, and he's tired of waiting. Five weeks of starving is enough. But if she never returns, the failure is more likely caused by mortality—a mate perhaps lost to a prowling leopard seal. Once the two-egg clutch is completed, the researchers check the nests every fourth day for losses, continuing until the chicks move away from the nest, and begin to crèche, at three to four weeks of age.

When Copa opens in late September or early October, the Adélies are streaming back. In some seasons, there may be considerable snow cover, which means that the penguins can't find their precious nest stones. Until there's a bit of melting, the breeding schedule may be delayed. This is also the time when much fighting occurs in the rookery. The male Adélies are very quick-tempered, really wanting to get on with business. There's little tolerance for passing birds who, potentially, might want to steal the slowly emerging stones. As a species, Adélies have selected a tight schedule, with the female expected to return very quickly to the previous year's nest site. But sometimes she's delayed. Eventually, when she finally returns, she may find her "ex" with another mate or, even more complicated, sitting on eggs produced with another spouse. The battles can be fierce, with blood shed readily and often. The resultant injuries are mostly surface wounds, but there's no question about the underlying tension.

Down the line, the researchers weigh all *repro* chicks at twenty-one days of age. This is accomplished with a small, spring-loaded scale, which is tubular in shape. The tube has a narrow opening on the side, calibrated to show how far the spring is stretched—and thus how much the object in question weighs. The chick is placed in a cloth bag and suspended from a hook at the bottom of the tubular scale, stretching the internal spring. After the roundup, fledging weights are recorded by weighing banded chicks-of-the-year on the beach, just before they head to sea.

Were Copa configured differently—say, in a fashion requiring all penguins to take the exact same route back and forth to the bay—different techniques might be used. For example, in the Australian Antarctic sector, there is an Adélie colony that has only a single ingress-egress path. Devices implanted beneath a penguin's skin are used to record that individual's comings and goings. It's just like at the local supermarket. The penguin reaches the narrow gap, passes through a bar-code scanner, and, instantly, the researchers know whether Joe or Mary has come or gone. Scales also can be installed so that every time the penguin passes the scanner it is concomitantly weighed.

The annual Copa sample of *repro birds* allows the team to ascertain annual averages for the various reproductive variables—fecundity, production, recruitment—and, further, to allow comparisons between any age class and in the penguin population as a whole. Some of the data are startling. Only less than 10 percent of Adélie chicks will make it back to attempt breeding for the first time in their third year. With gentoo chicks, less than 1 percent may return to begin breeding for the first time at age two, but in other seasons this rate has exceeded 30 percent. Typically, Adélie chicks won't return until age three to attempt breeding for the first time. In reality, the vast majority of chicks don't return at all. The survival of the banded penguins over the ensuing winter is used as an index of annual survival for each species' breeding population.

The procedure for gentoo and chinstrap repro sites is similar, but with some modifications to reflect different behavioral traits. For example, only one of the mates in the gentoo pair is banded. Gentoos are much more skittish than Adélies and chinstraps, and it is considerably more disruptive to force the issue. With little provocation, they will run off their nests and expose their eggs. Gentoos also change nest sites regularly, so keeping track of known-age and previous repro gentoos can be challenging. Some old breeders may be present, but around the corner—not exactly where they located the previous season.

The data cache is immense and helps to fill the picture. As Wayne suggests:

> There are definitely good and bad years—with certain parameters varying tremendously: How many chicks were produced? How much did they weigh? How much food was brought to them? We take these measures to indicate something about the food availability in the penguins' foraging ranges—probably within fifteen to thirty miles of the rookery during the chick phase. And by getting good baselines in place regarding facets of their lives that may be heavily impacted by food availability, we'll be ready when population changes are detected. We'll be able to make necessary comparisons and be in the thick of the effort to establish why the changes may have occurred.

There are two important, rookery-wide censuses carried out each season, the dates of which vary according to species. The first is a count of occupied nests, which is to be accomplished at the peak of egg-laying. This peak occurs when a majority of nests have two eggs. If all the nests have two eggs, the peak's been missed. From daily observations, the researchers can track the rate of egg production in each colony and have a precise sense of when this peak is reached. The second important count is chicks produced per occupied nest, accomplished at the peak of chick-crèching. This peak occurs when a majority of chicks have moved away from their nests and begun to assemble in larger groups. If the chicks have begun to move to the beach, this peak's been missed. The peaks for each of the species differ because the Adélies usually are two weeks ahead of the gentoos, and the gentoos two weeks ahead of the chinstraps. These were important clues that the three species might share the same prey resource—and might do so by having different peak demand periods, when the chicks hatch and require gobs of food.

All of the researchers carry their essentials into the field whenever they check their nests: A repro field book. A daily field logbook for recording daily sightings of known-age penguins and other noteworthy happenings. Calipers for measurements. Tally-whackers for counting and censusing. Scale and poly bag for weighing eggs and chicks. Large permanent black ink markers for marking eggs as they're laid—"A" or "B"—to note which came first. Pliers for fixing bands that have sprung from the penguins' left flippers. Mechanical lead pencils.

From years of collecting data in this fashion, Wayne and Sue began to discover differences and similarities among the three species. Like Adélies, chinstraps were migratory, but they arrived about four weeks after the Adélies. With chinnies, females usually took the first incubation shift, not the males—and the shift was shorter, a single week, not two. Once the chicks hatched, the chinstrap parents fed them more often, every sixteen to eighteen hours. The chinstrap chicks were a little older and a little heavier when they fledged.

The gentoos also showed important differences from the Adélie pattern. The gentoos at Copa were nonmigratory and did not engage in a lengthy fasting period before laying. In fact, both mates would forage during the day and return at night to build their nest and court. As first observed by Bagshawe and Lester at Waterboat Point in 1921–22, the gentoos had a completely different style. Four to five days before laying, the female would remain on the nest, with the male continuing his daily feeding runs. The gentoos' eggs normally appear two weeks after the Adélies' and two weeks before the chinstraps'. If Adélies or chinstraps lose their first or second egg at the exact time of laying, a third egg may be produced. Gentoos can relay up to two weeks after the first clutch is lost. Once the chicks hatched, gentoo mates would change over often and chicks would be fed every twelve hours. The changeovers were interesting because the mates seemed to recognize each other by sight, sitting birds often *hee-HAW*-ing to their quietly returning mates tiptoeing back to the nest. Only the gentoos were found to lay another clutch if the first set of eggs was lost.

The gentoo chicks also were found to be much less independent than the others. When Adélie and chinstrap chicks fledge and head to sea, their parental ties are cut, absolutely and forever. No more freebies from mom and dad. Gentoo chicks, by contrast, make test runs to sea at about eight weeks of age, then continue returning each night to be fed by their parents for another few weeks.

On average, Adélie males at Copa arrived about a day or two prior to the females. A very tight schedule. The chinstraps, collectively arriving about four weeks after the Adélies, had a looser regime—females arriving on average about five days after the males.

Gentoo mates seemed to be together much of the time. Being non-migratory, the mates also, potentially, spent the winter together in the Bay. There were further clues and inklings: Adélie males were very tightly tied to their nest sites—as if they were married to stones, not to their mates. Male Adélies proved to be 99 percent faithful to their nest site from the previous season. But they changed mates very frequently—only 63 percent of the mates re-paired the following season. At the other end of the scale were gentoos. These mates are very faithful to one another, previous mates re-pairing up to 90 percent of the time but highly prone to changing nest sites, only 65 percent of the pairs retaining previous territories. The chin-straps fell somewhere in between, showing an attachment to both mates and stones—94 percent of the pairs retained previous nest sites, and 82 percent retained their pair bond.

Wayne and Sue also considered the distribution of the three brushtaileds. While the ranges of all three appear to be Antarctic, there are important differences. The Adélies are truly polar: They concentrate around the far southern reaches of Antarctica, with the Peninsula being the most northerly aspect of their breeding range. The *high polar* proclivity means an adaptation to short summers and a premium of available nest sites. The gentoos are distributed in more moderate latitudes, extending to scattered subantarctic islands as far north as latitude 50 degrees south. The southern part of the gentoos' overall range is the Peninsula, with the absolute southern limit being at Petermann Island, at 65 degrees south, where Louis Gain studied them. By contrast to the Adélies, gentoos theoretically would have a wider choice of potential nest sites. The true Peninsula penguin is the chinstrap, whose distribution is concentrated in the

Scotia Sea area, which encompasses King George Island and Admiralty Bay. But in the Peninsula the weather is highly variable—some years clogged with ice and snow, other seasons blessed with relatively ice- and snow-free conditions. Indeed, the Peninsula represents a narrow band where all three of these penguins happen to overlap.

The Copa data suggested that the three species adapt differently to the plate they're served. The Adélies can't wait for either old mates or better weather. In evolutionary terms, they've selected for an early arrival on breeding territories and a synchronous arrival of both males and females. Again, the data showed only a one-day difference in arrival times. Males are not going to wait and will pair quickly with any available female. The schedule's tight and there's no time to waste. Moreover, Adélies must arrive fattened to the hilt. The males face at least five weeks of starvation, through the laying of the clutch and the male's first incubation shift. Both Adélie and chinstrap breeders lost considerable mass between the time of their arrival and the completion of their two-egg clutch. Much of the females' weight loss could be attributable to the eggs they were producing. For the males, though, the issue was starvation—or more precisely, coping successfully with the fasting regimes in their breeding schedule. The Adélie males had it the worst. The Copa data showed that Adélie males taking the first incubation shift are 27 percent heavier than females at that point in time. The males have serious work to do—and the timing has to click. So if the female Adélie doesn't return to relieve the male after the first two-week incubation shift, he bolts. By this point, his weight may have dropped 30 percent from when he first returned in the spring.

They've adapted to a schedule reflecting the very short summers at the *heart* of their breeding range. Good nests are hard to find, and male Adélies are attached to them. The nests are likely to be snow-free early in the season, and the males want the females to come to these prized locations and to get there on time. With only so much energy to burn, it makes no sense to retain a spectacular nest site if it takes "ex" another week or so to arrive home. That would translate to six or more weeks fasting after the male completes the first incubation shift, a price that Adélie males simply don't want to pay. Other studies had shown that while Adélie breeding success was improved by previous nesting experience, this had nothing to do with age or whether previously paired penguins reunited in subsequent years. So the Adélie pair bond is comparatively weak, its site tenacity strong.

The gentoos' schedule is exceedingly liberal, by contrast: Many possible nest sites. Generally ice- and snow-free conditions, removed from pack ice conditions predominating farther south. Gentoos don't need to be so picky about a single nest site—there are many possibilities. Also, they are nonmigratory and the mates tend to stay together—perhaps year-round. As a result, they've selected a more relaxed breeding schedule.

The chinstraps fall in between—selecting a bit of mate fidelity and a bit of site tenacity. The *heart* of their range is maritime Antarctica—the Peninsula, which is subject to significant climatological ebb and flow. Importantly, the maritime climate allows five to six months of decent weather to accomplish each season's breeding activities. Thus, chinstraps have some choices. It would be excellent to retain a previous, snow-free breeding site with good access to offshore feeding grounds. But if the variable climate produces a spring with lots of snow, rain, wind, and cold, the chinstraps have the option of holding off a few weeks until the weather clears. Also, the chinstrap can wait a while for its previous mate to appear, up to five days—five times longer than Adélie males. Chinstrap incubation shifts are also shorter in duration than those of the Adélies, which means that the overall fasting periods are shorter.

The Copa data showed similar breeding success among the three. There may be gross fluctuations from year to year, but over time breeding success averages to about one chick per pair. Wayne and Sue also noticed that the year-to-year variation in the number of breeders could be as high as 20 percent. Clearly, foraging success during the breeding season must have something to do with prey availability. All three species are major krill consumers in the austral summer, though gentoos' tastes are more catholic: They regularly eat substantial amounts of fish. But there were seasons when chinstraps switched to a substantial fish diet, and other seasons when Adélies ate large amounts of amphipods. There was also a suspicion that returning numbers of penguins may relate to winter food availability—or to other factors. Yes, the more Wayne and Sue looked, the more complicated the mosaic became.

They reasoned that some answers may be tied to how the three species exploited their offshore environment. This required more sophisticated equipment and techniques. In the late 1980s and early 1990s, Wayne and Sue pioneered the use of radio transmitters—TXs—and time-depth recorders—TDRs—to determine where these penguins were going, how long they were engaged in feeding during the chick-rearing phase, and to what depths they were going to find their prey. The whole package—a transmitter five inches long and two inches wide, with an aerial sticking out—is placed on the penguin's back, attached with a strong epoxy glue. Thin plastic cable ties are slipped underneath the feathers and tied around the transmitter for further support. The transmitter is easily removed when the bird returns, and any lost feathers will be replaced when the bird goes through its annual, pre-winter feather molt. These penguins, geared to the hilt with TDRs and TXs and looking like top-secret government spies, were dubbed the "bionic" penguins.

Overall, the conclusion was that during the chick-rearing phase gentoos usually foraged within four to five miles of their rookery, with a maximum of fifteen, and chinstraps within sixteen to seventeen miles, with a maximum of twenty. Adélies could wander to more than thirty miles offshore but seemed to prefer staying closer than twenty-five. Further experiments began to sort out the actual diving depths: The near-shore gentoos could exploit to more than 500 feet below the surface, Adélies to 250 feet, chinstraps to about 200. Gentoos also dived deep for longer periods—perhaps to two minutes or more, compared to the chinstraps' minute and a half. It was also known that krill swarms in the Bay and the Bransfield Strait could range from the surface to depths approaching 500 feet. So the gentoos proved to be the Greg Louganises of the brushtaileds, capable of feeding on the deepest swarms and for the longest amounts of time. These master divers could exploit krill and fish to a maximum extent, while the chinstraps and Adélies, apparently, would dive only so far and relied on a diet that was predominantly krill.

The experiments confirmed suspicions that the Copa Adélies, gentoos, and chinstraps had selected a very successful cohabitation scheme—staggering their peak demand for prey and employing different strategies for exploiting the offshore environment. They'd parceled out the periods when they'd need the maximum amount of food for their hungry chicks—that three- to four-week time frame prior to fledging, when the chicks needed to be fed constantly.

I remember one of my early Copa visits, which occurred at the height of this TDR work. The minute the bionic penguins hit the beach, returning from a feeding run, a computer alarm would ring and we'd spring to action. More often than not, this happened in the wee hours. These were days of little sleep. Catnaps were the routine, and much time was expended worrying about the penguins' losing one of these expensive devices. We'd race to the beach, Sue holding a portable aerial and beeper trying to pinpoint the penguin's exact location, Wayne hustling next to her with a big scoop net. The penguin would be found, captured, the TX and TDR unit plucked from its back, and its stomach gently pumped to check what it had been retrieving. After cleaning the device and attaching it to the computer, the data could be downloaded and, ultimately, there would be a complete readout of what the penguin had been doing—for however long it had been offshore. It was possible to determine when it was at the surface—resting or swimming, or making shallow dives, probably just searching—or when it was making long dives—actually capturing krill or other items. And how much time the bionic penguins spent performing all of these tasks.

The diet sampling led to these questions: What, precisely, had the penguin been eating? How much food had it taken by weight? If krill, what length of krill? If fish, could small remnant ear stones be specifically identified? The calcareous bits are called otoliths, and one of Wayne's graduate students, Nina Karnovsky, a three-season Copa veteran, was a master at identifying these characteristic fish parts. If squid, could the remnant squid beaks be specifically identified? Stomach lavaging is a very difficult field procedure, requiring unending patience and sensitivity to the penguin being handled.

Rob Dilling, who worked at Copa from 1993 to 1995, excelled at this—but he found it truly unnerving: "You really need to be careful. That tube has to go down the stomach, not the lungs. You really want to make sure the penguin is as comfortable as possible." In theory, the technique is simple: Fill the hot water bottle with warm water. It is sealed, topped by a long, flexible latex tube that gently needs to be inserted down the penguin's gullet. One of the researchers sits and holds the penguin, which is placed between the legs, face out, wings outstretched over the researcher's knees. You're constantly petting and stroking the penguin to keep it calm. Rob would then lean over, gently open the penguin's beak, insert the tube, and invert the bottle so the warm fluid would enter the penguin's stomach. Gentoos, with a much larger stomach capacity, might take about two thirds of a bottle, chinnies and Adélies about a half. The tube is then removed carefully and the penguin inverted over a plastic container. A finger in the penguin's mouth encourages the stomach contents to spew—for example, a mass of half-digested krill, undigested krill, perhaps other components. Sometimes, the procedure has to be repeated two or three times to get all of the stomach contents.

The stomach contents are then bagged and sealed, marked, and set aside for weighing and later analysis. The penguin by this time has been righted and carried upbeach to be released. Amazing: A twelve-pound gentoo might bring back almost a two-pound bellyful of food.

Stomach lavaging is a valuable research procedure, but it is done sparingly because it is stressful. The subsequent examination involves randomly measuring representative samples of prey items from each of the bags. Female krill have little red spots inside their thoraxes, allowing some individuals to be sexed. Adult krill will range somewhere between one and a half and two inches in length. In some years, the krill can be really large—up to two and a half inches— and in others the stomach samples may yield small, year-old krill—a half inch to one inch long. If research trawlers are working at the same time in the bay or the Bransfield, there can be comparisons to the sizes of krill the ships are catching. Are penguins taking what is available? Or are they seeking a specific size of krill? If the krill are small, it is likely that more energy is expended during foraging.

Wayne and Sue thought it clear that summer foraging success or failure, as well as the availability of prey and the penguins' ability to capture it, had serious implications. It affected the timing of nest reliefs. It meant the ability to survive long fasting periods. It directly affected whether chicks could be fledged and recruits added to the population. If food was readily available in summer, the incubation shifts would tend to be shorter and nest exchanges more frequent. If food was difficult to find in summer, the incubation shifts would be longer and nest exchanges fewer. In this latter scenario, the risk of egg or chick failures would be higher—and theoretically, fewer chicks would fledge, meaning less potential recruitment of new penguins. In evolutionary terms, stability means a penguin couple replacing itself over a lifetime. Population increases require new recruits above and beyond this simple replacement. Population declines reflect an inability to make even the simple replacement. Mortality, therefore, becomes a factor: How many adults survive the winter and return each spring? The Copa Adélies revealed a highly variable annual mortality rate, sometimes as substantial as 35 percent.

Which brought Wayne and Sue to questions about the most unknown time in the brushtaileds' life cycle. Were any of these parameters predetermined in an a priori fashion by conditions on the penguins' wintering grounds? One hypothesis was that winters of low prey availability might affect the composition of breeding populations the following spring. The unsatisfactory prey situation could be a result of distribution, declining numbers, or unusual ice conditions. After harsh winters, younger and less experienced penguins might return in poorer physiological condition, less able to endure their rigorous breeding routines—unable, even, to attempt breeding. The result would be the next season's breeding population skewing toward older, more experienced penguins who'd figured out how to exploit the depleted food supply and get themselves in proper breeding condition. Or, if winter conditions were really horrid, there also might be a deleterious effect on the numbers of experienced penguins returning the following spring. On the other hand, if there was sufficient winter prey to exploit, the following spring's breeding population would indicate many more younger and inexperienced penguins attempting to breed. Another factor: It takes inexperienced penguins a number of years of breeding attempts to get it right. Adélies might try to breed at age three but likely won't fledge any chicks until age six. These penguins might serve as effective monitors of the Southern Ocean ecosystem, but the ecosystem was proving vastly more complicated than expected.

Looking at the *whole* picture led Wayne, Sue, Bill Fraser, and David Ainley to reexamine one of the major hypotheses of Antarctic ecology. This theory linked the large increase in penguin numbers between the early 1940s and the late 1970s—especially regarding chinstrap populations—to an increase in prey availability caused by the excessive exploitation of Southern Ocean whale stocks. This excess was called the *krill surplus*. The reexamination challenged the notion of a surplus and suggested that whatever penguin population increase had occurred, it had ended in the 1970s. Populations may have doubled or tripled in this time but had now stabilized at these levels worldwide: two to three million pairs of Adélies, about seven and a half million pairs of chinstraps, and slightly more than three hundred thousand pairs of gentoos. The scientists sensed a new culprit: ice—especially the amount and extent of pack ice surrounding the Antarctic continent each winter.

There had been modeling suggesting that any surplus would have been taken by predators of similar size, meaning other whales. And during this time, minke whale numbers apparently had also increased. Another analysis noted that the diet of Peninsula penguins had not changed in this period, when more krill was presumably available. Gentoos, which are sedentary penguins, had maintained a stable population through these decades. Eyes and minds began to focus on new survey work establishing firmly that Adélies were winter denizens of the pack ice, linked closely to the ice edge, which they presumably used both for foraging runs and to rest. Chinstraps, notably, preferred open water in winter—the pelagic zone. Then came the Copa data: Large increases in Adélie numbers were coincident with large annual decreases in chinstrap numbers. More telling, these changes then tied directly to the extent of winter and spring ice cover—perhaps explaining differences in overwinter survival of Adélie versus chinstrap chicks, or why one species' population might vary considerably from season to season. The correlations were striking: If the winter sea ice was diminished—meaning more open water—there were increased numbers of chinstraps in the spring, and fewer returning Adélies. If the winter sea ice had been substantial—meaning more ice-edge habitat—there would be increased numbers of returning Adélies and fewer returning chinstraps.

The next step was analyzing weather and ice details, looking for trends over the decades. Unfortunately, there was no satellite imagery prior to 1973. Post-1973, however, the analyses of surface-air temperatures, ice imagery, and associated models indicated that there had been an increasing number of winters with relatively *minimal* amounts of sea ice. This suggested, therefore, favorable conditions for increasing numbers of chinstraps. The new hypothesis postulated that environmental warming over the last four decades had led to a reduction in the *frequency* of cold winters with extensive sea ice cover—thus favoring open-water versus pack-ice animals. Lean-ice winters would occur, on average, in no more than two of every five years.

At the time, Wayne notes:

That apparent population increase was over, and it may have ended even sooner than the 1970s. It's probably reasonable to assume that because of the very intense period during which the whales were so heavily hunted—culminating in the early 1960s—that there may well have been some food left over. If it helped the penguin populations at all, it was probably through the increased overwinter survival of the young chicks. But they may have adapted—along with the seals—very quickly to the new levels, and our data from the 1970s onward indicate no major changes. In our area, the comparative data between the 1940s and 1970s show doubling and tripling of numbers—yes, there appears to be a rise, but everyone quickly acclimated to new stable levels. Right now—though it's hard to say with any confidence—the penguins are probably right at carrying capacity. But in such a simple system, which has such huge variations from year to year, you don't get a stable rise and a stable plateau. We have data showing population changes of plus and minus 30 percent from one year to the next. So the physical impacts on things like survival of bird populations are tremendously variable, and it appeared that the driving force, among all possible factors, was the amount of pack ice in the winter. The more pack ice, the better chance for survival of Adélies. The less pack, the better for chinstraps and gentoos. Gentoos, of course, will winter in the bay if they can, taking fish, amphipods, and squid, if necessary.

More Copa data fit the emerging theory. It was believed that the breeding success of chinstraps and Adélies, including the number of inexperienced birds that attempt to breed, tended to follow the prevailing winter and spring ice conditions: Chinstraps doing well and Adélies poorly following winters of minimal sea ice. Adélies doing well and chinstraps poorly following winters of maximum sea ice.

The gist is that penguins need to return each spring with proper energy stores: If prey fluctuates with the extent of winter sea ice, there may be consequences—one species able to return sufficiently fattened for its parental duties, the other not.

Adélies also tend to live closer to ocean basins where sea ice persists throughout the year, suggesting a proximity to a preferred habitat. This factor tended to explain the curious Adélie distribution in the Peninsula, one population lying essentially in the Shetlands, the other south of Anvers Island—with a 250-mile gap in between. The northern Peninsula Adélies likely associate with the lingering pack in the Weddell Sea, the southern Peninsula Adélies with the pack in the Bellingshausen Sea. Adélies appear to cluster in areas where nesting sites open early in the spring—a consequence of prevailing wind, ocean currents, and north-facing slopes that receive considerable solar radiation, and which drain well. The necessary mix is having early access each spring to these top-drawer breeding sites, combined with the ability to reach lingering, favored pack-ice feeding habitats, where prey stocks are reliably found. The surmise is that the 250-mile gap is an area that theoretically lies too distant from ice habitats they'd prefer to graze, especially during times when nest reliefs and exchanges are crucial to a pair's breeding success. This was additional fuel for the notion that ice dictates the Adélies' rigid breeding strategy—necessitating a precise and early return to breeding sites, a long courtship fast, long incubation shifts, and proven access to prey when it's really needed in the early austral spring. In a sense the same is likely true in winter—that penguins rely on habitat where prey has proven dependable over aeons of time.

Chinstraps seem to have thrived in the gap where the Adélies are absent. Presumably less tolerant of heavy ice conditions, they've been able to adjust to fluctuating conditions. Certainly, the Copa data indicated chinstraps' ability to adjust the timing of their breeding schedule. If there's too much ice and snow early, they can delay for weeks, start late, and still fledge chicks. The chinstraps also showed a preference for oceanside breeding territories, suggesting and potentially confirming the notion that their focus is open-water krill swarms. Their gig is the pelagic zone, not the pack-laden seas where the Adélies roam in early spring. And indeed, returning three to four weeks later than the Adélies would allow for the early pack to dissipate, thus providing chinstraps easier access to preferred feeding habitats.

But in the 1990s new data have scrambled the analyses. Now, instead of annual changes in Adélie and chinstrap populations correlating to the fluctuations in winter sea ice, populations of *both* species are apparently declining. Something is happening. In the last fifty years, average year-round air temperatures in the Peninsula have increased by five degrees Fahrenheit, which computes out to about nine or ten times faster than the global warming rate. In midwinter, however, the rise has been higher—eight or nine degrees Fahrenheit. It could be a natural fluctuation. And it could be a fluctuation exacerbated by our spewing increasing amounts of greenhouse gases into the atmosphere. The atmospheric scientists tell us that global warming theoretically will be worse—and reveal itself earlier and more obviously—at the poles, before being detected elsewhere.

With respect to Adélies, the warming trends may be reducing their preferred habitat even further—increasing the distance from nests to pack-ice feeding grounds. With populations of both species trending downward, there emerges a view that global climate change—the Southern Ocean warming trend—is deleteriously affecting the standing stock of the penguins' major prey item, krill. Over many decades, winter pack ice would reach maximum levels in the Peninsula at six- to eight-year intervals, with reduced levels of winter sea ice occurring, on average, in no more than two of every five years. Now, reaching toward the millennium, lean-ice winters are occurring consecutively, two and three years running. In addition, the diminished ozone layer above the continent each spring allows increased amounts of deleterious UV-B radiation to seep through. The focus, then, turns to krill—*Euphausia superba*—the "power lunch" of the Antarctic, the mainstay of the entire food chain.

This extraordinarily long-lived crustacean—with a lifespan of seven years or more—lays a plethora of eggs in the austral spring and summer. These float to the bottom of the ocean, ultimately rising in various larval forms in winter. At that time of year, they seek the safety of the winter sea ice, which provides natural protection from foraging penguins, seals, and whales, and allows the larvae to graze vast algal blooms nurtured by the winter ring of pack ice surrounding the continent. In essence, the pack is a colossal krill nursery. Larval krill are not good swimmers. They're at the whim of the currents. As they mature and rise from the depths, the ice must be there. Otherwise they're likely to be eaten.

The new thinking postulates that massive reductions in the size of the nursery equates to entire year classes of krill—perhaps many *consecutive* year classes—being precipitously reduced. Two to three additional years down the line—when these year classes have grown to juicy adulthood and become prime, two-and-a-half-inch-long penguin fodder—there will be many fewer krill to exploit. Two consecutive, heavy-ice winters seems to ensure at least one large, annual cohort of krill. Then this complication: We can't find krill as reliably as penguins discover them. There have been seasons when Wayne and Sue's penguins come home with loaded bellies, while offshore trawlers are finding zilch. There's no question that penguins can chase individual krill and don't require krill swarms to do their foraging. The penguins have no problem going one-on-one—echolocating individual krill.

Estimates of krill population size and biomass in the Antarctic are not exact. Presently, there are best estimates of a standing stock of 6.5 billion metric tons of krill. It has been suggested that the world population of twenty-one million Adélies, chinstraps, and gentoos consume approximately five and a quarter million tons of krill annually. Factoring in early findings suggesting that the excess UV-B radiation seeping through the diminished ozone layer may negatively affect phytoplankton stocks by as much as 20 percent, it's not a far leap to suggest why penguin populations may be declining: Phytoplankton are krill's major grocery item. With less food at the store, there won't be enough to eat and, theoretically, krill stocks will diminish. That's one whammy. With many more lean-ice winters, the winter ice nursery for larval krill is itself diminished and that will translate to smaller annual year classes of krill. Whammy Number Two. Up the food chain, the deleterious bottom line is less food for the penguins. And if there's less food to exploit in winter, penguins may be returning in less than peak condition each spring, unable to withstand the rigors of their required breeding fasts. If summer krill stocks are diminished overall—or if they move because they can't find phytoplankton to eat—penguins may need to travel much longer distances on their feeding runs, may be unable to find any prey to exploit, and starving mates back home may then abandon eggs or chicks.

There are other consequences of a warming planet, which in and of themselves may delay the penguins' breeding activities, or cause egg and chick failures. Warmer air holds more moisture. So if year-round Peninsula temperatures have warmed by five degrees Fahrenheit in the last half century, that potentially leads to more frequent spring storms and precipitation. Snow and sleet, rain and wind, flood and mud—all may wreak havoc and retard the penguins' efforts to set up properly. If the precipitation is rain, nests can be swamped in meltwater. It's not uncommon at Copa to have eggs floating in water and later, when the temperature flips, to find the eggs frozen in ice.

Snow can bury incubating birds and their nests. I recall a freak heavy snowstorm that completely buried a portion of one Adélie colony at Copa. When sussing out the situation, we realized that we were walking over snow with penguins *underneath* our feet. But no damage was done, fortunately, because we didn't posthole down to the penguins. The next day, the snow had thawed and melted, and the Adélies were happy as clams, incubating as if nothing had happened.

Sometimes the snow leaves the penguins in unusual positions. I vividly remember Adélies who were totally buried with only butts and tails projecting out of the snow, raised straight to the sky. Or some in the reverse position, with only beaks and eyes showing. If Adélies in snow holes try an ecstatic display, they may get stuck— with their wings draped over the edge of the hole, finding it impossible to return them to their sides, as if they've fallen into a crevasse. Adélies trying to dive back into their snow hole, to get to the nest and eggs, sometimes miss and impale their heads in the snow alongside the hole.

The snow also produces sideshows. During their 1993–95 tenure, Gregor Yaneda, Tracey Mader, and Rob Dilling witnessed the Adélies' "snow madness"—when groups of returning or departing penguins would crazily drop prone and gobble the snow furiously, with almost reckless energy. Diving into the snow. Rolling in the snow. Absolutely mad about snow. It is well known that snow and meltwater are excellent water sources that penguins frequently partake of, but the drinking and slurping is usually done in more routine and less frenzied fashion.

Wayne and Sue would say: "Just the start of a *lot* more work." And the work continues. With the TDRs, exact foraging positions were uncertain. Now, the vogue is small satellite packs, which are slightly shorter and thinner, and allow penguins to be remotely sensed from high above. As a consequence, Wayne and Sue have been able to confirm a long-held suspicion that Copa Adélies might traverse considerable distances during the incubation period, when long absences from the nest are routine. Some of these round-trips to the eastern side of the Bransfield Strait have been impressive, involving hundreds of miles. And one male Adélie, during his first incubation shift, recently made a totally unexpected, greater-than-five-hundred-mile round-trip south to the Bellingshausen Sea, completely traversing the Adélie Gap. What's happening? Is the food situation so bad that they're extending their preferred less than twenty-five-mile range by almost two orders of magnitude? What about the notion that Adélies require easily accessible, proven food supplies?

With these weather considerations looming, Wayne and Sue have begun looking at penguin survival data, with surprising and unexpected results. They took a ten-year period, 1981–91, and examined the relationship between the survival of fledgling Adélies and the extent of the winter pack ice. Again, the backdrop is that the Southern Ocean shows an incredible ebb and flow of ice, a cycle of growth to a maximum of perhaps twenty million square miles, which then decays to a minimum of about four million square miles. And the greatest variations and changes occur in the Peninsula region of the Antarctic, where winter temperatures have risen by eight or nine degrees Fahrenheit. The six- to eight-year ice cycles are now characterized by two to three years of winters with extensive ice cover, followed by three to five years of winters with minimal sea ice. Prior to 1970, there would be extensive winter ice cover in three to four of every five years. Wayne and Sue expected to find that Adélie chicks fledging into winters with extensive pack ice would have significantly higher survival rates than cohorts fledging into low-ice winters. The assumption was that with extensive winter sea ice there would be a larger larval krill nursery, thus more available food for the penguins and greater returning numbers the next spring.

Rather, they found that survival was independent of the winter ice extent and fairly constant—a mean of 22 percent survival for the 1981–86 cohorts, then dropping significantly for the 1987–91 cohorts. Curiously, in both time frames, there were pulses of extensive winter sea ice. And lagging behind this drop in the survival of Adélie fledglings, Wayne and Sue found their overall Adélie populations declining from about ten thousand breeding pairs to five thousand. Simply not enough recruits being added to the population.

The emerging hypothesis was that survival is determined by the krill available to the fledglings as soon as they go to sea—when they leave the colonies in January and February. When Wayne and Sue examined their diet samples, they found that after a heavy-ice winter, Adélie stomach samples included small, year-old krill. Following lean-ice winters, only large, adult krill were found. Further, they theorized that the increasing frequency of lean-ice winters was decreasing the krill population significantly. The analysis suggested that krill would increase if a winter with a strong pulse of ice is followed by another heavy-ice winter. Wayne and Sue call this two-year production of krill a *super cohort*, which will carry the krill population through intervening and succeeding years of lean-ice winters. For a relatively stable krill population, it appears that there needs to be a *super cohort* produced at least once every seven years.

As a matter of krill biology, the first winter of heavy ice ensures good survival rates for larval krill and enhances the chance they will be recruited to the population at the age of one year. A second consecutive winter of heavy ice amplifies these effects by promoting early spawning by adults and enhancing conditions supporting the survival of larvae spawned the previous year. In other words, there needs to be a persistence of heavy-ice winters for krill stocks to flourish and to ensure that Adélie fledglings—perhaps the fledglings of all of the Copa penguins—will be able to find krill when they head to sea.

No doubt about it—you get your fingernails dirty with some local details and the theories, as well as the chicks, keep popping. As Sue describes, she and Wayne spend a lot of time thinking, thinking, thinking. The hypotheses are exciting, but they need years of testing and analysis, and in the end one is left with that overwhelming sense of humility. There's a lot going on that's very hard to explain, perhaps, even, impossible to reconcile. Much more work is presently needed on the penguins' winter food supply and range. While we have some notion of the Adélies' and chinstraps' preferred winter habitat—pack-ice edge versus open water—much remains unknown about their winter diet and general feeding ecology. To what extent do chinstraps and Adélies alter their basic, all-krill, summer diet? There need to be additional correlations to returning numbers and survival rates—indeed, more precise confirmation that minimal-ice winters and diminished cohorts of krill mediate the populations of penguins.

The memories of many Copa visits flash clearly. When you've spent enough time in one place you *see* changes. The Ecology Glacier north of Copa, which needs to be traversed to take that well-deserved post-roundup shower at Copa, is shrinking and receding. At low tide, the cobble fronting the glacier is relatively easy to walk. A decade ago, that was virtually impossible. As this glacier recedes, it exposes more and more of the underlying moraine. A similar recession is happening at the Baranowski Glacier south of Copa, on the way to the chinstrap colonies at Demay Point. In a short span of three years in the early 1990s, the beach fronting Baranowski has been dramatically exposed.

There are changes everywhere. At the Demay, Patelnia, and Uchatka chinstrap colonies at the southern end of Wayne and Sue's study area, large patches in these colonies lay fallow every spring and summer—the chinnie population is obviously dropping, dropping, dropping. Not yet to the point of concern, but, again—something is happening. And not yet to where you can safely toss the earplugs. On one recent December visit, I assisted Sue at Demay with egg measurements and weights. The protocol is to measure and weigh randomly twenty-five two-egg samples in each of the rookeries, all timed to coincide with the chinstraps' peak of egg laying. We were doing our work in a small cove with very steep and gnarly terrain—some very difficult footing and totally surrounded by chinstraps. The two of us were no more than three feet apart. The plan was simple: Sue lifted tails, plucked eggs, and did the weighing and measuring, and I kept the fieldbook and recorded the data she would yell out: *Length 66 mm, width 57 mm, weight 95 grams.* And I scribbled away. But even at a close distance it was practically impossible. Admittedly, both of us are tried and true chinnie fanciers. As Sue says: "I've got lots of friends in low places." Nonetheless, the racket was amazing. We simply couldn't hear each other. Until Sue bellowed: *Shut up, you guys.* A perverse calm settled in—but of course, for only about a half a minute. The racket renewed, ecstatic displays erupting at all the nests.

Many Copa incidents are emblazoned in memory: You may need to hold one egg or chick in your pocket—to keep it warm and out of the wind—while weighing the other. You can be awakened by juvenile gentoos loudly puttering over the front deck of the hut. You might observe young chinstrap males trying to mate with large Adélie chicks. Your work can be stopped dead in the tracks by amusing scenes: A whole line of gentoo nests. One gentoo leaning over to steal a stone from the adjoining nest, unaware of its neighbor on the other side stealing a stone from it, while a third gentoo snatches from the second, and the fourth from the third—and on and on, down the row.

And there are the flying birds that live near and sometimes interact with the penguins. Wayne notes:

You're so interested in studying the penguins and you don't want to upset them. Actually, the penguins seem to be totally naive and never quite get used to you. Some of the others, like the skua pairs that we've been working with for fifteen or sixteen years, seem very habituated to our presence. I just walk up to them at the nests like they're old friends, they're only half cawing at me, and you can just pick them up a bit, check for the presence of eggs and chicks, and you're off. Pat them on the head, say *Goodbye, good luck this year,* without muss, fuss, or bother. They're really tame. Other skuas, though, just get more and more hostile. They're always finding newer and better ways to make their living. There are lots of learned behaviors. We have one skua pair that predates nearby gentoo eggs and chicks in a special way. The male skua pulls on the tail of the penguin sitting in the nest, and when the gentoo turns to chase away this skua, the female skua grabs whatever is underneath the sitting bird. We lost the female in this particular skua pair a few years ago, and the new female is just learning the *snatch-and-seize* routine. Then, there are the sheathbills. They go for everything and anything. They'll sit in ambush of a penguin that's about to feed its begging chick. Just as the adult starts regurgitating, the sheathbill comes out of nowhere, flies in between the adult and the chick, the chick pulls back, and the adult, which can't stop, just drops a whole lot of krill on the ground. Since the chick doesn't recognize food on the ground, it just stays there. The adult penguin chases the sheathbill around for a while, after which the sheathbill circles back to scoop up its meal.

The action never stops. And this special place generates an inner grace and sense of peace. Says Janet Kjelmyr:

One does not live here without being touched by the uniqueness of the environment. Once immersed in these austere surroundings, perception changes. It has unquestionably changed my life. On many days what I know about Admiralty Bay is concise: wind, snow, birds, seals, and air as crisp as chilled vodka. Sometimes it's sapphire water and sky; sometimes emerald water and pale sky; sometimes glassy gray water and ashen sky just before a storm. Visibility can shift suddenly from complete obscurity to startling clarity. The weather changes hourly. A calm can be followed by a squall of icy rain, followed by a sunburst that turns the sea fog orange. Ivory glaciers sown with crevasses gently roll across the land until they abruptly meet the sea in magnificent ice cliffs. The wind can sing. It can also howl and scream. We have grown accustomed to the sounds of wind, surf, penguins, skuas, and elephant seals, until they become another form of silence. The night is so short as to be practically nonexistent. Light lingers, and the boundary between days becomes vague and the notion of time intangible. A curious state of suspension sets in. Often I do nothing but look and listen. I can't describe this privilege of simplicity, this luxury of peace. But the isolation sometimes overwhelms me. Everything goes along fine for a time, then the mood suddenly quivers and becomes fragile. Time bites, like the cold.

Time, endless time. For scientists studying Antarctic penguins, high summer represents a zenith—a culmination of effort when one last push is needed to complete that season's set of data and information. And to keep pushing the data forward, to unravel more secrets.

Copa endures. The work continues. Wayne, on reflection: "When I first came, I really fell in love with the place. I felt that if I could manage some funding for about ten years, I could do a very worthwhile piece of work. And I think that's happened. Whatever the future holds, I'll feel very good about the contribution we've been able to make. But, there's much more to do, and I hope that we can continue to be a part of it."

Let slick chicks pop—for seasons and seasons to come.

EIGHT

·····················

Two Blue Bags
and a Steamer

Being in a ship is being in a jail, with the chance of being drowned.

—*Dr. Samuel Johnson*

Penguins.

And the people who want to see them.

Perhaps inevitably, the population of human visitors to Antarctica continues increasing. It is the only venue on the planet where you can commune with truly unbelievable numbers of these almost-human fluffballs of short feathers, blubber, and sinew who constantly stoke our amusement and imagination. But everyone isn't *so* amused and *so* stoked. There's a lot of human diversity buying passage on these expeditions. In the 1997–98 Antarctic tour season, stretching from November across to the following March, the co-hort of visitors approached the ten thousand mark for the first time. These numbers present a challenge to the penguins who are trying to rear their chicks, as well as to expedition leaders and staff who are trying to minimize any potential disturbances.

It's hard to argue with the prospect of returning with many more Antarctic *ambassadors* who may be primed and poised to "spread the word" to others—friends, politicians, elites of all sorts, and ordinary citizens of all countries—that the relatively pristine Seventh Continent needs to stay that way. But the reality is a damned sight different if you've spent any time being an expedition leader on these trips. I know. I've done it—and the results are mixed. For those of us seeing Antarctica and its penguins as metaphors, symbols, or poetry representing a higher human calling, it can be daunting trying to impart a little emotion and substance to a too-high percentage of folks who are tuned out and high on other kicks. I don't intend to demean those whom Paul Bowles considered serious *travelers*, always digging in and consuming intently—and as much as possible—the culture, people, and surroundings into which they're thrust. I simply wish there were more of them.

Recently, these frustrations were reawakened by David Foster Wallace. His hilarious essay "A Supposedly Fun Thing I'll Never Do Again" describes a rather different shipboard experience—a weeklong Caribbean trip with twelve hundred fellow passengers on a supersleek luxury vessel. That kind of *posh* doesn't exist in the Antarctic shipboard expedition trade, but the same kind of people are potential customers. Wallace describes these rather amazing questions being asked at the ship's reception desk:

Does the crew sleep on board?

Does snorkeling mean getting wet?

What time is the midnight buffet?

The "crew" question is one I've been asked in the Antarctic. Another Antarctic favorite revolves around the fellow who approached the reception desk at 9 A.M. one beautiful Antarctic Peninsula morning, asking: *Where's the whale?* (The response: What do you mean, the "whale"?) *Well, last night I was out on deck and somebody said there was a whale at nine o'clock. So—have I missed it?* (Second response: Yes—you've missed it, but you missed it last night. We use the "watch dial" approach to let everyone know where the whale may be in relation to the bow—the bow, of course, being twelve o'clock.)

Here's another: *Where does the electricity come from?* (The not-too-serious response, intending to balance the preposterousness with some levity: Oh, haven't you noticed the extension cord we've been carrying behind us since we left Ushuaia? That's actually why we don't cross the Antarctic Circle. The cord won't reach that far.)

And after a couple of years you might think you've heard it all— but don't be deluded. The human capacity for this stuff is amazing. The latest iteration: *Is there such a thing as a female sperm whale?* (The response . . . well, there was no response initially because the person being asked was totally dumbfounded; then, in muted tones, came the correct—and fair—answer: "Yes.")

These tales are, admittedly, a form of self-denial. For most visitors and for a number of researchers, the only means of getting to the Deep South is on one of these ships. And being prepared for the occasionally clueless is a price that many have paid for the privilege of seeing penguins. There's no doubt that the vast majority of people going south are well-intentioned, impressionable folks, and I'm sure that many have the experience of a lifetime. Most get their penguin thrills, though the guano smell ranks high on the list of disconcerting annoyances. Some even may become dedicated Antarcticists, but my analysis over sixteen years indicates a steep, slippery, uphill slope.

In almost thirty years of Antarctic tourism, somewhere between one and two Super Bowls filled with tourists have visited Antarctica. I've led many of these trips and would rather point to the upside. Quite a few passengers are moved to the point of tears. Others become regular Antarcticophiles, showing regularly at lectures of the Royal Geographic Society in London or The Antarctican Society in Washington. Former Canadian prime minister Pierre Trudeau was moved to discuss T. S. Eliot's "Waste Land," knowing Eliot's reference to Shackleton in the notes to the poem's fifth section. The conductor Zubin Mehta came ashore clad in tails, baton in hand: "Toscanini only had ninety, I've got ten thousand." Even Apsley Cherry-Garrard, who apparently coined the word *Antarcticist*, realized that changing the entire world was impossible. But changing a few hearts and minds is a definite possibility.

One recent Antarctic Peninsula day, my colleague Louise Blight and I were trekking across the wide shoreline at Paulet Island in the northwest Weddell Sea. We were marveling at how the Adélies had rebounded from the previous season's breeding failure—virtually a total collapse of that year's entire complement of chicks. Something had happened when the majority of chicks were about two to three weeks of age. The detective work suggested either heavy ice and weather impeding the adults' ability to get to normal feeding grounds, or that the prey stock—krill—had for some reason unexpectedly disappeared or moved to an unknown location. But one year later all seemed normal, with the new cohort of chicks starting to erupt and make considerable noise. The shoreline was filling with adults and chicks, mud, and guano piles—back to the expected doses of noise, smell, and visual overload.

Upbeach, among the carcasses, we were approached by an elderly tourist posed in one of the ubiquitous red parkas the tour company issues to its passengers. Often, we call these folks "redhoppers"—a play on the name of rockhopper penguins, found on islands north of the Peninsula. This British gentleman asked if he might pose a few questions. No problem for us. We were happy to give it a go.

"Do penguins bury their dead?" he intoned solemnly.

For long seconds, Louise and I were somewhat flabbergasted and couldn't react. This was one we hadn't heard before. Carefully, respectfully, I replied: "No, sir, as you can see, they don't."

"Hmmm. Most untidy, most untidy." And with a disappointed air, head dejectedly bowed, he sauntered away from us.

It brought my days as an expedition leader back to focus. "Connecting to the planet" is the mantra of Antarctica—and expedition staff do their best to make these encounters as upbeat and meaningful as possible. When it happens, there is nothing more satisfying than enthusing a few more folks about the wonders of the Seventh Continent, its wildlife, and its history. Human nature suggests that everyone won't be hooked by this relatively unspoiled paradise, but with some people substantial links and emotions can be nurtured.

Then the sixty-four-thousand-dollar question is how long the newly forged Antarctic Spirit will continue blazing in these enlightened hearts and minds.

Like the Antarctic weather, people are people, and *really* strange things occur more often than not. Intended scripts aren't always followed. And there's one trip I will never, ever forget. Because I often have great difficulty remembering what I did yesterday, let alone what happened last month or even last week, my virtually total recall of those strange Antarctic days seems rather out of character. Then again, maybe I shouldn't be so surprised. With hindsight glances, those few days stay lodged in memory next to a single, undeniably appropriate adjective: *bizarre.* I recall this story with considerable amusement, but at the time and for a while it seemed as if our expedition was the Antarctic trip from hell. It was a microcosm of everything that's good or bad about tourism in this part of the world. And on top of everything else, there was a dog story rolled in for good measure, even though the dog in question wasn't of the shaggy, sledging variety normally associated with Antarctica.

All had gone rather well, until that fateful morning of January 24, 1984. Whaler's Bay, inside of Deception Island, was absolutely glorious. The Antarctic sky sparkled with a full, deep blue color. A black-green sea ran glossy flat and occasionally was rippled by swarms of porpoising chinstrap penguins. Deception's air blew cold and crisp, leaving invigorating ripples on one's cheeks. The enveloping volcanic scenery suggested a glimpse of primordial time, when fire and ice fought battles over the shape of the planet. These were the last few hours of a very pleasurable and exciting tourism expedition. Nineteen days ago, we had boarded the *Lindblad Explorer* in the far southern city of Punta Arenas, Chile, wound through the Straits of Magellan, then proceeded to the Falkland Islands, Shackleton's jumping-off spot of South Georgia, traversed the Drake Passage to the South Orkney Islands, and, finally, reached the Antarctic Peninsula. There had been numerous memorable moments.

The Falklands brought long walks over moors and among hordes of nesting rockhopper and magellanic penguins and alongside a slew of cliff-edge-nesting black-browed albatrosses. While penguins irritatingly squawked, sleek albatrosses rode thermals just barely over our heads and showed off their single chicks, which were becoming too, too large for their tall and narrow earthen nesting mounds. There was an opportunity to drink ale with local peat farmers—known as "kelpers"—at the Globe Hotel in Stanley and to discuss details of the very recently concluded Falklands-Malvinas War. Some of us had managed a tour of a battlefield above and behind Stanley, where soldiers who had participated in the conflict described using their "cold steel" to cut down marauding forces. Invading troops had removed detector caps from many land mines that they had placed, which was clearly in violation of international convention, so finding deadly mines quickly became hopeless and well nigh impossible. Much of the heathland beyond Stanley remained off-limits and was fenced by barbed wire because the military's bomb-defusing efforts had now ceased. Sheep and cattle still grazing the moors were being used, literally, as helpless cannon fodder. We heard numerous stories of these animals going "boom" at random times both day and night.

At the Bay of Elsehul, in the western corner of South Georgia, we had climbed wearingly to a colony of gray-headed albatrosses, despite an enveloping fog and rain. After avoiding a crowd of ill-tempered fur seals on the beaches below, we were surprised and alarmed to discover a bull fur seal occupying a vacant albatross mound at one edge of a cliffside colony. From this unusual perch, which gave us little maneuvering room on the steep slope, the bull snarled loudly and rasped his teeth just a bit too vigorously. Fortunately, he didn't charge. At the massive king penguin colony at South Georgia's Salisbury Plain—where my hero, Robert Cushman Murphy, worked—we thrilled seeing ten thousand pairs of immaculate, three-and-a-half-foot-tall birds weighing up to forty pounds, while many of their brown, hairy youngsters whistled and waddled about. While passengers went back for an evening meal, I and a few other staff members inspected a location called Start Point. Here, while lying prone and quietly on a stretch of cobble beach, we experienced these large penguins coming over to inspect us, then climbing on top of us for a more commanding view and to parade over the full length of our bodies. Before leaving South Georgia, we traipsed through the eerily quiet, fallow whaling station at Grytviken, visited Shackleton's nearby gravesite, and discovered a light-mantled sooty albatross nest high in the hills overlooking Cumberland Bay.

At Half Moon Bay, at Coronation Island in the South Orkneys, we found a nesting crevice where an immaculately white snow petrel showed off its few-days'-old chick, one half of an eggshell sitting close at hand. En route to Paulet Island in the northwest Weddell Sea, there was a huge penguinesque animal on a far distant ice floe, perhaps an immature emperor penguin. Paulet teemed with Adélie penguins. Many people climbed above Paulet's highland crater lake for an exceptional view of the penguin throngs below. Following

many shore landings in the Peninsula, we traversed down the Le-
maire Channel, reached our farthest-south point near Petermann
Island, made visits to the US Palmer Station and the British Faraday
Station, then proceeded to Deception.

This was my second season working these ships as a lecturer and,
in a sense, I was still "learning the ropes," trying to amass a wealth
of knowledge that my more experienced colleagues were earnestly
spewing to any and all questioning passengers. It hadn't taken long
for the Antarctic bacillus to settle and become a rather permanent
disease. The Little Red Ship was an excellent platform: 239 feet
long, about 46 feet abeam, a 2,500-ton displacement, and a regular
cruising speed between 11 and 12 knots. With a very shallow draft
of 15 feet and bow thrusters, *Explorer* could maneuver virtually anywhere. Our captain was Hasse Nilsson, a polished Swede who had
made many trips to The Ice and commanded inordinate respect
among both crew and expedition staff.

We were enjoying an expedition in what I now consider the
golden days of shipboard Antarctic tourism. These were heady times
when long, expansive schedules allowed plenty of leeway for complications forced by bad weather. The overarching goal was to spend
lots and lots of time ashore—as long as weather and sea conditions
cooperated. This was before the deluge of Antarctic shipboard passengers in the late 1980s, when economic competition prompted
operators to attempt more and more trips per season. In those hal-
cyon days of January 1984, the ship's itinerary tramped a very sensible pace, and the vagaries of weather and storms never seemed to
intrude too harshly. If weather wiped out one landing, we'd try
another. Simply put, flexibility was the essence of expedition touring.

The breathing room in our schedule meant that there would be very real chances to connect with locations and animals. Landings would sometimes continue for hours on end. In addition, our twenty-five-day schedule had this aura of going where others had never dared to tread, to try finding new, previously undiscovered and magical landing sites. And as if to evidence the prevailing expedition spirit, we visited a previously unexplored area in the Argentine Islands and penciled a new, albeit unofficial name—Nilsson Island—on *Explorer's* charts.

Passengers went ashore in rubber inflatable Zodiacs, the little boats large enough to carry twelve to fourteen people, as long as the sea wasn't welling up in strong lumps. The Zodiacs were reached by descending a long gangway from the ship's main deck, then bounding into the boat from a metal platform at the base of the gangway. There was much emphasis on a "forearm-to-forearm" grip as the Zodiac driver assisted passengers into the waiting boat, which one or more AB's—the able-bodied seamen—held fast by rope to the loading pontoon. These little boats were unsurpassed in their versatility and seaworthiness, and I soon realized that a truly successful Antarctic shipboard expedition practically devolved to one issue and one issue alone: the skill and abilities of the Zodiac drivers.

Before leaving *Explorer,* each passenger passed a wooden board and turned a specifically numbered tag from yellow to red, which documented that he or she had left the ship and gone ashore. The tag was supposed to be turned back to yellow when one returned to the tagboard, and was used by staff to track wayward passengers who just didn't want to return at the appointed time. But, as we were to discover later that fateful morning, tags might intentionally be left in a yellow, "on-board" position.

This landing routine was repeated as often as possible, so staff could show passengers as much of Antarctica as possible. I discovered when I became an expedition leader that the only problem with this "land-as-often-as-you-can" policy was coordinating with other departments on board, which had their own agendas and responsibilities to meet. Most important of these was the hotel staff, which was responsible for the three sumptuous meals per day advertised in the company's brochure. Any deviation or change in planned meal schedules usually required delicate and protracted negotiations with the hotel manager. But alas, this was a small price to pay for extended moments off of *Explorer* and in the lustrous vicinity of some of earth's most spectacular animals and landscapes.

Explorer carried a skilled staff of lecturers and naturalists, whose formal presentations were reserved for days at sea. Only a few passengers wished to spend their entire time in the Drake sorting through the nuances of identifying passing storm-petrels and albatrosses. Thus, some entertainment was needed to keep their minds off the long time this passage required—a minimum of forty rocking and rolling hours. Soon, the days-at-sea days would be a memory and those afflicted with seasickness could rise for fresh air. When we reached the Peninsula, the focus shifted to disembarking as often as possible. The expedition-cruising concept was unique and in this sense *Explorer* was truly a pioneering vessel.

She had been a substantial dream of her builder and long-standing owner, Lars-Eric Lindblad. From early beginnings on chartered vessels in 1959 and the early 1960s, Lars-Eric had turned his interest in visiting out-of-the-way and unknown places into a small, albeit very successful, aspect of the tour industry. However, by the time of this January 1984 trip, the oil crunch of the early 1980s had left its mark of havoc on *Explorer*'s already slim profit margin, and a period of considerable economic uncertainty began. Her trips became much more expensive to operate. *Explorer* had already been sold once, to a Swedish oil company that operated her through a new travel subsidiary, and on this particular trip we learned that, once again, she was going to change hands. Fortunately, such economic machinations were of little concern to us on board. From start to finish, *Explorer*'s go-where-we've-never-gone-before attitude prevailed.

She was designed for comfort and superb maneuverability in ice conditions. The Explorer Lounge, located in the bow of the vessel and on its main deck, was the primary area for socializing. Prior to an evening meal, this lounge was a locus for "recap" sessions during which staff and passengers would rehash highlights and lowlights of that day's landings. As often happened, with so many passengers and so much to see, recap sessions helped broaden the whole experience. Weird penguin behaviors, unusual animal sightings, and stupid human tricks—like falling into a pool of guano melt—were frequent topics. The expedition leader also would use these times to brief everyone about plans for the succeeding day or days.

The ship's lecture facility, one deck above and all the way aft, was called the Penguin Lounge. In the early days, it was adorned with an excellent penguin mural painted by one of the ship's regular lecturers, the naturalist and artist Keith Shackleton. Keith was a distant relative of Sir Ernest Shackleton, the great "Boss" of my Antarctic dreams, and this mural was a constant reminder of Keith's admiration and affection for both *Explorer* and its staff. No matter which waters *Explorer* plied, Keith's Adélie penguins pranced around this lectern, advertising the glories of the Seventh Continent.

No doubt, it all added up. This staff's reputation was well known and, in many respects, they become the expedition's true heroes. Staff had the most contact with paying passengers and had the best shot at inspiring these visitors to see things just a bit more clearly, to glimpse Antarctica for metaphors it truly represents. And for sure, raising the interest level of these travelers became a categorical imperative. In the first place, it wasn't hard to remember that these passengers were a privileged few, who had the resources and wherewithal to afford such an adventure. We on staff had the responsibility of honing and focusing these folks on broader themes and issues, which, given their usually conservative bent, could be awfully difficult. The group's average age was over sixty and we had on board only two relative youngsters: a willowy, late-twenties French woman, whom I'll call Françoise for reasons that shortly will become apparent, and a thirty-something American named Rob who was working in Alaska.

One special on-board guest was Ronald Lockley, an eminent writer and seabird ornithologist from New Zealand. I, being a devotee of storm-petrels, had just finished reading Ronald's book, and during the trip he and I had the pleasure one dusky evening of sitting and watching Wilson's storm-petrels returning to their nest crevices on Torgersen Island in Arthur Harbor. There were passengers from various walks of life and a number of them would become excellent and long-term acquaintances.

Moreover, this formidable collection was augmented by something of a canine stowaway. The unusual guest was a small puppy dog, a black-and-white terrier that simply had marched up *Explorer's* gangway at Punta Arenas and made herself right at home. One of the ship's second officers—we'll call him Martin for purposes here—seemed to recall that the dog had followed him back from an excursion into town. The little animal, which easily fit into one's cupped hands, quickly endeared itself to Captain Hasse, who decided that Steamer—which name seemed apropos to all of us—would be a fine companion for our journey. Its temporary name came from the smelly ducks that are common to the Beagle Channel and the Falklands, one species of which is totally flightless, and all of which skitter—or steam—across the top of the water with lots of splashing and thrashing. Hasse "arranged" for Steamer to bunk with Martin, who, I'd guess, now regretted mentioning how Steamer got on board. Martin clearly wasn't thrilled about housebreaking an ebullient little terrier in his private loo.

From the ship's expedition leader, Mike McDowell, through the No. 2 in charge, Judy Marshall, and lecturer emeritus Dennis Puleston, down to regular lecturers cum Zodiac drivers Alan Gurney, Peter Puleston, and Jim Snyder, it was an accomplished "A" Team that populated *Explorer* trip #4012. Aside from Dennis, staff ages ranged from the mid-twenties to the late thirties. The first I met was Geoffrey Gallagher, a childhood friend of McDowell's from Australia who was looking forward to spending some time with his old "mate." I immediately learned he was nicknamed "Snake," but for no obvious reasons. We shared a pair of seats on the plane heading south to Chile from Miami. After arriving in Punta, Snake and I rushed to *Explorer* and scrambled to the bridge, Snake wanting to find his long-standing friend, I just wanting to check in and say hello. Very quickly, I experienced a strange Australian ritual. Upon first sight, the two of them embraced in a rugby scrum, fell forward, and began pummeling each other as if they were wrestling on a Melbourne playground. Then, with blood flowing, they headed down to the Explorer Lounge for a drink, Mike bellowing, "Yeah, Ron, good to have you on, pal. Just settle in and join us." Which I did.

Mike was a tall, strapping fellow who had once worked for the Australian government as a geophysicist and had been part of a team that conducted seismic research on Macquarie Island in the sub-Antarctic. He was "discovered" and recruited to join Lindblad Travel staff while engaged in a two-year backpacking stint through South America. Company literature described Mike as one who showed "immense enthusiasm, seemingly endless energy, and easy accessibility to all." Also touted were his lengthy shore expeditions and an uncanny ability to improvise when necessary. After this trip, he was a prototype when thinking about the kind of performance I intended when I became an Antarctic expedition leader. Mike's credo was straightforward: Give folks as much as you possibly can, and use every possible opportunity to get them ashore.

I'd worked with Judy Marshall the previous season on *World Discoverer*. She had first gone to The Ice in 1978, also on *Explorer*, and was returning to the ship once this season. She'd done anthropological work in India and had been Lindblad Travel's lead representative in Cairo for a while. Judy was the operation's "nuts and bolts," keeping all passenger-oriented details in order and tending to various concerns—or complaints—that might arise. As bold and forward as

Mike appeared to be, Judy, by contrast, was calm—at least overtly— as she waded rather effectively through a torrent of minutiae, from luggage tags and boarding passes to dietary plans and bar bills.

Every morning, Judy and Dennis Puleston assembled at their "regular" table in the dining room for a quick breakfast of toast, coffee, and marmite, to begin a freewheeling evaluation of all events recent and forthcoming. Because Dennis was in charge of preparing the ship's log that would be given to passengers as a souvenir, I thought these little confabs were to ensure that few tidbits were left unturned for his journal. The reality, though, is that these two were long-standing colleagues and just simply enjoyed being with each other, on board, and in this indescribable location. Dennis and his son, Peter, like Judy, were Lindblad staff of many trips and seasons.

Dennis had been a founder of the Environmental Defense Fund. He was born and educated in England and became a student of biology and naval architecture. In 1931, he set out to navigate the world on a thirty-foot yawl, which, ultimately, took him six years. During World War II, he worked for the Office of Scientific Development and Research and participated in many operations in the Pacific and Europe. He happened to be the principal designer of the "duck" landing craft that were key to Allied successes in the Pacific Theater. After the war, he became the head of the technical information division at Brookhaven National Laboratory. Dennis was a skilled artist and a keen naturalist, which skills contributed greatly to the expedition log that he was preparing. Dennis had incredible energy for a man who was then in his seventies. Seeing him bounding over and through the tussock on Cape Horn Island, with his thick white hair flowing in the breeze, I thought that I'd like to be doing as well—and hopping about as easily—when I was just fifty. Dennis introduced me to lots of new "dickey birds," like thorn-tailed rayadito and tussockbird, and helped me sort through the correct identifications in some difficult seabird groups like prions and diving petrels. His son, Peter, was a skilled bone carver and had worked on ornithological expeditions for the American Museum of Natural History and the Smithsonian Institution, and had done archaeological work in Guatemala under the auspices of the University of Pennsylvania.

Another of our staff, Alan Gurney, was professionally a naval architect who designed racing yachts and cruising boats. He had raced the Atlantic a number of times and was a very keen birder, but his passion was Antarctic history. Gurney's historical lectures, using blueprinted charts and colored grease pencils, were a major highlight, which many staff tape-recorded to study finer points in their spare time. And there was Colin Monteath, who presented slide shows that were accompanied solely by music, and which successfully captured Col's emotional attachment to The Ice. At the time, it was impossible to imagine that, years later, he and I would collaborate on an Antarctic picture book, *Wild Ice*. Some seeds obviously grew from that one season's work.

It was patently obvious that Antarctica had inspired all of these people in a very special fashion. The group spirit was high and there was great camaraderie, despite a potpourri of individual quirks and variations. Everyone attended one another's lectures and spent much time sharing knowledge and expertise. They spent an equivalent amount of time racing around, making sure that no one on board lost out on anything—that no whale blow, no snow petrel sighting, no purple midnight sky, no beautiful iceberg was ever missed. If a rare seabird came sailing by, invariably there would be chases to find the few who weren't yet on deck. Often, for long stretches, staff would gather to reminisce about previous trips.

And then there was Jim Snyder, resident photographer, driver, and raconteur. Aside from his total immersion in and enthusiasm for photography, I was amazed to discover that many of Jim's stories were dead-on true, hardly embellished at all—for example, his story of the bloody shirt and how he was practically ripped to shreds by a fur seal at Elsehul. Jim regaled people with how he'd been protecting a group of visitors on the beach, while holding off a nasty fur seal with a wooden paddle from his Zodiac. Jim had aimed the paddle's flanged end toward the snorting fur seal as he slowly walked backwards toward the Zodiac, and as the passengers scampered quickly to safety. But then Jim slipped and—as he describes it— the seal was on him "fast," chewing hard on his backside. Oh yes, there were twenty or thirty stitches needed to close the wound, but his bloodied shirt from that bout was almost framed, and I understand that Jim still has it in his possession. Jim and another staff member, Christiana Carvalho, were always on deck waiting for "the next great shot," irrespective of the elements or sea state. They taught me how to use a rig called the Hosking Holder to steady my long-lensed photos. The camera and lens were mounted on a monopod and then inserted into a flag holder, which you see people in marching bands using. They had learned this setup from noted English photographer Eric Hosking.

Jim took his camera gear everywhere and hardly ever ceased thinking about pictures. And I know of only one time when he literally was stopped from taking photos. Jim's typical routine was to arise from his "B" deck cabin, in *Explorer*'s forward bowels, then to make his way up two long flights of stairs that proceeded directly from the laundry, two doors away from his cabin, right to the entrance of the Explorer Lounge. Yes, of course, he'd bring his camera bag topside because "you'd never know when something's going to happen." Usually, his gear stayed under one of the small reception tables at the top of the stairwell, while Jim trundled off to breakfast. One season I heard that some of the newer stewards were running late in their efforts to clean cabins before breakfast service had ended. They were changing lots of sheets and towels, and hastily dumping soiled items right next to and over Jim's camera bag. When the laundry—which, again, was right at the base of the long stairwell—opened and while no passengers were watching, the stewards decided to save some time by tossing everything in that big pile down two flights to "B" deck, including, of course, Jimbo's photo gear. Little survived this crash, and Snyder soon found a new stowage spot for his equipment.

I, too, was a denizen of the "B" deck bowels, on port side and in corner cabin #322, which was tucked between the laundry and the cabin that Snyder and Gurney occupied. My roommate was a British army officer from the fifth Royal Inniskilling Dragoon Guards, then Lt. Col. Patrick Cordingley. Both of us were billed as guest lecturers. Pat had just completed a book about Capt. Titus Oates, who had died on Scott's return trek from the South Pole in 1912, and who was a previous member of Patrick's distinguished army unit. These lectures interfaced nicely with Alan's history discussions. Patrick's military career blossomed considerably in subsequent years, when, in course, he became the leader of Allied tank operations during the Persian Gulf War.

Ours was one of the infamous "SODS" cabins in *Explorer*'s bow—smelly, unkempt hovels with bunk beds that weren't bolted to the walls. In addition, there weren't any straps to hold you in your bunk, all of which contributed to some interesting times rolling and pitching in the Drake, when our clanging bunks became a veritable nightmare of instability. Patrick and I learned that the acronym gracing our abode stood for the Southern Ocean Drivers Society, an honorary assemblage of Lindblad Travel hands who had "bonded"—that is, "all for one and one for all"—to ensure the aforementioned communality of spirit and purpose. Keith Shackleton claims that SODS "must be one of the world's most esoteric groups. Rallied under the motto *Per Macrocystis ad Littorum*—Through Kelp to the Beach—they are responsible for the ship's landing operations. Lamb's Navy rum is their formally approved beverage and comes aboard by special arrangement with the Falkland Islands Company at Port Stanley."

Newcomers like Patrick and me realized straightaway that SODS was the heart and soul of Mike's operation. If you could get people quickly and often to landing sites, you could be a successful expedition leader. If you could pull props and do stern-first landings, you could take passengers to high-swell beaches like Baily Head on the outside of Deception Island. In other words, if you had outstanding drivers, odds for a great trip rose substantially.

This staff played very hard and tried equally hard to share what they saw, impart their enthusiasm for Antarctica, and challenge the value structures and beliefs of some of the paying guests—

encouraging them to think a little bit differently. In the early 1980s, very few vessels brought visitors to Antarctica and shipboard tourism traffic was less than a thousand people per year. Now the number of vessels plying Antarctic waters has reached double digits and there are up to ten thousand or more visitors annually. Beyond the remaining numbers of keen, Paul Bowles–like travelers, the Seventh Continent is a strong lure for people who have been everywhere else and simply want to "tick" another continent. This raises a big red flag, and I wonder whether and if the consciousness of this particular cohort can be raised to new heights.

And I still wonder about the perils of navigating iceberg-strewn waters that aren't well charted. Indeed, *Explorer* has grounded twice. The first occasion was in Admiralty Bay, King George Island, on February 11, 1972. Her tourists were rescued by a Chilean vessel, *Piloto Pardo*, and *Explorer* was towed off by a German tug eighteen days later. The second event occurred when *Explorer* hit rocks off of Wiencke Island on December 24, 1979, and punctured her hull. Again, *Piloto Pardo* came to the rescue, along with the Soviet tug *Uragan*. At one point on this January 1984 trip, prior to our reaching Deception, I discovered Judy and Alan raising toasts as we passed the point where this last grounding occurred—now labeled Lindblad Rock on the nautical charts.

These incidents are unpleasant reminders, for sure, but risks usually stay hidden in the far recesses of memory, simply because Antarctica has a way of getting under your skin and blocking everything else from your mind. This January morning once again elicited some otherworldly feelings one comes to expect, as ninety or so expedition passengers and staff got ready to enjoy breathtaking geologic scenery at Deception Island. Here, one feels that the artist has really spun her palette. Traces of greens, oranges, and reds are speckled in reveling contrast to the dominant black-and-white cinder cast. At day's end, we would be heading back across the Drake Passage for a stop at Cape Horn, perhaps a visit in the Beagle Channel, then to Punta Arenas, Chile, and homeward flights.

Very early, Mike scrubbed a prebreakfast landing at Baily Head on Deception's southeastern coast. This was a shame, because I really wanted to spend some time with the huge numbers of chinstrap penguins I'd heard about. But sailing past, it was obvious that the swell was too high and the fog hadn't yet cleared, so Mike and Hasse felt more comfortable about proceeding through Neptune's Bellows and moving the group inside Deception's caldera. Another downer: Though the Baily Head colony also may be reached by hiking over from Whaler's Bay, there wasn't going to be enough time for such an extended excursion. None of us realized that one of the passengers had hiking plans of her own.

Once we anchored and the troops moved ashore, Mike provided me a substantial gift. Just to whet my appetite, he commandeered a Zodiac and drove me over for a brief peek at Baily Head's majestic, amphitheater-like scenery. We took the Zodiac into the small bay underneath the high rim and quickly hiked to the top. Through murky albeit lifting fog, I glimpsed endless rows of waddling, black-and-white bodies. Sadly, there was no time to linger. We had to get back and complete the landing at Whaler's Bay.

Deception has a mean elevation of almost one thousand feet. Mount Pond on its eastern flank rises to just over eighteen hundred feet, and Mount Kirkwood on its southern side tops out at over fifteen hundred feet. The eastern coast of Deception is fringed by a four-mile-long ice face. At some point in the island's geologic past, its caldera had sunk, and seas breached an entrance through the caldera wall, allowing water to gush through and to fill this vast sinkhole. The result was a giant, landlocked harbor that ultimately became a favored rest stop for vessels traveling the Peninsula. Typically, there are three locations tour ships tend to visit. The first is at Whaler's Bay and involves a sharp turn to starboard after the entrance into the caldera is passed. Much further inside, visitors may climb to a volcanic rim near Telefon Bay to inspect geologic changes from the most recent eruptions, as well as from current erosion or weathering, and visit steamy Pendulum Cove beach, where there are remains of a Chilean research facility that was destroyed and buried in the 1967 eruption. Here, perhaps, there may be an opportunity to go wading in the mixing zones between boiling water close to shore and subfreezing brew further out in the caldera.

Aside from the geology and the exploits of sealers, whalers, explorers, and early penguin biologists who came to Deception, there is considerable political history. Commander Henry Foster, on HMS *Chanticleer,* explored the Deception caldera in 1829 and Sir James Clark Ross also visited the area in 1843. British claims of sovereignty had proceeded from these events. But ignoring the British discoveries, Argentina laid claim to the South Orkneys in 1925 and Chile made a similar claim in 1940. In 1942, an Argentine expedition visited Deception and tried to take possession. A year later, the British sent a vessel to the island to remove any marks of sovereignty and to raise the British flag. During World War II, British vessels worked the area searching for enemy ships. In 1941, the British destroyed the fuel tanks and stocks of coal to deny these to any German ships seeking refuge. Once the Antarctic Treaty entered into force, these claims became back-burner issues that are not discussed. Under this regime Antarctica is, according to international law, unowned by anyone.

Deception's volcanic history is a long, equally calamitous record. In 1921, an eruption raised water temperatures so high that paint on vessels started to blister and peel. In 1930, an earthquake dropped the floor of the caldera harbor fifteen feet in some spots. The destructive potential is particularly evident because, at some places, geothermal activity causes the temperature of the ashy shoreline to rise to more than 110°F just a few inches below the surface. Strange mosses and liverworts have colonized these damp areas. Crumbling wooden buildings are lone remnants of the British research station that bore the substantial brunt of the most recent eruptions. Lately, it has been quiet—but you can't take this hot spot lightly. It will blast again.

Descriptions of eruptions in the late 1960s are horrific—volcanic bombs dropping at random, clouds of noxious fumes streaming upward from the center of the eruption, and men from both the British station at Whaler's Bay and the Chilean base at Pendulum Cove racing around—and panicking—for their lives.

So, under a fast-clearing sky, the first landing this morning was inside Deception's large, protected harbor, mostly to explore and pay our respects to the whaling and scientific stations that had been destroyed in that last burst of fire and bombs. Immediately, a visitor

is awestruck by this primordial black landscape, and by gases bub-
bling and rising from the warm black beaches. Some people examined the station ruins. I joined Dennis in leading others uphill in a
corner of the bay to examine some nesting pintado petrels. Alan,
Jim, and Pete began a concert of sea chanteys and bawdy songs
inside one of the boilers, taking advantage of its excellent acoustics.
Snake and Colin, occasionally relieved by the concerteers, resumed
a shuttle of passengers from shore to ship, while McDowell strolled
the beach, keeping tabs on passengers scattered everywhere. He was
starting to fend off rapidly emerging questions about homeward
travel, luggage tags, and airline reconfirmations. Martin, Steamer's
cabinmate and the officer on watch, strolled on deck, binoculars
strung around his neck, watching the ship's anchor line and making
sure that it was holding, and occasionally querying Mike whether
passengers would make the last Zodiac back to *Explorer*. With
less than an hour to go in the landing, Martin raised Mike over
Channel 16 on the handheld radio: "Hey, Mike, this is Martin, do
you copy?"

"Sure, Martin, take it over to six-nine. What's going on?"

Martin switched to the other channel: "How are you doing,
Mike?"

"Just fine, pal—are you just wanting to shoot the breeze?"

"Well, not exactly, Mike. What are you doing right now?"

"Martin, I'm standing here making sure these folks get into Zodiacs and get back to the ship. Not a wanker in this bunch. Is
everything OK back there? What are Steamer and Hasse up to? Is
the anchor holding?"

"Sure, sure, all's fine. But Mike, I think we have a problem."

"What do you mean, a PROBLEM? Everybody's smiling, having a good time. What's happening?"

"Well, Mike, can you turn around and look up into the hills?"

"Huh? Well, of course I can. What SHOULD I be looking at?"

"Now, Mike, just hold on. I've got you in my glasses. Turn just a little more to port from where you are. Yes, yes, that's good. Now look up—way, way up on the hillside. That's right. Look higher. Yes, you should have it."

Mike had now swiveled enough to be facing to starboard of the wrecked buildings, in the general direction of screaming Antarctic terns patrolling nests at the base of the cliffs. With a slightly scornful, albeit amused tone, Martin continued: "Now, Mike, if all's going so well, can you explain why one of your passengers—the lady in the trenchcoat with the two blue bags—is halfway up the mountain, and is still going straight uphill?"

There wasn't time for an answer, even if Mike had some explanation for two little blue bags and a plastic raincoat heading right toward the crest of Deception. He loudly belched a stream of expletives and ran crazily toward the Zodiacs Snake and Colin were driving back to shore. I was returning from my hike to the pintado nests and, with a small group of passengers, tried to take in the emerging tumult. Mike flipped his radio back to Channel 16 and barked orders for Snake and Colin to meet him immediately on shore. He raised Martin once more and asked him to round up the ship's doctor, who, presumably, had returned on board, and to send him—with full kit—immediately to the beach.

As soon as they had tied up their boats, Mike dispatched

Snake and Colin uphill, with orders to check out what was happening. Most important, they were to bring this wayward passenger back—safely—to the ship. They had no idea what they were up against. Mike quickly—but not too obviously—gathered remaining staff and asked that we basically proceed as usual, that all was likely to be well in hand, and reminding us that we still had another landing to do before heading back across the Drake. "So," he said, "let's get everyone back on board, as planned. There's really no need to panic." He didn't sound completely confident, because as yet, there hadn't been any news from Colin and Snake. They were still scaling the caldera slopes. Most passengers returned to the ship rather unsuspectingly. Things stayed calm for a while, but as time for our expected departure to Telefon Bay came and went, it became more and more obvious that something strange had happened.

Colin and Snake discovered that the passenger with the blue bags was Françoise, the young woman from France. Confidently, Françoise asserted that she wasn't intending a "jolly" and the guts of it was that she'd decided to stay in Antarctica! She told them that she was basically sick of humanity and that she was ready to try something new and vastly different. She, too, had read the history of Deception and knew that researchers and whalers had lived here, so she was convinced that she'd be able to get by and find a steady supply of penguins to capture and eat. Occasionally, of course, there would be visiting scientists and tourists, and the abandoned buildings would offer some protection from the elements. She'd obviously been planning this little scheme for a while.

"WHAT DID SHE SAY?" Mike screamed incredulously when

Snake and Colin reported in, after which the two of them had quite a struggle coaxing Françoise down. Mike and the doctor met them partway up the incline. Almost immediately, Mike had to contend with the doctor, who, sensing some serious psychological ramifications, insisted on injecting Françoise with everything he had in his medical bag. Mike sternly advised the doc to back off and tried himself to reason Françoise out of her determined position. By now, they had reached the Zodiacs, but Françoise was nonplussed by Mike's description of what life at Deception might *really* entail once the austral winter set in. They managed to get her into the Zodiac, but just a few yards out from shore, Françoise jumped into the freezing water and tried swimming back to shore. Snake dived in and grabbed her, and all of them managed to get Françoise back into the Zodiac as quickly as possible. Mike now added hypothermia to his list of concerns. Once retrieved, Snake knelt on the now very blue-skinned Françoise to prevent her from jumping out again, and the Zodiac crew was greatly relieved when they reached the gangway.

Many passengers were eagerly watching the emerging scene from *Explorer*'s various decks. Worse, Mike was starting to receive more advice than he needed. Suddenly unabashed doctor-passengers were cornering Mike with numerous and sundry theories. But first things first. Shivering violently, Françoise was speedily escorted back to her cabin on "A" deck, one level below the main deck. Mike entrusted Françoise to her roommate, Elsa, the grandmother from New Jersey who happened to be one of our favorite passengers. Elsa had been unaware of the unfolding scene, yet instinctively and quickly she sensed the predicament, and dutifully ensured that Françoise enjoyed a hot and very long shower. And, I'm sure, Elsa offered Françoise more than a few hugs and kisses.

Mike was into full-fretted worrying about the Drake. Judy checked Françoise's documents and discovered that she had no return air tickets to France. It was also discovered that she hadn't turned her landing tag to red, so, if it hadn't been for Martin's successful watch, Françoise's plan might have succeeded. Rumors began spreading, and it was time to tackle the entire situation head-on. Mike first called a staff meeting and advised us that we were going on round-the-clock watch at night outside Françoise and Elsa's cabin until we got back to Punta. He also wanted to know why no one had noticed Françoise bringing her two blue suitcases into the Zodiacs: "What did you think they were—camera gear?"

His next stop was the Explorer Lounge, to which everyone had been summoned by Judy's announcement. Mike dispelled fast-igniting stories by explaining that we had a very unhappy passenger on board but that all was OK and that there was no reason for this incident—or Françoise—to disrupt the rest of the trip. Mike said that he expected everyone to act normally around Françoise and to treat her just as they had up to that point. And with *Explorer* under way, it was time to get ready for the last landing at Telefon Bay.

Then came Mike's best move. As passengers started filing out, Mike took Rob, the young American, aside. Mike had known that Rob and Françoise were spending some time together at the bar, though it was unclear whether or not their friendship had proceeded much beyond the talking stage. Mike's deal was a straightforward offer to cover all of Rob's bar tab and other on-board expenses if he'd spend every remaining, waking moment of this trip with Françoise, when she wasn't sleeping or in the shower. Thus, with Rob in public areas, staff in hallways, and Elsa in the cabin, Mike felt there was a decent chance of getting Françoise back safely across the Drake.

The short story is that Mike's strategy worked. After a long, warming shower, Françoise seemed to understand that her "dream" to move to Deception was lost, and she began to relax. As a result, we had a relatively happy crossing, except, as might have been expected, for Snyder. That first night across the Drake, Jim had the 2-to-4 A.M. shift outside of Françoise and Elsa's cabin. When Jim relieved me at 2 A.M., it had been an uneventful evening, and there was little reason to suspect anything unusual. Jim had been up in the Explorer Lounge and he was somewhat energized, seemingly eager for his two-hour stint. As it happened, though, Jim started nodding off around 3 A.M. and he was awakened only by a "vision" he saw and felt moving around a corner.

"OH MY GOD, I'VE LOST HER!" was all that crossed his mind as he raced up and down, through all of the inside passageways, up and down from deck to deck, around all outside deck space, but nowhere was Françoise to be found. After about twenty minutes, Jim was spent. It was time to report the tragedy to the officer-of-the-watch. Jim trudged up to the bridge, pulled the heavy door, and proceeded inside. As he approached the third officer, then in charge, to tell his tale of extreme woe, Jim failed to notice a second person in the wheelhouse, who was quietly watching the Drake churn by. After hearing Jim's frantic case, the third officer smiled, then introduced Jim to a man he called the "sleepwalker," who came to visit the bridge *every* morning at about this same time— and who, he added, had a cabin right down the hall from Françoise and Elsa!

Jim's cries of relief were no less substantial and audible than a collective sigh that erupted when we tied up in Punta Arenas, our full passenger complement happy and definitely accounted for. I can't say that I have any recent word on the Françoise-Rob liaison, and I'd like to believe that our long ride back across the Drake allowed them to steal more than a few intimate moments. By this time, the company had contacted Françoise's family and the last information had Françoise spending a few days in town, waiting for money to arrive for her homeward flight.

Our last night at sea was special. Patrick and I were much surprised to find ourselves formally inducted into SODS. Each of us was presented with a plaque, which contained a SODS coat of arms that Dennis had painted, and we were required to down a glassful of Lamb's Navy rum in front of the assembled crowd in the Explorer Lounge. Still, we had one final round of night watches, which I recall being very easy because Françoise and Rob spent a very long and late evening at one of the lounge tables.

But sadness crept in. I always find the end of these trips to be emotionally difficult, when you're leaving friends behind, and especially if the trip's gone well in terms of animals and experiences. My heart wasn't into it, but I had to get ready to escort this group back home. I began throwing clothes into my duffel, and nagging doubts about the worth and value of these trips reared up once more, disquieting concerns about the promise of nature tourism and how it really might produce a cohort of people who have really *touched* and *connected* with the planet. Or is it only the elite among us who get to ponder such matters? It is a challenge inspiring people to higher ground, and I was sure that we'd really been able to reach some of those on board this trip.

Elsa was one prime example—a senior citizen who had stumbled into birds for the first time. The situation with Françoise aside, Elsa had gotten hooked on wildlife and she took in every last second with albatrosses and giant petrels in the Drake. She *loved* penguins. Years later, she was still chasing birds when we crossed paths in Alaska. But what about other passengers who seemed glued to the bar? Some of these denizens of the Explorer Lounge certainly had "ticked" their last continent, but I felt some failure because my interactions had produced very little appreciation of fitting Antarctic pieces into the global puzzle.

It always comes back to feeling that a true measure of these adventures depends on "yes" answers to these questions: Are we bringing back a committed group of "ambassadors" who thoroughly understand conservation and scientific needs of the location just visited? Or at least a few such people. Are these folks destined to continue proselytizing about their experiences? Will they encourage others to visit these places, or will they somehow contribute to working on that location's conservation issues? Over the years, many travelers have indeed connected. I remain in close contact with scores of people who've become dedicated Antarcticists and kept fully up to speed on the latest political and scientific developments. I am fortunate to have met some very special individuals who have gone out of their way to assist my research in the Peninsula.

In one manifestation, ecotourism means going to wild places—not to human-created attractions like amusement parks, beach hotels, or sporting clubs—and studying or enjoying scenery and plants and animals that might be found. But can some of these places be studied or enjoyed too much? Passengers may be provoked to a self-conscious critique of our human place in the grand scheme of things, inspired by the grandeur lurking in the antics of penguins and the unspoiled beauty of Antarctic landscapes and seascapes. But providing that inspiration in Antarctica may become harder and harder.

The breathing room that existed in the expedition schedules during old *Lindblad Explorer* days has evaporated. A regular rotation of seven to eight days cruising and visiting the Peninsula has shrunk to three to five. Fast turnarounds and a greater emphasis on amenities translates into less time to work with visitors and to nurture their connections, which returns us to basic issues: Are these expeditions—and those of us leading them—really changing attitudes and opinions? Are connections lost as soon as participants return home? How might awareness be translated into something more long-lasting? Skilled expedition staff can do the nurturing, but how many open-minded Elsas are there?

The ecotourism movement continues to grow, but it is hardly entrenched. It remains tied to a fickle economic base. Profits *qua* profits still seem to be an overriding maxim. The comfort, I believe, is that as long as the companies ensure an experienced complement of expedition leaders and staff who readily can identify the animals and explain their behavior, know the history, and understand the science—and who bare their souls about the places being visited—there's a chance. We needn't be so bold as to think we can change the *whole* world, but knowing that we've influenced even a few hearts and minds is worth it.

With bags finally packed, it was time for goodbyes and for resolving one last, important order of business: What to do with our canine acquaintance, Steamer? *Explorer* was next embarking on a so-called "circumnavigation" around to the New Zealand side of Antarctica, and New Zealand's strict quarantine laws prevented Hasse from bringing his bridge buddy along for another ride. As reported to me, it was a somewhat emotional moment. Hasse just didn't have the heart to return Steamer to Punta's streets, from whence the dog presumably originated. So Martin, who had tended Steamer for more than three weeks, was summoned to captain's quarters and ordered to do the nasty deed. The housebreaking experiment in Martin's loo was thankfully over and no doubt would end rumors that the stewards had refused to clean his cabin for weeks. Thus, Martin was only too happy to comply with Hasse's order, and he hardly restrained his enthusiasm.

But Martin had other designs. He was one of the virile young officers you'd expect on such a voyage, but no "significant other" had emerged to conciliate Martin's normal urges. Martin believed it was time to kill two birds, so to speak—his and Hasse's—with one proverbial stone.

Martin gussied up with some of his best civilian clothes, while Steamer was passed around staff and crew for a long string of *au revoir* hugs. It's difficult to imagine what might have been going through Steamer's little head, but we hoped that this time on board had allowed for any number of puppy highlights, whatever these might have been. Some of the lowlights were well known. For example, Steamer had a really difficult time dodging the skuas, which occasionally buzzed down to threaten an attack, and was visibly terrified by the huge elephant seals, especially when they reared up and growled menacingly. On the upside, though, Steamer always wore this slurpy little dog smile when she was in the wheelhouse with Hasse, her front paws propped up on the forward windows, ears erect, and tail wiggling vigorously.

Martin and Steamer strolled down *Explorer*'s gangplank and began their long walk into town. Neither looked back. Martin's gait was quick and determined, yet Steamer had no difficulty keeping pace. And it wasn't surprising to learn that Martin's compass was set directly for Mama Teresa's, one of Punta's more famous institutions, in fact, one of the most renowned houses of sometimes ill repute in all of South America. I say "sometimes" because there are varied points of view. Martin definitely had some physical pleasures in mind. But Teresa's is a rather unusual bordello, with a remarkable absence of pressure. If you just wanted to unwind after a trip and have a *cerveza*—while ignoring other possibilities—no problem. In addition, Teresa's was always considered the safest place in this rough-and-tumble town, and its reputation continues, even after Punta's vast military buildup in the last decade. This safety factor made a big difference to many Antarctic researchers who, between trips or before the end of their austral summer research projects, left their precious field notebooks with Teresa for protective keeping. Lots of science apparently had its genesis in data that Teresa guarded.

Martin walked straight to Teresa's front door and banged loudly, with Steamer standing just a few feet behind and shaking her tail energetically. In reality, Steamer started getting agitated and anxious, and began bouncing up and down on her front paws. Martin had to knock again.

Finally, the door opened and three of Teresa's regulars peered out.

"Good to see you ladies again," beamed Martin, who was almost crushed as the three stormed past him to the now frantic Steamer, yelling: "Susie, Susie, Susie, where have you been? It's been weeks. Where have you been? We missed you so much."

The three embraced the terrier, tears streaming down their cheeks. They began to dance in a circle, hugging one another, hugging Steamer, Steamer licking back—all totally ignoring Martin and proving, no doubt, that what the customer sometimes taketh, the customer sometimes returns to the fold.

So, now, whenever I return to Punta Arenas, a wry and rather substantial grin strikes my face, much like this city's prevailing and overpowering wind gusts. The smile broadens and I can't help thinking of Françoise, and wondering whether or not she ever made it back to France. I hope so. And why hadn't we noticed those blue bags when we took her shoreward in the Zodiac? Oh well, she probably wouldn't have enjoyed eating penguins even if she had succeeded in staying at Deception. I think of the SODS and of Snyder's camera gear being tossed to the laundry, and, yes, there will always be dreams about visiting chinstraps at Baily Head. And I happily think about Elsa, who not only provided some helpful comfort to Françoise, but whom we were able to nurture to that higher level, full of flapping and gliding seabirds and dreams of penguins and wildness. How many more Elsas are there? I trust there are many.

And perhaps my fondest memory is of little Steamer, heartily wagging her tail and bragging about the most extraordinary Antarctic trip that any puppy from Punta has ever accomplished.

NINE

....

The Burial Pool

In order to arrive at what you do not know
   You must go by a way which is the way of ignorance.
In order to possess what you do not possess
   You must go by the way of dispossession.
In order to arrive at what you are not
   You must go through the way in which you are not.
And what you do not know is the only thing you know
And what you own is what you do not own
And where you are is where you are not.

                  —*T. S. Eliot*

February begets closure. It is shut-down time.

    Antarctic Peninsula slopes and plains sprout pillows of shorn white feathers.

At Baily Head, adult chinstraps huddle in lava ravines or in rocky crevices—wherever they can shield their shivering, weakened bodies from the winds and developing storms. It's a meager prize for a damned fine job, two relentless months of nonstop activity—finding mates, defending nest sites, copulating, incubating eggs, raising and fledging chicks. Disconsolate, they bow heads and shed their feathers. All of them. All at once. Not gradually as in other birds. They've properly managed their incubation shifts and nest reliefs, and now, the chicks have exited to sea. Perhaps never to be seen again. The adults' annual feather molt is a painful, two- to three-week process that saps whatever energy they may have left. Soon, they, too, will depart and head north. The planet still spins.

I've sat in the upper reaches of Baily Head at these times, huddled near a barren, dry streambed where a hundred chinnies have taken shelter. They're tucked on the leeward side, out of the wind, shaking a snowstorm onto the brown, pockmarked ground. They are disheveled shadows of their gallant, noisy selves. Earplugs are no longer needed. Clumps of feathers sprout randomly. The feathers drop in mounds at their feet. If gusts swirl through the amphitheater, myriad tossed plumes lift like dust in sunlight, scattering over the island's reaches. Weakly, the chinstraps turn to one another, make a half bow, occasionally snort, then resume an upright, albeit slumped, posture. They can hardly move. Eyes blink. Days pass. This pain soon will end. No more raucous, rookery-wide ecstatic displays. No more copulations. No more bowing and hissing between mates. I have no idea what may be passing through their penguin consciousness, but if anything, I'd bet on dreams of two-inch-long morsels full of protein and energy.

At Copa Beach in Admiralty Bay, gentoo chicks and adults still roam widely. The chicks have gone to sea, but not for long. They return for some final meals, extending their parents' duties for a few more weeks. The adults then head to sea to feed, some for more than a month, before returning to Copa to molt. Other adults, standing in place, have already begun dropping a steady stream of short white feathers to the ground.

But at Paulet Island, it is as quiet as the city morgue. The remains of dead chicks from previous seasons poke through the guano slime. Over a week's span, a hundred thousand Adélie chicks jumped away, speeding to krill riches and the pack ice, tempting lives of dodging predators and surviving howling winter storms and weather. In succeeding days, most of the adults followed. Only a few have lingered. Adélies usually don't molt where they've bred, preferring other turf or to wait until they've reached the pack ice.

The days are shortening noticeably and the weather becomes more inclement. Along beaches and into canyons, the penguins assume different airs and my senses are scrambled. Penguins litter the ground with their old, spent fluff, shivering, scampering away weakly when I approach. They are virtually defenseless. They can't go to sea until their new feathers are in place. For the next ten days to two weeks, they endure and starve. At these strange times my penguin-cognition delusion turns 180 degrees. Instead of numbers that defy counting, a silence emerges that defies comprehension. Suddenly, everything flips to a different mode. Landscapes once filled with unending levels of penguins lie obliterated of life. Absence, not presence, is the password. The Sturm und Drang of a fevered, two- to three-month breeding cycle metamorphoses to docile tranquillity. I feel dispossessed.

I've enjoyed a very productive field season. Much data and information have been collected, and today's visit to the Aitcho Islands is literally the swan song. Tomorrow, the Drake Passage and my reverse migration. Unavoidable reflections pound my radar screen.

There is incredulity: I've grabbed the same string that began with Louis Gain and Charcot at Petermann Island, and with Bagshawe and Lester at Waterboat Point. I can hardly believe that my work, my life, is the same territory these people worked, the same creatures they examined. I connect to a fertile legacy of penguins. No protective barrier or pane of glass physically separates me from them. The window is *open*. I'm privileged to inhabit a front-row seat on their turf and observe these high-strung packets of sinew and muscle firsthand, nose-to-nose, as their lives of joy and pathos unfold.

There is gratitude: Many visitors come to Antarctica, and to most of them it's a once-in-a-lifetime occasion. Most people don't come at all. Because I've come regularly and often, and because I've scrutinized the entire onshore cycle of chinstraps, Adélies, and gentoos, sometimes in excruciating detail, I feel extraordinarily lucky.

There is perspective: After chasing penguins and associated Antarctic mysteries for sixteen seasons, the complexity emblazons my vision as clearly as penguins spewing guano. Answers will be difficult to tease out of a morass of data, and even then, today's theories likely will give way to future, presently unknown correlations. Today's achievements are tomorrow's history. I accept the complexity, welcome it—believe it keeps us curious. If we lose our inquiring minds, we might as well be dead.

In the early 1990s, the extent of the winter pack ice surrounding Antarctica was identified as the important factor mediating the returning numbers of penguins, favoring chinstraps in lean-ice winters, Adélies in heavy-ice winters. In the late 1990s, we realize better how the ebbs and flows of winter sea ice link to global processes affecting the entire planet—processes that we cannot control, though our industry and mechanization may contribute to some of the negative effects. Penguins are a constituent element of this complicated jigsaw puzzle, whose disparate pieces we may never fully understand. There can be no assurance that the pieces will continue to fit as they may appear to connect at this point in time. We scratch the surface, believe we've identified relevant elements of the puzzle, but the picture never completely fills. Penguin-counters need to continue counting and Antarctic science, generally, needs to continue chasing the mysteries.

It is an irrelevancy that my other home, Washington, actually lies 8,910 miles from the South Pole, 7,230 miles from Louis Gain's stomping ground at Petermann Island, and 7,180 miles from Heroína Island in the northwestern Weddell Sea. The distance is physical, not emotional. I feel not one step removed. One questions nags: Will there be more or fewer penguins to count next season and decades hence? If and when changes are detected, will we have sufficient data or intuition to discern the natural variations, let alone to identify whether we humans are contributing to the flux? We are just a few degrees of separation removed—linked in a fashion belying the physical distance that lies between.

Consider *our* chlorofluorocarbon production and these chemicals' release to the atmosphere, which has damaged the ozone layer. The ozone layer still thins each austral spring and has not yet repaired, despite international efforts to cease CFC production and use. The damage will take decades to mend. Meanwhile, a surfeit of UV-B radiation slips through—a predicate for other dominos falling. Some initial studies suggest the excess UV-B may be affecting standing stocks of phytoplankton and zooplankton by as much as 20 percent. Less phytoplankton means less food for krill; fewer krill mean less bounty for penguins, seals, and whales. Just a few steps from us and our CFCs to them.

Or consider the planet's premillennial warming trend. How do our greenhouse gas emissions fit into this equation? Are we exacerbating the trend? The warming may simply be a natural variation in earth's weather—with another ice age in the offing once this bout of warming ceases. With winter temperatures in the Antarctic Peninsula having risen eight or nine degrees Fahrenheit in the last decade—the predicate for more lean-ice winters—that means diminished annual cohorts of larval krill and, as recent news has described, diminished numbers of chinstraps, Adélies, and gentoos. Are these penguin declines serious? As yet, we're told that none of the Peninsula penguins is particularly threatened, not to the point of being endangered in any kind of way.

But that is this year's expert opinion. Tomorrow is another matter. In global terms, the weather will continue changing dramatically—our climate and the penguins'. One of my penguin gurus, Frank Todd, optimistically hopes "that good sense will prevail, and that these wonderful animals will be preserved for future generations to marvel at. Most people acknowledge that they will never see penguins in the wild. But just knowing that they are there is enough." My fear is that admiration truly isn't enough—that many admirers don't thoroughly appreciate the close nexus between us and them, how linked our fates actually are. The penguins are sending messages and these signals leave me discomfited. It's wonderful knowing that penguins exist, but that's no different from saying we humans are pretty terrific, too. We can't stop innate global processes, but we can recognize that what affects us, affects them. The supposed degrees of separation are blurred and diffuse.

Admittedly, I'm not a dispassionate observer: I've held them, counted them, chronicled their behavior close up and firsthand, relished them at the peak of their virility, and been chastened by their injuries and deaths. I have different antennae—a penguin barometer that senses things differently. February's truth is seeing clearly what these withered adults and fattened chicks represent. Each stage unveils instants of wonder.

There is the setup:

Two eggs are the normal clutch, though brushtaileds occasionally will lay a third egg, and gentoos may double-brood if a pair's first clutch of two is lost. The penguins exhibit a strong, unrelenting tendency to brood their eggs, and sometimes they'll attempt to haul in extraneous eggs. In a steep colony like Baily Head on Deception Island, I've observed a chinstrap trying to incubate five eggs. I'd doubt if more than two of these would hatch. Clearly, these eggs weren't produced by a single couple. Some had undoubtedly rolled in after a disturbance uphill.

Then, precious bounty:

The penguins may continue incubating, even after eggs seem doomed. On a visit to the Aitchos I made earlier in the season, there was a miserable rainstorm holding forth and the penguin-counting was a messy quagmire of slips, slides, and mud. I was counting the chinstrap nests on the eastern heights when I came across a penguin incubating in a pool of water. Using my field notebook, I distracted the chinnie sideways to examine whether it really had eggs. Its mate ran up, squawking in typically loud chinstrap fashion. I found one egg in the hole, almost completely covered by water, and discolored a horrid shade of blue. I felt confident the egg was addled. The incubating chinstrap got very annoyed and hopped out of its pool, and I grabbed the cold egg and set it in front of its mate, figuring it would find the urge to incubate irresistible. Bingo. It immediately hopped on the blue egg, snuggled it into its brood patch, and sat prone on the turf. Sometimes eggs can survive a few days in melt pools. Maybe this one could be revived. As I backed away, the original chinstrap returned to the pool and immediately sat down in the water, up to its neck, completely oblivious to the egg's removal. I proceeded upslope, looked back, and the wet chinnie was still there, happily bathing in its cold water.

Properly incubating birds often will rise, stretch, and "show" their eggs—perhaps every twenty minutes or so, which is believed to provide the developing embryos an important exchange of respiratory gases and water through the eggshell's pores. During the stretching routines, penguins often expose the interior of their brood pouch, which in the case of chinstraps reveals vibrant purple-colored skin. The parents endure long stints maintaining these sacks of evolutionary jewels. While the incubation period for all three species is similar, the timing of the nest reliefs varies. Adélies may be away from nest and mate for up to two weeks, and chinstraps for up to ten days, while gentoos change over daily.

Next, pips and babes:

After a month and a few days of incubation, the chicks emerge. The egg tooth at the end of the chick's beak is used to pip the shell. The chick nibbles, breaks, and stabs until it emerges, usually within twenty-four hours. These little souls are almost totally naked and helpless, which biologists technically label *nidiculous*. In these very early moments, all of the *nidiculous* chicks resemble ridiculously fragile, small, bald extraterrestrials from another galaxy. They bear only a very thin cover of down and are hardly able to move, and will be almost fully dependent on the parents for three to four weeks, technically described as *semi-altricial*. They are considered *precocious* if they buzz forth and immediately, innately, start acting like grown-ups.

The scenes are tender: Adélie parents rearing back slightly, the wobbly chick attempting to lift its shaking head upward, chirping, quickly touching and bobbing against the parent's beak, inducing the parent to open its beak—where ready morsels await. Chinstrap parents projecting wild-eyed yellow stares at their doddering youngsters, from the get-go brainwashing their babes that they're going to be infinitely more raucous than the other brushtaileds. Gentoo parents opening beaks as wide as possible, the chicks laying their necks and heads inside the extended lower mandible and disappearing from view.

Until the chicks gain more feathering and fatten up, they can't maintain the requisite metabolism and body temperature by themselves. The parents use their brood pouches to protect the chicks.

The parent keeps them warm by crouching in a prone position. The chicks' metabolic capabilities improve rapidly, with chinstrap and gentoo chicks being well on the way by ten days and fully able to thermoregulate at fifteen to sixteen days. While the Adélies and chinstraps are prone to long incubation shifts, the chick-feeds occur at a more rapid rate, every twenty-four hours with Adélies and twelve to sixteen hours with chinstraps. Gentoos feed their chicks every twelve hours.

The brood pouch extends longitudinally down the penguin's belly, and both male and female penguins develop one by the time the clutch of eggs is completed. Penguins don't carry their babes around in these pouches. They just cover them. There's plenty of room inside—so much so that when censusing nests early in the season, you might see a bit of one egg exposed in front of an incubating bird, but it is impossible to see a second egg fully tucked within the pouch. This cavity opening is lined with feathers and is about six inches long. Inside the special compartment the skin is bare and the interior walls very efficiently transfer body heat to the naked chicks, and it is sufficiently large to shield both fragile new-borns from the elements.

Immediately after hatching, the chicks are fed frequent small meals—one to two ounces of regurgitated mush at a time. Initially the chick's eyes are closed and the begging is stimulated by the sounds and calls associated with its parent's changeover routines or the movement of the brooding adult. The chick begs by raising its beak to nibble the parent's bill. The parent often encourages the chick to feed by nudging down to touch it with its bill, or by nestling the young one closer. Within five days, the chick may yawn

and stretch regularly and begin to move stones around the nest—
some early practice for later nest-building efforts. Apparently from
observing their parents' mutual displays, both Adélie and gentoo
chicks will employ modified and simplistic versions of these displays
when begging for food. Within ten days the chick begins preening,
cleaning, and maintaining its feathers. Adélie chicks, though, won't
start to rub oil into their feathers until about a month of age. Adélie
siblings also are known to fight with each other when less than two
weeks of age.

Then, day-care arrangements:

The chicks grow so rapidly they quickly outgrow their parents'
protective pouches. Some scenes are amusing: Too-large chicks still
may be able to tuck their heads under a parent, but with chubby
stomachs thrust outward and bums hoisted skyward. Shortly, the
chicks become too large to hide any body parts, and they'll stand
or lie prone next to the nest or parents. The parents continue watching them closely for another week or so. This early segment of life
is called the *guard phase*, and it extends for three to four weeks. In
this time, the chicks will have replaced their initial down fragments
with a somewhat thicker, down garb. The Adélie chicks' guard coat
is sooty gray, the chinstraps' is pearly gray, and the gentoos' is a
darker gray-and-white combination.

Next, a future with crowds:

After four weeks, both parents cease to guard the chicks, which
begin to move away from the nest and to collect in groups. Technically, this *crèche phase* begins when the chick assumes some independence and begins to wander short, then progressively longer
distances from the nest. When they first crèche, the chicks are one

half to two thirds the height of the adults and their down has grown much fluffier—a thick bouffant arrangement, no doubt accentuated by their substantial weight gain.

The Adélie chicks are the premier crèche-addicts among the brushtaileds. Sometimes these groups comprise scores and scores of chicks, and the numbers seem to swell when the wind and weather are bad. The chicks generally crèche within a radius of twenty-five to forty feet from their nest. Chinstrap and gentoo crèches, however, are more loosely organized and don't become as large and compacted.

There is maximum caloric intake:

By the time the guard stage ends, the chicks are receiving meals ten times greater than their initial nibbles. Each parent is capable of returning with more than a pound of food. A twelve-pound gentoo is perfectly capable of returning home with two pounds of krill and fish in its belly. Adélie chicks grow much faster than chinstrap and gentoo chicks. This likely reflects the Adélie's high polar distribution and the fact that it has the shortest of windows of time to rear its chicks. During the guard phase, Adélie chicks receive meals of about three and a half ounces each, which for two chicks amounts to a total of just under a half pound. This will double and triple during the crèche phase to individual meals of ten and a half ounces each, or a two-chick total of a pound and a third. At Copa Beach, Adélie chicks reach a peak weight of almost eight and three quarter pounds at two months of age, which is about 75 percent of an adult's weight, then lose about 5 percent of that mass before fledging and heading to sea.

Chinstraps also grow phenomenally: At Copa they weigh about

five and a half ounces at three days, four pounds at three weeks, and seven and a half pounds at five weeks, building to a peak of almost nine pounds at eight weeks, which represents 90 percent of an adult's weight. Overall, chinstrap chicks grow a tad more slowly than Adélie chicks, likely reflecting their Peninsular, maritime distribution. Gentoo chicks grow very slowly and reach a more robust weight than chicks of the other two species—to twelve and a half pounds. They will go to sea weighing more than their parents weigh at the end of the nesting cycle.

During crèche, Adélie chicks balloon to fat blobs of blackish down. At this stage, chubby chinstrap chicks are light gray above and white below, and gentoo chicks are plump little dirigibles, dark gray above, white bellies below. Somewhere underneath, a juvenile penguin lurks. The thick down is difficult to keep clean. Clear skies occasionally appear, but inevitably there is more flood, mud, and assorted crud with which to contend. This muck cakes and clumps the chicks' down and turns these fluffballs into sorry, pitiful sights. The Adélie chicks become especially slimy and guano-fied. The chicks are trapped: Until they've molted to their first juvenile plumage, they are neither waterproofed nor insulated for life at sea. They can't wash off.

They live to eat—and to the point of exhaustion. A common sight is overly sated chicks sprawled prone and forward, wings and legs akimbo, totally wiped out. So fat they're simply immobilized. But the torpor doesn't last long, and the chicks rise, anxious for another handout.

Next, races and chases:

The parents return with bellies full of protein, the only difficulty then being: *Where are my chicks?* How are one pair's chicks separated from the others among this conglomeration of yearlings? The pace is frantic enough, with so many chicks milling about—noisily scurrying here, rushing there, ever alert for the next feed. At the same time, you, the penguin-counter, may be seriously bounding the perimeter of the crèche, trying to count the horde as best you can, when you're brought to a full stop by the manic, hyperkinetic feeding routines.

A returning Adélie adult porpoises in, swims to the edge of the beach, and hops out—blooming fat from its obviously successful run. It stops, preens momentarily, then begins to hobble slowly toward its nest site. It utters a few croaks and calls, which its chicks apparently recognize. And other chicks, not its own, hear and see that the food truck has parked. The adult nears the crèche of chicks in the vicinity of its nest site, croaks a few more calls, and six to fifteen or more hungry chicks furiously and in single file begin chattering and rush after it. The Adélie's eyes bulge at the approaching throng and it scampers wildly away, down the beach, attempting to outrun the chicks. It is a game of sorting its own from the masses. The chases are chaotic, often disrupting other groups of standing chicks and adults. The parent continues running, every so often letting up to turn around, check how many chicks are continuing the chase, peck away some of the impostors, and then resume the scamper. It will be that parent's chicks who persist and who ultimately get fed. To the tenacious go the spoils.

Bill Sladen's seminal work in the 1950s proved that Adélie and gentoo parents feed only their own chicks during the crèche stage. Feeding chases account for 14 percent of the time Adélie parents and chicks spend together, and at times may extend to a thousand feet away from the nest site. But much still needs to be learned. To some extent, the chases allow the parent to do its work away from the crowds. Once its two chicks are sorted, the parent can apportion the bounty between the two with less wastage and spillage. The Adélie and chinstrap feeding chases are much longer if the parent has two mouths to feed instead of one. There is speculation that this apportioning also allows the parent to give favored treatment to the hungrier of its chicks, and in times of scarcity to ensure that the stronger chick survives to fledging. Another hypothesis is that the chases allow the chicks to become more familiar with farther reaches of their natal rookery. Many Adélie feeding chases end at the waterline, while chinstraps tend to head away from the shore.

All chases don't end in feeds. Some of the returning adults are so alarmed or discombobulated by the chasing swarm, they escape by making a quick U-turn to the water. It must be somewhat exhausting, if not annoying, to be swarmed by the chick paparazzi. Many parents who have completed their feeding duties grab a blow by moving a considerable distance from the crèche and the crazed chicks, seeking some uninterrupted rest and sleep.

Annoyance aside, the crèche phase is important for the chicks' parents. It represents the first opportunities they've had in almost two months—after more than a month of incubation and a three- to four-week guard phase—to feed *simultaneously*. Until then, it has been a rotation of effort with both sexes sharing the brooding and the feeding responsibilities. Likely, both members of the pair are hungry as hell. Gentoo males, slurping the food, may jump from twelve and a half pounds during the guard stage to almost fifteen pounds once the chicks crèche. During the same period, female gentoos may jump from ten and a half pounds to thirteen pounds.

Crèched chicks have grown too big to be individually plucked by predatory skuas, and the collective size of the crèche further deters these flying marauders. When explorers and biologists first described crèches, there were suggestions that these assemblages are tended by "baby-sitters"—for example, nonbreeding adults or failed breeders who patrol the edges and shoo the skuas away. However, studies by Bill Sladen and Lloyd Davis determined that the masses *qua* masses were the deterrent, not alleged au pairs and nannies. By this time, chicks have gained some necessary skills—aggressively staring down skuas flying above, stabbing at those walking about.

Yet, some skuas score:

It's rare when an entire colony is totally *synchronized*—meaning "on schedule"—so there always seem to be some late breeders whose small chicks represent potential snack food for alert and fiendish skuas. Reality often intrudes. I recall a day at Copa Beach when the chasers and the chased were thoroughly oblivious to a scrawny, guano-laden Adélie chick who had strayed too far from the crèche and was cornered by a pair of skuas. The bulky skuas thrust their thick bills repeatedly at the chick's head and eyes. Finally, there was a direct hit and the chick stumbled forward, gasping. Three adults resting nearby were aroused by the noise and dashed the skuas with beaks agape and voices at fever pitch, wings shaking, attempting a diversion that unfortunately came too late.

The skuas go right for the meat, and the chicks they predate have their bellies and chests plucked out and devoured. The heads and wings and tail often remain. By contrast, leopard seal kills are virtually shaken out of their skins, literally chewed and turned inside out. Neither adult penguins nor their chicks are dominant food items for either predator. The skuas will take eggs and chicks if available, but otherwise make their living by fishing. Similarly, leps will take penguin adults and newly fledged juveniles, if available. One was observed taking six penguins in seventy minutes. Leps usually take penguins in the water, though occasionally they will lunge through brash ice or onto an ice floe to grab one. But leopards eat everything, and penguins aren't an exclusive dietary staple. Their diet is believed to comprise one third krill, one third fish, and one third penguins, other seabirds, and other seals.

The spikes and peaks of egg and chick loss correlate to important events in the breeding cycle. Adélie egg loss is highest in the first few days after laying, which links to skuas' seizing eggs that were infertile or addled. If food's unavailable at the instant of hatching, the chicks may survive for as long as six or eight days, becoming weaker with each passing hour. But even when the food is on time and available, and the feeding runs and changeovers well synchronized, the nest exchanges have to be performed smoothly. If the mates expose the eggs too long or too obviously, skuas may swoop in. Another spike relates to nest desertion by the starving birds incubating well past the expected time of relief. There are many reasons why a mate fails to return: Killed by a leopard seal. Lost in a freak storm or accident. Or just plain stuck because an established krill location unexpectedly turned barren, protracting the feeding run by many days, perhaps weeks. If food can't be found, the schedule falls apart. And the skuas wait—ready in a flash to pounce on eggs or chicks that are abandoned.

Timing, experience, and proper nest sites are really big deals:

At Copa Beach, the long-term average productivity of approximately one chick per nest masks what, in actuality, have been wide swings from year to year. Chick production may be high one year and decline by more than 30 percent the next season. In Adélies, mistimed nest reliefs—either during incubation or during the guard phase—are the major cause of loss. The fasting bird waits only so long before deserting and exposing the egg or chick to the cold and to predators. Once the chicks are demanding food—and lots of it— a mistimed return means a ruinous fate. The chicks may be abandoned, left to starve or become skua fodder. Other adults won't feed the abandoned chicks. If the chicks wander aimlessly from their nest sites, they may be pecked to death by other penguins. But all is well when mates work complementarily and have their shifts fully synchronized.

Some pairs may adjust the lengths of their shifts to accommodate perturbations caused by diminished food supplies and longer-than-expected feeding runs. Chinstraps, with females doing the first incubation shift, might have a sequence of six-day, ten-day, eight-day, five-day, and quick shifts over the last three days until hatching. If krill is harder to find, an experienced pair may adjust to an eight-day, twelve-day, ten-day, two-day sequence intended to end precisely when the first chick hatches at thirty-two days. In the end, it's critical that food arrives and is available when the chicks hatch.

Also, variation in annual breeding success has much to do with the breeder's experience. Young, inexperienced penguins take years to learn and perform the sequence of breeding routines and behaviors. Many penguins attempting to breed for the first time will return reasonably early in the spring, but will be underweight—insufficiently fattened during the winter and therefore incapable of successfully managing the long fasts associated with incubation. These inexperienced breeders hardly leave the starting gate.

Has the best nest site been chosen? Also, interior breeding sites within a colony often are more successful than nests on the periphery. Chinstraps generally go for the high ground, gentoos the flats, and Adélies in between. But sometimes it's not so easily sorted. One season at Copa Beach, some chinstrap males expelled a number of Adélies that had chosen some prime, elevated turf above the beach. At Copa, chinstraps generally arrive later than Adélies, and at a time when Adélies are just past the peak of egg-laying. As the Copa Adélie population expanded, inexperienced Adélies began to occupy territories at the periphery of the colony, claiming sites that experienced chinstrap males, generally arriving a month later in the season, preferred. So what ensued was a battle between older, significantly heavier chinstraps in their prime and young, inexperienced, underweight Adélies. After being tossed, these displaced, inexperienced Adélies returned in succeeding seasons and chose different nest sites nearby. Ultimately, they learned the ticket to success. They began arriving significantly earlier and fatter—at the same time as established Adélie breeders—and were successfully able to maintain breeding territories. Many seasons later, as Adélies kept expanding and more and more of them gained the skill and experience to time their spring returns properly, fattened to the hilt, they were able to displace and fight off competing chinstraps.

Experience ups the ante. With Adélies, breeding success improves until the birds reach seven years of age, and in gentoos it has been demonstrated that both egg and chick survival rates are much lower with younger, first-time breeders. With increasing age, gentoo females produce larger eggs and, overall, experienced gentoos that have bred at least once produce more eggs and chicks.

The transition from guard phase to crèche is terribly tenuous for underweight chicks. In addition to their meager size, they are no longer guarded by their parents and become prime candidates for predation. In a broad sense, chick weights at the time of crèche indicate the availability of prey that season. A slew of skimpy, undernourished chicks suggests a problem with the stocks of the penguins' favored prey items. Even if there's a high amount of synchrony in the colony, there may be a number of inexperienced breeders who either start late or haven't mastered their foraging skills. Consequently, chicks from these inexperienced breeders are malnourished. And there are seasons when there's a total lack of synchrony, with wide swings in the number of chicks in crèche. That's a nightmare for a penguin-counter attempting a chick count at the peak of crèching.

Nonetheless, much is sorted by the time of crèching: If the chicks successfully make it into crèche, they're likely to survive to fledging. In general, penguins are long-lived seabirds that typically delay breeding until they've reached a certain age, and which exhibit a low annual mortality of adults. We know something about annual survival of Peninsula penguins because of their *philopatry*—their tendency to return to specific nest sites in a colony, or to a nearby colony in the rookery. By banding sufficient numbers of adults and ascertaining how many known-age penguins return each season, a measure of survivability is obtained. A high return rate is tantamount to high annual survival.

Will there be a bright future?

Adélie and chinstrap chicks hold crèche until they're about seven weeks of age, before moving to the beach and heading to sea. Once to sea, they don't return that season. Adélies may return as one-year-olds, in late January or February of their post-fledging season, perhaps to scout surroundings. Chinstraps may return to their natal colonies and form a pair bond at age two. With gentoos, the system's a bit different: Gentoo chicks hold the crèche much longer and don't go to sea until ten to eleven weeks of age. And even after hitting the water, they will continue returning to be fed until fourteen to sixteen weeks of age, by which time their parents have begun to molt and canceled the meal plan.

For chicks that survive, successful breeding does not happen immediately. Generally, the average age of first successful breeding is one to three years subsequent to the first attempt, with females tending to breed earlier than males by one to two years. Gentoos will start breeding at age two, and by the age of three to four years most will have bred. Chinstraps may form pair bonds at age two, but don't have success initially.

Additional work by Bill Sladen and Robert LeResche confirms the Adélie's step-by-step maturation from juvenile to first breeding attempts. Pre-breeding Adélies typically spend their first and likely a second year at sea or in the pack ice. They may return briefly to their natal colony for a little inspection tour—single, unpaired, and not exactly attached to any particular site. They're just wanderers.

A vast majority of surviving, inexperienced birds will have visited their natal colony by the age of four. In future years, they will begin to claim territories, build a nest, *keep company,* and form an initial pair bond. As the penguins age, they return in greater numbers to their natal colony, earlier and earlier each season, and progressively for longer periods. Their wandering years drawing to a close, they begin to focus on a particular breeding site, which is typically within six hundred to seven hundred feet of the area where they hatched. As they gain experience, they begin to show a greater fidelity to a particular nest site and an increased tendency to retain the same mate. The age of first breeding for Adélie females is four to five years, for Adélie males, more than six years. Some may not breed for the first time until age seven.

After their first precarious year, mortality rates appear to lower until the penguins begin to breed, and may increase again until they become established breeders. The annual survivorship of first-time breeding, three-year-old female Adélies may be a mere 25 percent, and only 36 percent with respect to four-year-old male Adélies. This compares to a 61 percent survivorship with respect to established breeders. By the same token, breeding takes a toll regardless of age. Nonbreeding Adélies may have an 18 percent higher survivorship than successful breeders. Adélie penguins surviving to old age tend to have failed more often than not, or may not have bred for the first time until a much later age.

Against this background, evolutionary success or failure ultimately depends on the number of chicks reared to fledging over an entire breeding lifetime. Adults in the wild are lucky to live to a decade, though there are many records of successfully breeding sixteen- to twenty-year-old Adélies. Some work on lifetime reproductive success has been done with little penguins in Australia and New Zealand, but more data in this regard are needed with respect to Antarctic Peninsula penguins. The Peninsula penguins are difficult subjects for a study of lifetime reproductive success because of the vagaries of site-fidelity and mate-fidelity. In theory, a population will remain stable if the average lifetime productivity of breeders equals two replacements per pair. The population grows if breeders generate more than two replacements per pair, and suffers if breeders can't replace themselves.

In penguin population dynamics, however, a high annual survival of adults is generally balanced by a relatively low survival of juveniles, particularly in the first year after fledgling. Up to 89 percent of Adélies may survive from season to season, but only 51 percent of first-year birds. Population changes reflect the tradeoff between breeding productivity and the number of penguins departing the population through mortality. How many penguins are recruited versus how many penguins die. A 5 percent change in juvenile survival to breeding age produces only a 1 percent population increase, while a 5 percent change in adult survival generates a more whopping 5 percent population increase.

Take my chicks, please:

The comical appearance of the chicks and the fun and games of chases and races obscure how wearying the last two months have been for the parents. Being married with penguin children is an ordeal. The parents can't wait to get the kids out of the house.

Chinstrap and Adélie fledglings will head to sea at seven to eight weeks. Gentoo fledglings head off to sea at ten weeks but keep returning to be fed until the parents molt. Through the crèche period, the age of the chicks can be estimated by the amount of down they bear. There is a bona fide juvenile penguin underneath these fluffy coats, but it takes weeks to molt the wispy tufts. They exhibit a crazy-quilt mix of old and new feathers, a plethora of weird hairdos and patterns. Adélie chicks may resemble teenaged boys with mohawk haircuts. Gentoo chicks may look like gigantic toy dolls without feet, composed solely of heads, wings, and fat stomachs.

Finally, they go. I recall one Adélie fledgling who clearly was attempting its first trip. A very few tangles of down remained on its head, but it otherwise seemed healthy and all set. It stood on a small ice cake stuck on the shoreline, and it waited long, long minutes before making a plunge. It bent low, almost as if to sniff the water. It looked to see what others were doing. Some fledglings were jumping in playfully and whisking away; others were mired on the beach, totally apprehensive about departing. The chick finally dived in and immediately hopped right back out, returning to its ice perch. Was it too cold? It shivered a bit, then resumed its sniffing and peering routine. Three minutes later it tried once more—and on this occasion bolted back even faster as a leopard seal lurched from the surf, jaws agape, trying to snatch this little prize. *Never saw one of those before.* The chick ran with all its strength up the beach, screaming uncontrollably at the top of its lungs, and moving as far from the surf as it possibly could get. I'm sure its heart was pounding wildly.

Until the Adélie's first adult molt, at fourteen months—assuming it survives the leps and myriad other calamities—it will have a distinctive white throat and black eye ring. From that point forward, it bears the adult's characteristic black throat and white eye ring, which enhance its tuxedoed appearance. The chinstrap's first adult molt also occurs at fourteen months. Until then, it looks like an adult except for a dingier face caused by dark spotting near the eye. Gentoo juveniles resemble the adults except many have discontinuous white patches—fillets—on top of the head. In adults, the white patches are joined by a slim line of white-colored feathers.

And then, more pain for the adults:

With chicks rushing to the beach, the brushtailed parents must complete their annual total-feather molt. The renewed feathering is critical. The adult's feathers have worn substantially from a year of work, particularly over the last two months rearing the chicks. Without a renewed insulation, they will be unprotected in the coming winter. The molt is incapacitating, so the first order of business after the chicks are independent is to take a long, offshore feeding run to replenish energy. If the premolt feeding run goes well, the penguins will attain their heaviest weight of the year: Gentoo males to seventeen and a half pounds, females to sixteen and a half. Adélies to fifteen pounds, chinstraps to almost twelve pounds. And they'll need every ounce of it. During the two- to three-week molting period, they cannot go to sea—in fact, they'll be almost totally immobilized, hardly able to move.

Penguins are warm-blooded animals that maintain a specific body temperature of 100–102°F. through a range of air and water temperatures. When the air or water drops below this *thermoneutral* range, penguins must increase their metabolism to survive. Walking and swimming are locomotory activities that ordinarily would help them thermoregulate, but these won't help during molt. Without sufficient feathering, they lack proper waterproofing and insulation, and entering the water at this time would be fatal.

Molting is a thermoregulatory nightmare. Feathers are lost and the penguin's rate of heat loss increases dramatically. Moving about is unusually painful and difficult, and there are few options for keeping warm. Muscle contractions and shivering generate some heat but are inefficient because the heat dissipates too easily. The better, more effective route is to bulk up substantially before dropping a single feather, then to rely on these increased energy stores though the two- to three-week fast. Gobs of fat will be burned, translating to a loss of 25 percent of the penguin's mass. A fasting male gentoo might weigh seventeen and a half pounds at the start of its molt, and barely fourteen pounds at the end. A molting female gentoo might reduce from sixteen and a half pounds to twelve and a half. They've been in weight training all season. A male gentoo may weigh just over twelve pounds at copulation, the female just over eleven, and 5 to 10 percent of that weight will be lost through the end of the guard phase. At the end of the crèche phase, the gentoo male might weigh fourteen and three quarter pounds; the female, thirteen.

The gentoos' premolt feeding sojourn may last from twelve days to more than four weeks, during which they're adding three or more pounds of mass to survive the two- to three-week molt. For successful Adélie breeders, the pre-molt sojourn may be only nine or ten days or can last two weeks. The mandala turns and turns.

And the season is over. It has spanned the penguins' spring return through defending nest sites, courtship, laying, incubating, hatching, arduous feeding runs, chick-fledging, and the big change of feathered clothes. Shutdown time arrives, when the entire process may be summed and tallies added—both statistically and emotionally.

In February, among molters and any lingering chicks, my snapshots merge like connect-the-dot puzzles, generating motion pictures of entire, manic lives. Tick, tock, up and down and forward we go, marching to a special drumbeat. I, too, will soon return north and continue dreaming, wondering about another return next season—if I survive and if my work continues. Antarctica makes you think. You can't simply go out and take it, call it your own, say it's a special experience. I'm inundated with collateral messages. I link to a primeval wildness that existed long before I arrived—and I stand alone, shedding the real world like penguins shed their old, worn feathering, trading for another beginning.

It is a typically overcast day at the Aitcho Islands—and uncharacteristically, enjoyably windless. After a huff and puff up the island's eastern slopes, I shuck layers of clothes and crave crisp, fresh air to whisk my sweat away. The chinstrap chicks are beginning to shed lots of their down and pace about nervously. The crèches, loose to begin with, are collapsing. A few parents continue to deposit slurries of krill into their chicks' gullets. Below, with much less synchrony, there are gentoo chicks well past crèche and others still full of down, and a few adults have begun to molt. I'm sure that many adult gentoos are offshore relishing their premolt feeding forays. I notice a gentoo uncharacteristically lose its footing and—wide-eyed with wings spread—slide down a nearby mud slope on its back. At the bottom, it does a couple of somersaults, then rights itself. A wayward Adélie appears onshore, disoriented. It takes a breather, perhaps notes the abundance of chinstraps and gentoos, and departs. No more room at the inn.

This is one of my favorite locations. This group of small islands lies in the northern entrance to English Strait, between Robert and Greenwich Islands. My work concentrates on the small, unnamed island that is the principal visitor stop in this string. The Aitchos were charted and named in 1935 by the Discovery Investigations run by the Falkland Islands Dependencies Administration, and named to honor the United Kingdom's Admiralty Hydrographic Office—the "HO." The visitor site is relatively easy to work. The islands are often windswept and shrouded in mist and fog, and it may be inconvenient for expedition ships to anchor. But there's an excellent slice of Peninsula life to partake. The site isn't overrun by thousands of penguins. It offers a bit of solitude.

You can sit quietly on five-hundred-foot-long Whalebone Beach, on the southeastern end of the island, and simply watch the world go by—gentoos, chinstraps, perhaps some Weddell seals on the beach, and bergy bits sloshing offshore. Gentoos nest among the remnant whalebones. Above Whalebone Beach, on the eastern end, there are masses of nesting chinstraps, which require a steep, sixty- to seventy-foot climb to reach. Island-wide, there are more than three hundred pairs of nesting gentoos and almost four thousand pairs of nesting chinstraps. The two-mile hike to the southern elephant seal wallow on the island's western end is relatively easy but complicated by the extensive patches of moss, which in late summer seem to erupt everywhere.

The chinstrap chicks are moving around the tops of the slopes, looking for a pathway to the sea. The angled slopes have become totally slippery and are clearly more difficult to negotiate than is usual, whether climbing or descending. The upside is that the eastern end won't see many visitors and the chinstrap colonies likely will prove excellent *controls* whose reproductive success may be compared in future years to the productivity of the chinstrap groups closer to the landing beach. *Prasiola* erupts in much of the unoccupied space, tingeing the misty rocks with vibrant green color. A few adults, undoubtedly failed breeders, have begun to molt. Below and to the west, down Whalebone Beach, gentoo fledglings are scurrying about, waddling here, waddling there, first swims just a few days off.

When a field season concludes—and the censuses are done, orientation maps corrected, and site descriptions revised—I seek communion with a few molting adults and fattened chicks. I can't simply hike back to the Zodiac, return to the ship, write up my notes and data sheets, drink a couple of beers, and forget it. Another long season is now history. Another data set needs to be processed, collated, filed, and analyzed. I'm elated that the work's continued and that it's gone well, but I have no bloody idea whether any of this season's information ultimately will prove anything. That's the risk: Hypotheses need to be tested. Baselines need to be compiled. New scripts inevitably connect to those compiled by Gain and Bagshawe and Lester and Bennett and the Trivelpieces. And we penguin-counters and Antarcticists keep returning, decoding the puzzle one dot at a time. An eerie, inanimate calm, a quiet desolation, takes over. The molters and chicks tell us something about how much, when, how, and why—but they also provide inspiration of times to come and new paths to explore.

I came as an outsider and we've tested each other. And because of their innate curiosity, we've struck a bargain. I've had the chance to go one-on-one, face-to-face, with creatures framed totally differently than I am, and who are thoroughly inclined to other tactics. By assuming a low posture and reducing my threat to them, I've tried defining some common ground. The risks have led to closer and closer encounters, numerous tête-à-têtes with creatures I'm only beginning to understand. As they inspect me in inimitable, penguinesque ways, their body language suggests a freedom I barely comprehend. I'm still a *rookie*, still scratching the surface. The answers lie deeper and I want to continue clawing and digging.

I tuck away my camera gear, notebooks, and tally-whacker. It's getting late, the light is failing, and there's no more than forty-five minutes left before I need to return to the landing beach, the Zodiac, and head back to the ship. All my work is done for the day— indeed, for the season. I simply want the panorama to fill my head, let the whole of it pass by, however unobtrusively or presumptuously it chooses to flow.

I slowly move down from the heights, intending to check a small group of chinstraps nesting just below the slopes and just up from the water. These chicks are a bit younger than the ones above, and still holding their loose crèche. On the edge, depressingly, I catch a glimpse of an adult chinstrap shivering uncontrollably, gashed open on the left side and bleeding from a leopard seal bite. Its two chicks, about five to six weeks of age, beg inconsolably for food. They probably scooted out of the crèche when the parent returned, expecting the usual handout. But today, there is no feeding chase and there won't be any feeding at all.

This chinstrap won't survive. Blood slowly oozes from its wound and drips slowly to the ground. Otherwise, it is fairly clean. It was likely nabbed on its close approach returning to the island. And I conjure that its mate rushed immediately to sea, assuming that the chicks would be tended. But the penguin cannot move. After the leopard strike, it innately returned to its last space on earth, to its last issue. There's some hope its mate may return with another meal—and that the chicks may survive another week or two, and actually make it to fledging. But with only a single parent now bringing the goods, their chances of survival are lessened.

The chinstrap grimly and proudly holds its space, head up and eyes peeled forward—staring into the open, breathing steadily. It is hurting badly, but refuses to give in. The chicks nudge closer, squealing, bobbing, and nodding to their parent—but it is clearly too pained to move. The chicks retreat a few feet and glumly cease their chirps. This chinstrap has done its job, weeks upon hard weeks perpetuating the gene pool. And somehow it has wiggled from the lep's grasp, but not quickly enough. It won't return next season. It waits. This last, noble stand. A life is over. This compelling sight.

I move back and head away, shivering and suddenly chilled through and through. I feel exposed yet curiously fulfilled, connected indelibly to this single penguin. I turn back every minute or so to check, but the chinstrap's mate hasn't yet returned. Waiting still. It will stand until it can no longer breathe. Like all of these penguins, it stands with its life in front of it and never looks back. The view is always forward, never behind to what has happened or what might have been. Its vast gaze is powerful.

For most people visiting or working in the Banana Belt of Antarctica, the reactions and commentary normally extol the profusion of life one inevitably encounters every spring and summer. But the more I investigate my field of dreams—and absorb all of the rhythms from October through February—the more clearly I see a profusion of both life and death. The full cycle inspires my humility.

John Ruskin, perhaps the most influential essayist of the nineteenth century, espoused a particular raison d'être: that the "greatest thing a human soul ever does in this world is to *see* something, and tell what he *saw* in a plain way. Hundreds of people can talk for one who can think, but thousands can think for one who can see. To see clearly is poetry, prophecy, and religion, all in one." I understand. I won't claim anything overtly religious, but I firmly believe our psychological well-being might benefit from an honest concession that we don't steer the planet. We'd do much better if we simply savored our moments, which unasked, unrequested, we nonetheless have.

The pathology is startling. Insatiably, we consume *virtual* reality—whatever inventions our alleged, perhaps oxymoronic, Human Development brings. I worry about technological obsessions becoming so au courant they suffocate our connections to the planet. My angst, bluntly, is that I don't want the last penguins to be the ones downloaded onto my computer screen. Too few of us are smelling the guano—the *real* guano.

I recall the season at Paulet Island when most of the Adélie chicks died. There are between sixty and a hundred thousand breeding Adélie pairs within a mile of the landing beach, and it was a death camp—the most staggering penguin crash I've ever witnessed. Bodies were strewn in all directions, stiff and embedded in guano. Very few chicks made it past the guard stage. Something happened—a penguin apocalypse. The ice was extensive that summer and perhaps impeded the adults' ability to find necessary amounts of food for the chicks. Or perhaps the krill supply had moved. Or perhaps, with the krill having disappeared, the penguins switched to less nutritious amphipods or copepods. But everything returned to apparent normality the next year. One season down, the next up. There are always changes, nuances.

On another occasion, I almost stepped on an adult Adélie crouched prone in my path. I'd never encountered a penguin that simply wouldn't move, absolutely wouldn't budge without some kind of display or noise. But there was a reason: It had just expired. I held it in my arms, touched its fading warmth, felt its body slowly chilling and stiffening. There were no leopard bite marks, no signs of injury, and it was sufficiently plump. It appeared perfectly healthy and clearly hadn't starved. Holding a ten-pound tuxedo, its white eye ring still clean, its sharp black plumage still glistening, I examined the feathering around its beak, the long claws, and simply wondered: Why? I returned the bird to the position in which I'd found it, and moved ahead.

I've seen numerous Adélie chicks ripped by skuas. Chinstraps flipped and shaken out of their skins by leopard seals. Gentoo chicks with broken wings who have tumbled from nests above into crevices below, unable to escape. All of these instants help me see clearly, remind me that the mysteries I chase and the picture I wish to fill represent a fragile, complicated *balance*.

My hero, Robert Cushman Murphy, had a similar epiphany at South Georgia. He was working the higher reaches of Salisbury

Plain, where he found a group of gentoos nesting miles from the landing beach. He also discovered the gentoos'

romantic sepulchre. Near the summit of a coastal hill I came upon a lonely pond in a hollow of ice-cracked stones. Several sick and drooping penguins were standing at the edge of this pool of snow water, which was ten or twelve feet deep. Then, with a tingling of my spine, I perceived that the bottom was strewn, layer upon layer, with the bodies of gentoo penguins that had outlived the perils of the seas to accomplish the rare feat among wild animals of dying a natural death. By hundreds, possibly by thousands, they lay all over the bed of the cold tarn, flippers outstretched and breasts reflecting blurred gleams of white. Safe at last from sea leopards in the ocean, and from skuas ashore, they took their endless rest; for decades, perhaps for centuries, the slumberers would undergo no change in their frigid tomb.

I've chased this burial pool. The landscape is dotted with numerous tarns and snowmelt pools. Above, many gentoos gambol through snow or explore the edge of a glacier. I can imagine them getting stuck, dying in place, and then tumbling downhill with the next thaw. It's a common occurrence. One large pool lines up well with Murphy's photographs, but the water is murky green, thick with algae blooms, and no dead gentoos appear. But all around me, gentoos are present—and full of life. Some approach the green pool to drink. A few rest along the edge, staring for long minutes into the gloaming. One waddles slowly, clockwise, around the pool's circumference, its intentions unclear. Another jumps in and starts bathing.

I actually don't believe that gentoos or any of the penguins go off to die—that sacred, gentoo burial territories exist. Rather, penguins continue living, breeding, fighting, and feeding until they literally drop. At sea, giant petrels will slurp the remains. On land, the bodies will be scavenged by skuas and then wither. At most, in the penguins' dust, we'll find their distinctive tarsometatarsi. To succeed, they've selected full lives and large doses of what we'd describe as both hope and sadness. I doubt that penguins actually feel these emotions, which are human constructs. I admire them greatly—just for being penguins. Aeons hence, should land predators for some reason be introduced in Antarctica, I'm confident that the penguins—the aerially challenged—will evolve some new motions in geologically short order.

Penguins never retire. Every moment counts. They teach me a reverence for life, wherever it is found. So the symbiosis I see clearly is to experience life—including its uncertainties—as vastly as I possibly can, looking ahead and not behind, standing naked with whatever moments earth's animals and landscapes might provide. George Gaylord Simpson captures this feeling: "What good are penguins?" he asks. "It may be crass to ask what good a wild animal is, but I think the question may also be legitimate. That depends on what you mean by good. If you mean *good to eat*, you are perhaps being stupid. If you mean *good to hunt*, you are surely being vicious. If you mean *good as it is good in itself to be a living creature enjoying life*, you are not being crass, stupid, or vicious. I agree with you and I am your brother as well as the penguin's."

The burial pool I fear is disconnecting from the bigger picture and missing the penguins' signals altogether. Penguins have become part of my ethos. Initially unknown and now welcomed, they continue exposing me to the unfamiliar, to new unknowns I might embrace without objectifying everything in my path. It is a full circle.

I saunter over toward Whalebone Beach, for one last glimpse of the little gentoo dirigibles. I remember walking this beach a number of years ago with my good friend Charles Swithinbank, one of Antarctica's leading experts on glaciology, and a noted Antarctic explorer and geographer. We were trying to locate Charles's wife, Mary, who had hastened down the beach, as Charles put it, "looking for some special moments." It was an extremely foggy day, and Mary was nowhere to be found. But as we neared a bend in the shoreline, we heard recorder music and discovered Mary perched on a rock, serenading a recumbent and very soundly sleeping Weddell seal. The seal's loud breaths kept a fair pace with Mary's inhalations and exhalations. "Oh well," she exclaimed, "my backyard hedgehogs are more responsive than this." But it was a mild complaint. We headed on and she insisted on staying. The stillness was precisely what she'd sought.

And at the end of another field season, I desire the same. As Proust describes, an "hour is not merely an hour, it is a vase full of scents and sounds and projects and climates, and what we call reality is a certain connexion between these immediate sensations and the memories which envelop us simultaneously with them—a connexion that is suppressed in a simple cinematographic vision, which just because it professes to confine itself to the truth in fact departs widely from it—a unique connexion which the writer has to rediscover in order to link for ever in his phrase the two sets of phenomena which reality joins together." I craved some end-of-season sights and sounds and smells.

Twenty or more fat gentoo chicks roam the beach, wearing substantial down and not fully molted, and certainly not ready to go to sea. They chirp constantly, prancing about in what Murphy calls their "uncertain, wobbly fashion." It's not simply the end of another penguin summer, it is a new envelope holding additional clues. Open it.

Four of them set off to the west, bobbing left, bobbing right, hustling quickly for some undefined purpose, then abruptly stopping to chat and bow to one another. Their curly thick, second down is substantially matted and beginning to shed in random clumps, yielding a dumpy, unkempt appearance. Their juvenile plumage emerges underneath. Murphy said the shedding process "superficially resembles the peeling of the velvet from a deer's horn. By the middle of February, or toward the close of the moulting period, clinging tufts, collars, or topknots of down give the otherwise smooth young penguins the appearance of clowns and *pierrots*" (characters in French pantomimes who dress in floppy white outfits).

Above the scattered whalebones, I drop my bag of gear, untie the parka from around my waist, and sit. Infrequent, insubstantial gusts of wind aspirate the calm. Two eight- or nine-week-old gentoo chicks nibble the *Prasiola* at the base of the nearest bones. One spies me and slowly saunters over. My legs are outstretched and I'm sitting up with my arms propped behind me. The bird waddles to my boots and begins to peck gently. Every few seconds, it raises its head, shows me its orange beak and emerging white fillets, and nervously extends the beak toward my face. I can't quite figure it out. It nibbles up my leg, goes for my crotch—gently, fortunately— then claws its way up into my lap. I'm generally a fair space away from them, but this chick can't be bothered. By keeping absolutely still, I've encouraged a close encounter of the most special kind. The chick raises its head to mine and browses through my scraggly beard with its beak. It finds my wire-rims rather interesting but doesn't peck or stab.

It is very difficult not to move—and not to laugh during this tickling, micro examination. My acquaintance begins rocking and swaying against my chest, then rears back, allowing a spectacular eyeball-to-eyeball moment, mere inches apart. I see its dark, star-shaped pupil. Perhaps it notices its own reflection in my glasses. Murphy first introduced me to these gentoos' disposition, when he discovered

that the general attitude toward such a strange visitor as myself was one of indifference or of curiosity unmixed with fear. Then I pulled on leather mittens for safety's sake, seized a passing penguin, lifted it off the ground, and tried with all my might to prevent it from struggling. The outraged bird screeched, beat a tattoo with its flippers that stung even through thick polar garments, bit, squirmed, kicked, and fought like a demon. The tussle continued for about a minute, and I was just about to give up and drop the furious armful when it abruptly quieted down. There it rested in the crook of my elbow, unhurt, bright-eyed, and as contented as a well-fed baby. I stroked it from head to tail and it seemed fascinated or hypnotized. I placed it gently on the ground, whereupon it looked up serenely, as though nothing unpleasant had occurred between us.

I have no interest in any new grabbing experiments. The chick immediately settles to serenity mode. What a feeling. Nibbling concluded, it dabbles and pats its feet against my privates, turns clockwise, faces the sea, and leans backward, resting its back against my chest for support. Our heads are at the same level. Its breaths chime noticeably. Every so often it turns and its beak bumps my nose. We stare outward, for long moments inhaling the view. Every so often it raises its wings, wiggles its tail, then returns to this erect and relaxed position. For a few seconds, I stroke its back up and down, with no adverse reaction.

Here is a new creature to the planet, about to embark on its own great adventure, encountering a somewhat older creature, still sorting through a flood of unanswered questions. This chick is beautiful: A spiffy gray-and-white down coat. Another week or so to shed its fluff before heading to sea. It coos and grunts, alerting the other chick-of-the-year, perhaps its own sibling, who waddles over and starts pulling the rubber tip of my left boot. The breeze kicks up slightly, and some of my lapmate's wisps of down begin swaying and blowing away. The second chick is quickly disinterested and leaves. My lapmate relaxes further, squats on its haunches, and fills my lap with its very fat belly. We continue perusing the surf beyond. I feel its heart tapping, and remain as still as I possibly can.

What if anything parses this penguin's consciousness? I can hardly describe what's going through mine. Is this little gentoo so hardwired it doesn't have time to think? I am merely another new item that's invaded its very brief life. Perhaps it will draw some good conclusions from this smooth encounter. We're up to six minutes—and I don't want it to end. Alone on this beach, at peace, with the object of my work. It's a different kind of reward. I admire these tough animals, realize their scurrying, crazy lives have become my focus—that they are my research subjects. And along other, emotional avenues, they inhabit me.

This chick's parent or parents will soon return. Feeds will continue for a few weeks and the chick will continue growing, ultimately hitting full independence slightly heavier than its parents. When it entered crèche, its feet were 86 percent of adult size, its flipper 66 percent, and its culmen—the bill—54 percent. In very short order, however, the extremities will be adult-sized. From the Aitchos, there is easy access to the sea and there will be lots of open water when winter strikes. It will stick close, I'm sure, return for a site inspection and perhaps a first breeding attempt by age two. In three to four years, it will integrate along the edges and become part of the Whalebone Beach family. Or maybe it will move toward the western end of the island, seeking a little more space and less frequent disruptions. I wish I had Mary's recorder with me, to see how it might respond.

The next small wave brings two adult gentoos whizzing ashore, just back from a feeding run. They shake away excess water with vigorous head and body wiggles, then shimmy along the cobble, clean and sleek. The chick is greatly aroused by the new arrivals and briskly hops down, bounding toward them and chattering loudly. I remain glued and stunned. Off it goes, never looking back.

Waves quietly, delicately, tap this forlorn beach. Above, the slopes bask in a similar, awesome silence. Offshore, newly fledged penguins test flippers and wings, practice feeding runs, and preen—wiling away youthful moments. Molt concluded, a weary tribe of elders descends from the heights and parades slowly to the surf. Shrunk from weeks of fasting, they must regain their strength before migrating north. Days shorten and the Peninsula dusk enlarges to a substantial, darker night. A full moon swells in round display above the ancient pinnacles, shedding starry glints over an immutable, enduring scene. I swing lazily back and forth, in my own ecstatic display, allowing the crisp air to fuel my lungs. Nearby, a deliberate and endless glacier reaches the sea, its ride not quite done. Penguins new and old ripple the moonlight, their ride just beginning. I notice the sensation of blood moving through my forearms, the regular thumping in my chest.

I feel all of these taps and ripples.

That I'm here is pure accident.

But the sky is mine, I have no boundaries—and I am not quite finished.

The Next Generation

Beauty and grace are performed whether or not we will or sense them. The least we can do is try to be there.

—ANNIE DILLARD

Another season begins.

And with an abundance of ice.

The November 10 Bellingshausen Ice Analysis from the National Ice Center in Washington, DC,—the infamous *ice chart*—indicates heavy pack on the Weddell Sea side of the Peninsula. But the Antarctic Sound, the passage over to the Weddell, doesn't appear blocked, nor does the approach up to Paulet Island, which is always an excellent place to visit. So we'll give it a try. Maybe the stars will be with us.

Maybe not.

Ice charts lie. In the first place, they're not actual satellite snapshots of a precise moment in time. They are composite analyses of many recent satellite photos. And by the time each of these weekly summaries is faxed through to the ship, it may be ten days old— in real time. So you take your chances, and you pray.

On *Explorer's* bridge, well before breakfast, the expedition leader, Matt Drennan, isn't a happy camper. None of us are. Captain Uli Demel is already pacing. The ice is bad enough. The dense fog banks make it worse.

I'm usually up early, keeping close tabs on the schedule, where we're heading, and when the landings are actually going to occur. Also, it's virtually the only free and quiet time to catch up with my good friend Matt. The Inventory project usually collects a profusion of data when we work with him and I have the highest regard for Matt's leadership abilities. He knows the Peninsula exceedingly well and the ship regularly logs at least two landings, or Zodiac trips, per day when Matt's in charge. And barring weather and other assorted calamities, Matt usually gets me and my field teams where we need to go. Even better, when there have been two or three additional survey sites near to where the tourists are visiting, Matt has been extraordinarily helpful driving us around. I admit that my compliments mask some selfish pride. I was *Explorer's* E. L. when Matt made his first trip to Antarctica, and now he's taken the baton forward—by light-years. There's usually a lot of banter back and forth about places we've visited, new places we'd like to visit, and a plethora of shipboard gossip that hasn't got a bloody thing to do with penguins. The Antarctic represents a very tight family, and returning each November is like coming home. Returning to our holy cathedral of penguins.

If we ever get there. Dealing with this ice and fog is excruciating.

For *Explorer*—the Little Red Ship—this is season number twenty-eight. She fuels many memories. I was working on board when Françoise from Paris tried to leave the ship, intending to stay in Antarctica. That was the same trip with Steamer, the stowaway puppy from Punta Arenas. And during the years I led Peninsula trips, *Explorer* was my vessel of choice. It carries a reasonable number of passengers—up to ninety—has excellent visibility and maneuverability, top-drawer officers and seamen, and continues to carry one of the best staff contingents in the business.

This morning's ice is much worse than expected. Our location is approximately fifteen miles from the western entrance to Antarctic Sound, at the northern tip of the Peninsula. We're moving at a snail's pace, nudging carefully through a *six-tenths* concentration of annual sea ice. There are small floes up to sixty feet across and a few large floes extending for miles, but only a smattering of leads. Our chances for making it to the other side are fading quickly.

The standard for measuring and evaluating ice concentrations is a scale of tenths: Ten tenths means that you have concentrated, compact, or very close pack ice totally blocking the way. Seven to eight tenths means *close ice,* still no bargain for navigation. The *Explorer* is an ice-reinforced ship, but not an icebreaker. She can push annual ice and brash if necessary, but whatever a ship's strength may be, captains avoid ice like the plague. No one wants to be the Southern Ocean version of *Titanic.* At a concentration of four to six tenths, which is considered *open ice, Explorer* would have a chance—

and that's what the most recent ice chart indicated west of the Sound. But obviously, things change.

Matt wants to get the passengers ashore and this will be a real challenge. At 7:30 A.M., just before Matt makes the wake-up call, he wags his finger and asks me to join him on starboard side. "I don't know, Ron," he hrumphs, peering over the nautical chart. "Don't know what we're going to do. What do you think?"

He knows and I know that there are few options.

"What's the time situation?" I ask.

"If we turn, it means at least seven or eight hours back across the Bransfield to Deception. We're something like ninety nautical miles away. And even if we make good speed and the weather doesn't turn to crap, we can't get ashore until late this afternoon. Maybe we'll just ride it forward until after breakfast. If the ice clears, we may be through the Sound by mid- to late morning. Then, Paulet—maybe, after lunch."

"Yeah, but what about something on this side of the Peninsula? Brown Bluff? Hope Bay? Unfortunately, all the alternatives I know are on the other side of the Sound, or south of Astrolabe Island on this side."

"Don't know, Ron. There's not a lot of choices. The ice looks pretty messy. I'll wake everyone, and we'll reconvene at nine. You never know. This stuff could clear and Paulet's a helluva lot more interesting than another day bouncing in the Bransfield. These folks are tired of lectures. I'd love to get them off the ship."

It is a prime example why expedition-leading causes hair loss, stomach acid, and sleepless nights. Weather and ice are constant miseries in the Peninsula, especially early in the season. At the end of the summer, the days get shorter, and then the wind somehow blows even harder than it normally does. If you want to be a good expedition leader, it's like getting to Carnegie Hall. You must practice, practice, practice. You ride the seat of your pants more than you'd like, and there's a premium on knowing the sites well. For Matt's sake, because I've endured the same kind of misery, I hope there's a break.

Two hours pass—and no improvement. The ice scenery is beautiful, and the carpet on the bridge wears thinner from the excessive pacing back and forth. Again, Matt wags me to starboard.

"What do you know about this place?" he whispers, pointing to a page in *The Penguin Bible*. It's a listing for Adélies: Gourdin Island, two colonies, and a rough estimate of three hundred pairs, from thirty years ago.

"Don't know it at all. We didn't fly that far north with *Endurance*."

We look at the chart. Gourdin Island is a very tiny blip surrounded by shallow water. The *Geographic Place Names of the Antarctic* indicates that it is the largest of a group of islands and rocks located one mile north of Prime Head, which officially is the northern tip of the Peninsula. It was discovered by d'Urville's expedition in 1837–40 and is named for Ensign Jean Gourdin of the d'Urville's flagship vessel *Astrolabe*. The Falkland Islands Dependencies Survey charted the island in 1945–47. The *Antarctic Pilot* provides further tempting bits: About a mile from north to south, with a rounded summit at three hundred feet. Offshore of the northern end is a narrow and distinctive rock pinnacle.

Matt flips the pages of *The Penguin Bible:* Gourdin also has one chinstrap colony, designated *B*—no estimates available—but an accompanying remark notes it is a "large colony." For gentoos, there's an estimate of fifty breeding pairs.

"Let's go for it," Matt exclaims. "We'll do some of that good ole expedition-cruising. The sun is out and I don't want to diddle in here anymore. It looks like it's more open down to the southwest. If we go bust, we'll do Deception very, very late." It will take a couple more hours to reach Gourdin. Passengers are invited to enjoy the ice scenery or take in another lecture.

By 11 A.M. the sun has burned more of the fog and blue sky begins to show, a welcome sight for tired eyes. Gourdin and its neighboring islands can be discerned on the horizon. The bridge is crowded, all of us with binoculars pinned to eyes, trying as best we can to suss it out. Matt is glued. Slowly, surely, we move closer and closer. About two miles off the northeastern end of Gourdin, we finally see one slope covered with penguins, presumably Adélies. Just slightly west of this first group are more penguins. The whole of the island seems surrounded by a massive overhanging ice foot. The tide has dropped—by at least six feet. At one spot, Adélies are racing to the edge of the foot, nervously spinning back and forth, then clambering on the edge, waiting for one brave soul to jump.

"There are *more* than three hundred Adélies," Matt utters excitedly. He lowers his binos and flashes a characteristic wide-eyed, big-smile grin. "The only problem is I can't figure out where we're going to land."

He consults with Uli and the first officer, Peter Skog, and Peter radios Villaruel the boatswain to arrange for a scout boat to be lowered posthaste. Matt races to his cabin and within ten minutes he's on his way. The Zodiac disappears around the corner. Steve

Forrest and I race to get ready. There is hardly any swell, the visibility's improving by the minute, and I'm growing confident we'll be counting penguins very shortly. If we can climb ashore.

Fifteen more minutes pass, Matt radios back. It's a *go*. The only problem is the ice foot. The northwestern end of the island has a protected cove and will be the best place to land. A lot of cobble is exposed, but the ice foot rims the entire island.

"Bring shovels, an ice pick or ice axe, and ladders. We've got to cut some stairs. Oh, yeah. I almost forgot. There are penguins up the ying-yang. And I mean all of them: Chinnies. 'Délies. 'Toos. Lots of them."

Music to my ears. Matt wants to prepare the landing site before bringing folks ashore. Lunch is moved forward to accommodate some long hours ashore. Hopefully. More boats are dropped and Steve and I head in with Matt's staff. As we round the tip, the rock pinnacle described in the *Pilot* comes into view. The sun breaks through in all its glory, shining on an amazing mass of penguins. Indeed, they are everywhere. Because of the low tide, the penguins have lost their easy access to the sea. When the tide is up, the water laps the ice. But for the next few hours, it will be complicated. Today they will be platform divers. Along the entire ice foot, numbers of penguins are scampering back and forth, trying to find a decent launching pad. When one promising spot is discovered, all of the penguins waddle over and line up, waiting for one to go. And it does. Then others. Little missiles plunging headfirst into the water—bang, bang, bang. Kamikaze penguins, all.

It's a very low tide, necessitating a fifty-yard walk over the cobble tide flat to reach the ice foot. Using ice axes, Matt and some of the others have made the top of the ice foot. Initially standing on backs and shoulders, we're pulled to the top. Matt's team begins digging a stairwell above the cobble and through the ice foot, allowing folks an easier and safer means of reaching the penguins. Steve and I drop our life jackets in a pile and begin sorting gear. It is another Heroína situation—except, if the weather holds, we'll have much more time, perhaps four or more hours to pull the data. Steve's GPS machine is warming up, our tally-whackers are zeroed out, and off we go. Steve wants to start at the highest point and then spread out over the island. I will proceed with tally-whacking and fistfuls, starting with the chinnies on the pinnacle end.

Another bowl full of penguins—a dreamworld. To reach the chinnies, I must wade through a large throng of Adélies. There are groups ranging in size from twenty to a few hundred nests. There are gentoos to the side and upslope, with chinstraps in the far distance. All three of *my* penguins—right here, and in numbers. I'd later discover that the estimates in *The Penguin Bible* derive from a brief 1969 visit to Gourdin by British Antarctic Survey personnel. Clearly, the numbers are going to rise substantially. This is an excellent find—more penguins that we really didn't know much about, more fodder for the database. In the Peninsula, it is a rare circumstance to find all three brushtaileds nesting in close proximity. Copa Beach and Stranger Point on King George Island, and Ardley Island—in a bay on the southwestern end of King George—are three examples, but all of them are off-limits areas under the Treaty. Gourdin, therefore, is a special treat.

Or a culmination. A trance sets in. The work proceeds, religiously and systematically—the chinstraps near the pinnacle, loose assemblages of gentoos scattered here and there, with Adélies over much of the remaining space. When I finally reach the top of the island, two hours into the survey, I discover a cement stanchion or signal tower, perhaps the remains of a trisponder setup from previous *Endurance* work. I'll have to check the records in *Endurance*'s hydrography office, next time I'm on board.

The fog returns. Far to the south, I hear but cannot see another bleating group of raucous chinstraps, their *duh-ARGH'-ARGH'-ARGH', duh-ARGH'-ARGH'-ARGH'* calls carrying for hundreds of yards. The chinstraps, Adélies, and gentoos generally have sorted into species-specific groups, but there is one spot where all three species are nesting within twelve feet of one another. Some of the gentoos are nesting at higher elevations than the chinstraps. And despite the generalized segregation, some Adélies have mixed with chinstraps, some with gentoos. All are on eggs, though the Adélies are a bit ahead and will hit the peak of egg-laying before the others. In the end, we will estimate fourteen to sixteen thousand Adélie pairs, more than a thousand chinstrap pairs, and between five and six hundred gentoo pairs.

It is a behavior factory. I meet one gentoo closely and can hear its squeaky hiss, which is a prelude to its regular *hee-HAW* call. Skuas prance through the Adélie groups, attracting nasty pecks and stabs and frequent, aggressive stares. At the craggy lofts, a few chinstrap pairs are copulating, then like a spreading disease scores detonate their volcanic, wing-waving ecstatics. On my closer approach, two chinnies bow very low with their necks extended. Then they slowly, deliberately, raise themselves and weave their heads upward, snake-like, spewing hissing *awwhhhhhhhs*. More *awwhhhhhhhs* slither from the other side of this high chinstrap lek. One chinstrap waves its wings and stretches its neck far forward, parallel to the ground, then yawns with a full gape.

No one has examined Gourdin like we have on this visit. And whether the blizzard of the century, the melt of the millennium, or the mother of all katabatic windstorms—the penguins will continue their business. The cycle goes on and on and on. The baton passes to future generations of penguins and penguin-counters and expedition leaders.

When I reach the beach, there's a totally engaging sight. The returning penguins, smart and clever as they are, have reconnoitered the ice stairs that Matt and staff carved. They're massing and lining up in orderly fashion, taking over this most convenient route back to nests and mates. *Boing, boing*—one by one they hop upward to the top of the ice foot.

I head east, following a narrow path over the cobble, between the six-and-a-half-foot-tall ice rim and a grounded, onshore berg. Under the ice foot, the meltwater dribbles in long streams to the cobble below. Thirty yards away, the walkway terminates at a large, deep pool of seawater. All along the path, marching in the other direction, are spiffy clean chinstraps, Adélies, and gentoos who've just returned from offshore jaunts. Small waves break over the exposed cobble on the seaward side of the pool, and only gentle ripples tumble in. Two thirds of the circumference of the pool is overslung by long flanges of the ice foot.

I find a position at one end of the pool, immediately below the overhanging ice. Every few seconds, directly over my head, an individual Adélie or chinstrap or gentoo peers over the edge, totally oblivious to my presence.

Straight out and across the pool from me, a line of penguins—all three species—edges closer and closer to the outside extremity of the ice foot. The agitation is palpable. One brave Adélie takes a chance, extends far over the edge, stares bug-eyed at the pool below, then inexplicably retreats, obviously nervous. The others scatter, then regroup.

I hear scratching claws directly above, look up—and a chinstrap launches, straight away, beak forward, wings extended, and legs stretched behind. It bombs into the pool and the splash explodes with a loud *plop*. A string of additional kamikazes sails forth.

The news spreads, instantaneously.

Penguins across the pool, their fears displaced, start to jump.

Now, from all edges of the ice foot, endless numbers follow suit—and the water surface obliterates with soaring penguins.

I also soar.

And they fly.

Acknowledgments and Notes

Apsley Cherry-Garrard wrote that "polar exploration is at once the cleanest and most isolated way of having a bad time which has been devised." Also, many of us Antarcticists indubitably recognize that our mania for this isolated place and its bounteous creatures—particularly the time we spend "in the field"—may be the cleanest and easiest means of generating bad times with those whose lives we share, and whose support for our work and dreams is constant. So to Ellen and Alex, four heartfelt words: I love you dearly.

There are many people whose conversations, interactions, suggestions, stories, and advice greatly assisted my writing. I thank them immensely for their patience, occasional scolding, and regularly clear thinking: Wayne Trivelpiece, Sue Trivelpiece, Bob Headland, Frank Todd, Tom McIntyre, Rob Dilling, Janet Kjelmyr, Geoff Geupel, Charles and Mary Swithinbank, Wally Herbert, Matt Drennan, Megan McOsker, Allan Borut, Barbara Heffernan, Anne Kershaw, Denise Landau, Victoria Underwood, Ruth Norris, John Huyler, Herb Horowitz, Harold Sigall, Alexander Ralph, Mohan Ambikaipakur, Praful Saklani, John Rowlett, Bill Wadsworth, and Christopher Merrill.

My compatriots in the Antarctic Site Inventory project—Rosi Dagit, Louise Blight, Steve Forrest, Brent Houston, and Richard Polatty—deserve special kudos. These top-drawer "data troopers" banded together to ensure that our work proceeded expeditiously and rigorously, and they were an unending source of opinions and ideas when we discussed the lives and times of penguins. May you always have lots of guano whizzing past your lens caps.

My great thanks go to all officers, expedition staff, and budding Antarcticists I've met and with whom I've shared innumerable, pleasurable moments on board (*Lindblad, Society,* and now, simply, *The*) *Explorer, World Discoverer, Livonia,* and *Alla Tarasova.* Work on the Antarctic Site Inventory project was the impetus for many of the penguin escapades described in *Waiting to Fly.* The project had been sustained, in various ways and means, by the generous support of The Tinker Foundation, the U.S. Marine Mammal Commission, the U.S. National Science Foundation Office of Polar Programs, the U.S. Environmental Protection Agency, the U.K. Foreign and Commonwealth Office, the German Umweltbundesamt (Federal Environmental Agency) on behalf of the German Federal Environment Ministry, the International Association of Antarctic Tour Operators (IAATO), and private contributors. My thanks to all. I especially acknowledge Dr. Mike Richardson of the U.K. Foreign and Commonwealth Office, and the officers and crew of HMS *Endurance* for their unique contribution to the Inventory project. May all of you continue to have penguins prancing in your dreams and across your radar screens.

This book would not have been realized without the tireless enthusiasm and confidence of Howard Yoon and Gail Ross. They were believers in me, penguins, and the stories I wished to tell—and I always will be grateful for their diligent nurturing. I am enormously thankful for the ebullience and cooperation of my editor, Henry Ferris, and everyone at William Morrow & Company who so willingly and eagerly embraced this book, and who turned my special dreams into a very substantial reality.

Acknowledgments and Notes

Woven through these tales are a considerable amount of data and information about the lives of chinstraps, Adélies, and gentoos. Because my locus is that special paradise known as the Antarctic Peninsula and South Shetland Islands, I've relied as much as possible on the scientific literature emanating from this region. Though attempting, carefully, to transcribe these facts and figures, I take full responsibility for any errors that may have infiltrated the manuscript.

Selected Bibliography

In describing the lives and times of Antarctic Peninsula chinstrap, gentoo, and Adélie penguins, and the exploits of the researchers who studied them, these references were particularly valuable.

Books and Monographs

Ainley, David G. et al. *Breeding Biology of the Adélie Penguin.* Berkeley: University of California Press, 1983.

Bagshawe, Thomas Wyatt. *Two Men in the Antarctic: An Expedition to Graham Land 1920–1922.* Cambridge: Cambridge at the University Press, 1939.

Cherry-Garrard, Apsley. *The Worst Journey in the World.* London: Chatto & Windus, 1952.

Croxall, J. P., and E. D. Kirkwood. *The Distribution of Penguins on the Antarctic Peninsula and Islands of the Scotia Sea.* Cambridge: British Antarctic Survey, 1979.

France, Anatole. *Penguin Island.* New York: Random House/The Modern Library, 1949.

Gurney, Alan. *Below the Convergence: Voyages Toward Antarctica 1699–1839.* New York: W. W. Norton & Company, 1997.

Matthews, L. Harrison. *Penguins, Whalers, and Sealers: A Voyage of Discovery.* New York: Universe Books, 1977.

Murphy, Robert Cushman. *The Oceanic Birds of South America.* New York: American Museum of Natural History, 1936.

———. *Logbook for Grace.* New York: The Macmillan Company, 1947.

Simpson, George Gaylord. *Penguins: Past and Present, Here and There.* New Haven: Yale University Press, 1976.

Todd, Frank S. *The Sea World Book of Penguins.* San Diego: Sea World Press/ Harcourt Brace Jovanovich, 1981.

Williams, Tony D. *The Penguins.* Oxford: Oxford University Press, 1995.

Woehler, E. J. *The Distribution and Abundance of Antarctic and Subantarctic Penguins.* Cambridge: Scientific Committee on Antarctic Research, 1993.

ARTICLES

Bagshawe, T. W. "Notes on the Habits of the Gentoo and Ringed or Antarctic Penguins." *Transactions of the Zoological Society of London* 24, pt. 3 (1938): 185–291.

Fraser, W. R., and W. Z. Trivelpiece. "Factors Controlling the Distribution of Seabirds: Winter-Summer Heterogeneity in the Distribution of Adélie Penguin Populations." In *Foundations for Ecosystem Research in the Western Antarctic Peninsula Region,* edited by R. Ross, E. Hofman, and L. Quetin. Washington, D.C.: American Geophysical Union, pp. 273–85.

Fraser, W. R. et al. "Increases in Antarctic Penguin Populations: Reduced Competition with Whales or a Loss of Sea Ice Due to Global Warming?" *Polar Biology* 11 (1992): 525–31.

Gain, L. "The Penguins of the Antarctic Regions." In the 1912 annual report of the Smithsonian Institution, pp. 475–82.

Loeb, V. S. et al. "Krill and Salp Dominance in the Antarctic Food Web." *Nature* 387 (1997): 897–900.

Naveen, R. "Brush-Tails, Tuft-Heads, Emperors, and Kings." *The Antarctic Century* 5 (1990): 1–6.

———. "Interview: Wayne & Sue Trivelpiece." *The Antarctic Century* 5 (1990): 7–10.

Palmer LTER Group. "The Western Antarctic Peninsula Region: Summary of Environment and Ecological Processes." In *Foundations for Ecosystem Research in the Western Antarctic Peninsula Region*, edited by R. Ross, E. Hofman, and L. Quetin. Washington, D.C.: American Geophysical Union, 1996, pp. 437–48.

Trivelpiece, S. G., and W. Z. Trivelpiece. "Antarctica's Well-bred Penguins." *Natural History*. December 1989.

Trivelpiece, W. Z. et al. "Adélie and Chinstrap Penguins: Their Potential as Monitors of the Southern Ocean Marine Ecosystem." In *Ecological Change and the Conservation of Antarctic Ecosystems: Proceedings of the Fifth Symposium on Antarctic Biology*, edited by K. Kerry and G. Hempel. Berlin: Springer-Verlag, 1990.

Trivelpiece, W. Z., and W. R. Fraser. "The Breeding Biology and Distribution of Adélie Penguins: Adaptations to Environmental Variability." In *Foundations for Ecosystem Research in the Western Antarctic Peninsula Region*, edited by R. Ross, E. Hofman, and L. Quetin. Washington, D.C.: American Geophysical Union, 1996, pp. 273–85.

Trivelpiece, W. Z., and S. G. Trivelpiece. "The Courtship Period of Adélie, Gentoo, and Chinstrap Penguins." In *Penguin Biology*, edited by L. S. Davis and J. Darby. New York: Academic Press, 1990, pp. 113–28.

Volkman, N. J., and W. Trivelpiece. "Growth of *Pygoscelid* Penguin Chicks." *Journal of Zoology* 191 (1980): 521–30.

Index

Index

Index

Index

Index